# STEVE SHEINKIN

# BOMB

## THE RACE TO BUILD—AND STEAL—THE WORLD'S MOST DANGEROUS WEAPON

ROARING BROOK PRESS

NEW YORK

*For Mom, my first and most patient writing teacher*

Text copyright © 2012 by Steve Sheinkin
Published by Flash Point, an imprint of Roaring Brook Press
Roaring Brook Press is a division of Holtzbrinck Publishing Holdings Limited Partnership
175 Fifth Avenue, New York, New York 10010
mackids.com

Library of Congress Cataloging-in-Publication Data

Sheinkin, Steve.
  Bomb : the race to build and steal the world's most dangerous weapon / Steve Sheinkin.
    p. cm.
  ISBN 978-1-59643-487-5
  1. Atomic bomb—History.   2. World War, 1939–1945—Secret service—Soviet
Union.   3. World War, 1939–1945—Secret service—Great Britain.   4. World War,
1939–1945— Commando operations—Norway—Vemork.   5. Operation Freshman,
1942.   6. Atomic bomb—Germany—History.   I. Title.   II. Title: The race to build and
steal the world's most dangerous weapon.

UG1282.A8.S235 2012
623.4'5119—dc23

2011044096


Roaring Brook Press books are available for special promotions and premiums.
For details contact: Director of Special Markets, Holtzbrinck Publishers.


First edition 2012
Book design by Jay Colvin
Printed in the United of America by RR Donnelley & Sons Company, Crawfordsville, Indiana


1  3  5  7  9  10  8  6  4  2

# CONTENTS

Prologue ............................................................. 1

Part 1: Three-Way Race .................................... 5

Part 2: Chain Reactions ..................................... 43

Part 3: How to Build an Atomic Bomb .................... 89

Part 4: Final Assembly ...................................... 143

Epilogue ........................................................ 227

Race to Trinity ............................................... 237

Source Notes .................................................. 243

Quotation Notes .............................................. 249

Acknowledgments ............................................ 260

Photo Credits ................................................. 261

Index ............................................................ 262

# PROLOGUE: MAY 22, 1950

**HE HAD A FEW MORE MINUTES** to destroy seventeen years of evidence.

Still in pajamas, Harry Gold raced around his cluttered bedroom, pulling out desk drawers, tossing boxes out of the closet, and yanking books from the shelves. He was horrified. Everywhere he looked were incriminating papers—a plane ticket stub, a secret report, a letter from a fellow spy.

Gold ripped the papers to shreds, carried two fistfuls to the bathroom, shoved them into the toilet, and flushed. Then he ran back to his bedroom, grabbed the rest of the pile, and stumbled on slippers down the stairs to the cellar, where he pushed the stuff to the bottom of an overflowing garbage can.

The doorbell rang.

Gold walked to the door. He took a few deep breaths, trying to slow his heartbeat, then opened the door and saw the men he expected: Federal Bureau of Investigation agents Scott Miller and Richard Brennan. They'd been questioning Gold for days, showing him pictures of known spies, demanding information about his connection to these people. Gold had admitted nothing, insisting he was what he appeared to be: a simple, hardworking chemist who lived with his father and brother, and had never been far from his Philadelphia home. Unconvinced, the FBI agents had come to search his house.

Gold led the way to his room. Agent Miller sat down at Gold's desk and started opening drawers, sifting through paper piles. Brennan went to work on the sagging bookshelves, packed tight with math and science volumes, and stacks of paperback novels.

Brennan flipped through a paperback, stopping to inspect something stamped on the inside cover: the name of a department store in Rochester, New York.

"What's this?" he asked Gold, holding up the open book.

"Oh, I don't know," Gold said, "must have picked it up on a used book counter somewhere. Lord knows where."

Then, from a desk drawer, Miller pulled a train schedule for the Washington-Philadelphia-New York-Boston passenger line. Another clue that Gold wasn't the homebody he'd described.

"What's this, Harry?" Miller asked.

"Goodness knows," Gold said, shrugging. "I probably picked it up when I went to New York." *This is bad*, he said to himself. *Bad, but not terrible.*

Then came the body blow.

Gold watched Brennan slide a thick, tattered copy of *Principles of Chemical Engineering* from the shelf. Nausea swelled Gold's throat as he saw a light brown, folded street map drop to the floor. To Gold, the map seemed to scream its title in the silent room: "New Mexico, Land of Enchantment."

*Oh God*, he thought.

"So you were never west of the Mississippi," said Brennan, bending down to lift the map. He opened it and saw, at the spot in Santa Fe where the Castillo Street Bridge crosses the Santa Fe River, an *X* marked in ink.

"How about this, Harry?" demanded Brennan.

Miller spun from the desk, stood, and watched Gold.

Gold needed to speak quickly, needed to offer an explanation. But he froze.

"Give me a minute," he managed, falling heavily into his desk chair.

Brennan offered him a cigarette, which he took. Brennan lit it, and Gold drew deeply.

"A torrent of thoughts poured through my mind," Gold later said of this moment. The map could easily be explained—he'd just say he loved Western stories, which was true, and that, out of curiosity, he'd sent to a Santa Fe museum for the map. Surely they didn't keep records of such requests; no one could prove he was lying.

But then he thought about what would happen if he continued claiming innocence: "My family, people with whom I worked, and my friends whom I knew, my lifetime friends—they would all rally around me. And how horrible would be their disappointment, and the letdown, when finally it was shown who I really was."

Harry Gold had been living a double life for seventeen years. Overwhelmed by exhaustion, he turned to the FBI agents. They were still waiting for an answer.

"Yes, I am the man," Gold said.

He slumped a little lower in his chair.

"There is a great deal more to this story. It goes way back," he said. "I would like to tell it all."

KNUT HAUKELID
Norwegian
resistance
fighter

FRANKLIN
DELANO
ROOSEVELT
U.S.
President,
1933-1945

HARRY GOLD
courier and
spy for the
Soviets

LEO SZILARD
physicist,
helped
initiate
Manhattan
Project

EUGENE WIGNER
physicist,
helped initiate
Manhattan
Project

# PART 1: THREE-WAY RACE

OTTO HAHN AND
LISE MEITNER
discoverers
of fission

ALBERT
EINSTEIN
world-famous
physicist

# SKINNY SUPERHERO

**HARRY GOLD WAS RIGHT:** This is a big story. It's the story of the creation—and theft—of the deadliest weapon ever invented. The scenes speed around the world, from secret labs to commando raids to street-corner spy meetings. But like most big stories, this one starts small. Let's pick up the action sixteen years before FBI agents cornered Harry Gold in Philadelphia. Let's start 3,000 miles to the west, in Berkeley, California, on a chilly night in February 1934.

On a hill high above town, a man and woman sat in a parked car. In the driver's seat was a very thin young physics professor named Robert Oppenheimer. Beside him sat his date, a graduate student named Melba Phillips. The two looked out at the view of San Francisco Bay.

It was a fine view, but Oppenheimer couldn't seem to stay focused on the date. He turned to Phillips and asked, "Are you comfortable?"

*Robert Oppenheimer poses at the front of his classroom at Princeton University, December 17, 1947.*

She said she was.

"Mind if I get out and walk for a few minutes?"

She didn't mind.

Oppenheimer got out and strolled into the darkness. Phillips wrapped a coat around her legs and waited. She waited a long time. At some point, she fell asleep.

She woke up in the middle of the night—the seat beside her was still empty. Worried, she stepped onto the road and waved down a passing police car.

"My escort went for a walk hours ago and he hasn't returned," she told the cop.

The police searched the park, but found nothing. They notified headquarters, and a wider search was begun. An officer drove to Oppenheimer's apartment to look for useful clues.

He found the professor in bed, sound asleep.

The cop shook Oppenheimer awake and demanded an explanation. Oppenheimer said he'd gotten out of the car to think about physics. "I just walked and walked," he said, "and I was home and I went to bed. I'm so sorry."

A reporter for the *San Francisco Chronicle* got hold of the story and wrote an article with the headline: "Forgetful Prof Parks Girl, Takes Self Home."

No one who knew Robert Oppenheimer was the least bit surprised.

HE'D ALWAYS BEEN DIFFERENT. A girl who knew Robert as a child in New York City described him as "very frail, very pink-cheeked, very shy, and very brilliant."

Oppenheimer was a tougher critic. "A repulsively good little boy," he said of himself. "My life as a child did not prepare me for the fact that the world is full of cruel and bitter things."

He was constantly getting sick, so his nervous parents tried to protect him by keeping him inside. While other boys played in the street, Robert sat alone in his room studying languages, devouring books of literature and science, and filling notebooks with poetry. Around kids his age he was awkward and quiet, never knowing what to say unless he could bring the conversation around to books. Then he would let loose annoying bursts of learning.

"Ask me a question in Latin," he'd say, "and I'll answer you in Greek."

Hoping to toughen up their stick-skinny fourteen-year-old, Robert's parents sent him to a sports summer camp. But he was an awful athlete and simply refused to participate. Then the other campers found out he wrote home every day, and that he liked poetry and looking for minerals. That's when they started calling him "Cutie."

Robert never fought back. He never even responded. That made his tormentors even angrier.

One night, after dinner, Robert went for a walk. A group of boys waited for him in the woods. They grabbed him, dragged him to the icehouse, and tossed him on the rough wood floor. They ripped off his shirt and pants, dipped a brush in green paint, and slapped the dripping bristles against his bony body.

Robert never said a word about the attack to camp counselors. "I don't know how Robert stuck out those remaining weeks," his only friend at camp later said. "Not many boys would have—or could have—but Robert did. It must have been hell for him."

Science saved him. Robert dove deep into chemistry and physics in high school, graduated from Harvard University in 1925, then earned advanced degrees at top universities in Britain and Germany. Even in classes with some of the brightest students in the world, "Oppie," as friends called him, never lost his know-it-all style. He interrupted physics lectures with his own theories, sometimes charging to the chalkboard, grabbing the chalk and declaring. "This can be done much better in the following manner." Classmates got so annoyed they actually signed a petition asking him to allow others to speak in class. After that, Oppenheimer calmed down. A little bit. "The trouble," a friend said, "is that Oppie is so quick on the trigger intellectually, that he puts the other guy at a disadvantage."

He'd lucked into a thrilling time in theoretical physics. Physicists were just beginning to figure out what atoms look like, and how the tiny particles inside them move and affect each other. Theoretical physicists were the explorers of their day, using imagination and mind-bending math to dig deeper and deeper into the surprising inner workings of atoms. Oppenheimer knew he'd found his calling.

When he returned to the States, schools all over the country tried to hire him. He picked the University of California, in Berkeley, where he quickly built the country's best theoretical physics program. Students who came to study with Oppenheimer quickly realized they were in for a wild ride. "When you took a question to him," one student remembered, "he would spend hours—until midnight perhaps—exploring every angle with you."

"He generally would answer patiently," another student agreed, "unless the question was manifestly stupid, in which event his response was likely to be quite caustic."

While sitting in on other professors' lectures, Oppenheimer was known to squirm impatiently. "Oh, come now!" he'd call out. "We all know that. Let's get on with it!"

Oppenheimer's own lectures, according to a student named Edward Gerjuoy, were lightning bursts of ideas, theories, and math on the blackboard. "He spoke quite rapidly, and puffed equally rapidly," Gerjuoy said. "When one cigarette burned down to a fragment he no longer could hold, he lit another." Oppenheimer paced as he lectured, his wiry black hair sticking straight up, his large blue eyes flashing, as he furiously wrote, erased, wrote more, talked, puffed, and bobbed in and out of a cloud of white smoke.

During one lecture, he told students to think about a formula he'd written. There were dozens scrawled all over the board, and a student cut in to ask which formula he was talking about.

"Not that one," Oppenheimer said, pointing to the blackboard, "the one underneath."

There was no formula below that one, the student pointed out.

"Not below, *underneath*," snapped Oppenheimer. "I have written over it."

As one of Oppenheimer's students put it: "Everyone sort of regarded him, very affectionately, as being sort of nuts."

"I NEED PHYSICS MORE THAN FRIENDS," Oppenheimer once told his younger brother. Lost in his studies, Oppenheimer paid little attention to the outside world. He didn't hear about the stock market crash that triggered the Great Depression until six months after it happened. He first voted in a presidential election in 1936, at the age of thirty-two.

"Beginning in late 1936, my interests began to change," he later said. There were a few reasons.

For one thing, the country's ongoing economic troubles began to hit home. "I saw what the Depression was doing to my students. Often they could get no jobs," he said. "And through them, I began to understand how deeply political and economic events could affect men's lives. I began to feel the need to participate more fully in the life of the community." Oppenheimer started going to political meetings and discussion groups. He began giving money to support causes like labor unions and striking farm workers.

But it wasn't only events in the United States that caught Oppenheimer's attention—he was also alarmed by the violent rise of Adolf Hitler and his Nazi Party in Germany. Hitler took over as chancellor of Germany in 1933 and started arresting political opponents and tossing them into concentration camps. With complete control of the country in his hands, Hitler began persecuting German Jews, stripping them of their legal rights, kicking them out of universities and government jobs. Oppenheimer, who was Jewish, still had family in Germany, as well as Jewish friends from his student days. When he heard that Hitler was harassing Jewish physicists, Oppenheimer dedicated a portion of his salary to help them escape Nazi Germany.

At the same time, the German dictator built up a huge military and started hacking out what he called a "Greater Germany," a massive European empire that Hitler insisted rightfully belonged to Germans. He annexed neighboring Austria in 1938, then demanded a huge region of Czechoslovakia. Britain and France were strong enough to stand in Hitler's way—but they caved in to his threats, hoping to preserve peace in Europe.

"This is my last territorial demand in Europe," Hitler promised.

A few months later, he sent German troops into the rest of Czechoslovakia. Just twenty years after the end of World War I, it looked like a second world war was about to explode.

Oppenheimer followed these terrifying events from his home in California, burning with what he described as "a continuing, smoldering fury" toward Adolf Hitler.

But how was a theoretical physicist supposed to save the world?

# THE U BUSINESS

**ACTUALLY, THEORETICAL PHYSICISTS** were about to become more powerful than Oppenheimer had ever imagined.

In late December 1938, in the German capital of Berlin, a chemist named Otto Hahn set up a new experiment in his lab. By the late 1930s, scientists like Hahn understood that everything in the universe is made up of incredibly tiny particles called atoms. They knew that atoms themselves are composed of even smaller particles. Atoms have a central core, or nucleus, made up of protons and neutrons packed tightly together. Surrounding the nucleus are electrons.

Scientists also knew that some atoms are radioactive. That is, their nucleus is naturally unstable—particles break away from the nucleus and shoot out at high speeds. This was useful to experimenters like Hahn, because they could use radioactive elements as tiny cannons.

Hahn began his experiment with a piece of silver-colored metal called uranium. He placed the uranium beside a radioactive element. He knew that neutrons would speed out of the radioactive material. He knew that some of these tiny particles would hit uranium atoms. The big question was: What happens when a speeding neutron crashes into a uranium atom?

The answer was shocking. Hahn was sure he'd made a mistake.

As expected, some of the speeding neutrons hit uranium atoms. What staggered Hahn was that the force of the collision seemed to be causing the uranium atoms to split in two. According to everything scientists knew in 1938, this was impossible.

AT ONCE EXCITED AND DISTURBED, Hahn needed help. He turned to his former partner, Lise Meitner, a Jewish physicist who'd been forced out of Germany by Hitler. Hahn wrote to Meitner at her new office in Sweden, describing the strange results of his experiment.

"Perhaps you can suggest some fantastic explanation," Hahn said of the splitting uranium. "We understand that it really *can't* break up."

Meitner responded immediately, agreeing that the news was amazing, but adding: "We have experienced so many surprises in nuclear physics that one cannot say without hesitation about anything: 'it's impossible.'"

A few days later Meitner's nephew Otto Frisch, also a physicist, came to Sweden for a visit. Over breakfast, she showed him Hahn's letter.

"I don't believe it," he said. "There's some mistake."

The two went outside to discuss the mystery. "We walked up and down in the snow, I on skis and she on foot," Frisch recalled.

They talked over an idea proposed by the great Danish physicist Niels Bohr. Bohr had recently suggested that the nucleus of an atom might act like a "wobbly droplet" of liquid. If that were true, they asked each other, what would happen if a speeding neutron hit the nucleus of a uranium atom? Could the force of the collision cause the uranium nucleus to stretch and stretch—just like a liquid drop—until it split?

They brushed the snow off a fallen log and sat. Meitner pulled out a scrap of paper and pencil, and Frisch sketched a diagram of a circle stretching into a long oval shape, and finally breaking in two.

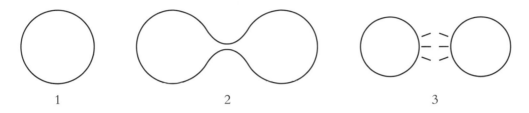

"Yes," said Meitner. "That is what I mean."

They agreed: this must be what happened to the uranium atoms in Hahn's lab. Meitner took the pencil and paper and began working out the math.

"If you really do form two such fragments," she said, "they would be pushed apart with great energy."

An atom splitting was incredible enough. But what made this a world-changing discovery was that if atoms really *could* be split, they would release energy as they broke in two. How much energy? Just enough, Meitner and Frisch calculated, to make a grain of sand jump. That doesn't sound like much—but keep in mind how tiny atoms are. With 238 protons and neutrons, uranium is the largest atom in nature. Still, each atom is incredibly small. A single ounce of uranium has about 100,000,000,000,000,000,000 atoms.

What if you had a twenty-pound lump of uranium? A fifty-pound lump? What if you were able to get all those atoms to split and release energy at the same moment? You'd have *by far* the most powerful bomb ever built.

"I feel as if I had caught an elephant by its tail, without meaning to," Frisch wrote to his mother. "And now I don't know what to do with it."

NEWS OF THE DISCOVERY SPREAD QUICKLY within the small world of theoretical physicists. Otto Frisch rushed to Copenhagen, Denmark, catching up with Niels Bohr just as Bohr was boarding a ship for America. Frisch began telling

Bohr that uranium atoms could split in two and was halfway through his explanation when Bohr slapped himself on the forehead.

"Oh, what idiots we have all been!" shouted Bohr. "Oh, but it is wonderful. This is just as it must be!"

Bohr was so excited, he ran home to get a blackboard. He set it up in his cabin on the ship and spent most of the two-week Atlantic crossing exploring this new discovery. By the time he reached New York City in January 1939, he was convinced—uranium atoms really could split in two. He took the news to a physics conference in Washington, D.C., where it leaped from one physicist to another.

"Bohr has just come in," one scientist announced. "He has gone crazy. He says a neutron can split uranium!"

A newspaper reporter attending the conference described the news in a short article, which was picked up by papers across the country. The next morning a young physicist named Luis Alvarez was sitting in a barber shop in Berkeley, California. While the barber snipped his hair, Alvarez grabbed the *San Francisco Chronicle* from a pile of papers beside the chair. "In the second section," he remembered, "buried away some place, was an announcement that some German chemists had found that the uranium atom split into two pieces."

Alvarez put down the paper.

"I got right out of that barber chair and ran as fast as I could." He sprinted to the campus of the University of California, where he taught, and ran from lab to lab with the news, soon bumping into one his fellow professors, Robert Oppenheimer. Alvarez told Oppenheimer that uranium atoms split in two—scientists were calling it fission.

"That's impossible," Oppenheimer said.

Alvarez explained what little he'd read about fission. Oppenheimer quickly agreed it must be true. "It was amazing to see how rapidly his mind worked," said Alvarez.

"The U business is unbelievable," Oppenheimer told a friend a few days later—U is the chemical symbol for uranium. Like all the scientists involved in the discovery, Oppenheimer was fired up by new ideas in physics, deeper glimpses into the weird inner world of atoms. The thought of making weapons of mass destruction had never occurred to him.

But now, suddenly, he couldn't shake it from his mind: fission might make it possible to build a whole new type of explosive.

"Within perhaps a week," recalled a student, "there was on the blackboard in Robert Oppenheimer's office a drawing—a very bad, an execrable drawing—of a bomb."

ROBERT OPPENHEIMER realized something else right away. If it was obvious to *him* that an atomic bomb might be possible, it was also obvious to everyone else in the global community of top physicists. This would not usually be a problem. In normal times, scientists from around the world freely shared new ideas and theories. But in 1939, normal times were rapidly coming to an end.

Adolf Hitler was demanding a big piece of Poland, claiming it rightfully belonged to Germans. Britain and France finally faced the fact that Germany would continue gobbling up territory until stopped by force. At Poland they drew the line. A German attack on Poland, they warned, would mean war with Britain and France.

Hitler waved his fists and raged, "I'll cook them in a stew they'll choke on!"

Calling his military chiefs to Berlin, Hitler announced: "Further successes can no longer be obtained without the shedding of blood." He ordered the German military to prepare an all-out invasion of Poland. Hitler knew this might ignite a much wider war, but he was not worried about taking the blame.

"In starting and waging a war," he told his generals, "it is not right that matters, but victory. Close your hearts to pity! Act brutally! The stronger man is right!"

17

# FINDING EINSTEIN

**ON THE HOT SUNNY MORNING** of July 16, 1939, a Dodge coupe pulled to the sandy side of the road in the oceanfront town of Patchogue, New York. Out of the car climbed two sweat-soaked men.

The men looked around, then began walking down the town's main street. Speaking with European accents that locals couldn't quite identify, the visitors asked for directions to "the cottage of Dr. Moore." No one in town knew of such a place. The men went into stores and gas stations. No luck. They hiked back to their car and collapsed into their seats.

"Perhaps I misunderstood the name 'Patchogue' on the telephone," the driver said. "Let's see if we can find some similar name on the map."

Visibly irritated, the man in the passenger seat unfolded a map of Long Island. He ran his finger along town names in tiny print.

"Could it be Peconic?"

"Yes, that was it," the driver exclaimed. "Now I remember!"

He started the engine. They got back on the road.

• • •

DRIVING THE CAR WAS EUGENE WIGNER; in the passenger seat sat Leo Szilard. Both were Hungarian-born physicists, both about forty, both Jews who had fled from Europe as Adolf Hitler rose to power. Both were tormented by the same question: What had German scientists told Hitler about the possibility of building atomic bombs?

They had no way of knowing. But this much was clear: fission had been discovered in Berlin. Probably, German physicists were already working on an atomic bomb. This was a terrifying thought. Especially since six months had already passed since Hahn's discovery, and the American president, Franklin Roosevelt, still had no idea that such a thing as fission even existed.

Szilard and Wigner were determined to tell him. Step one of their plan was to find Albert Einstein, the world's most famous scientist. If Einstein sounded the alarm about the danger of a German atomic bomb, President Roosevelt might just listen.

Wigner had called Einstein's office that morning. He was told the great man was on vacation, staying at a beach house he rented from someone named Dr. Moore, in Patchogue. Or was it Peconic? Something with a *P*.

About an hour after leaving Patchogue, Wigner and Szilard pulled into Peconic. Once again they asked around for the home of Dr. Moore. Again, no one knew.

"Let's give it up and go home," Szilard sighed. "Perhaps fate never intended it."

Wigner shook his head. "But it's our *duty* to take this step," he insisted. "It must be our contribution to the prevention of a terrible calamity."

So they drove slowly on, passing dunes and cottages.

Szilard had an idea. "How would it be if we simply asked where around here Einstein lives?"

Wigner spotted a young boy, about seven, walking along the side of the

19

road holding a fishing rod. He pulled over. Szilard leaned his sweaty head out the car window.

"Say," he began, "do you by any chance know where Einstein lives?"

The boy looked up, and said, "Of course."

ALBERT EINSTEIN stood on the porch of his rented cottage, looking cool, tan, and relaxed in loose pants, a T-shirt, and slippers. His famous mane of white hair was windswept from a morning of sailing on Long Island Sound. He welcomed the weary Hungarians, inviting them to sit down and have some iced tea.

After a few minutes of small talk, Szilard and Wigner brought up the subject they'd come to discuss. They told Einstein about the newest discoveries in fission and explained how uranium might be used to build devastating bombs.

Einstein hadn't been following the fission research. He took a minute to process the science. Then he said, "I hadn't thought of that at all."

Einstein quickly realized that with atomic bombs, Adolf Hitler would be absolutely unstoppable. "And Einstein was just as horrified as I was by that prospect," Wigner recalled. "He volunteered to do whatever he could to prevent it."

Wigner got out a pen and a piece of paper. He took notes as Szilard and Einstein worked out the text of a letter to President Roosevelt.

SIX WEEKS LATER, on September 1, 1939, Germany launched a massive invasion of Poland. Using a new style of attack known as blitzkrieg, German for "lightning war," Hitler's planes, tanks, and soldiers slashed deep into Polish territory. Britain and France had promised to protect Poland—they had no choice but to declare war on Germany. They did, but it had no effect on the German charge. Hitler's troops poured into Warsaw, Poland's capital, in late September.

On October 11, in Washington, D.C., an economist named Alexander Sachs showed his ID to security guards outside the White House. He walked into the building with Albert Einstein's letter in his briefcase.

Sachs was a former aide to President Roosevelt, and a personal friend. He also knew Leo Szilard, and he'd told Szilard he could get Einstein's letter directly into Roosevelt's hands. The start of World War II had made it tough to get an appointment with the president, but he'd finally made it.

Sachs was ushered into the Oval Office, where the president was seated behind his desk.

"Alex," Roosevelt said, flashing his famously big smile, "what are you up to?"

Sachs sat down. He asked Roosevelt to listen very carefully to what he had to say. Roosevelt poured two glasses of brandy, got comfortable in his chair, and motioned for Sachs to begin.

Sachs explained the warning in Einstein's letter. "The element uranium may be turned into a new and important source of energy in the immediate future," Einstein had written. "One day man will release and control its almost infinite power. We cannot prevent him from doing so and can only hope that he will not use it exclusively in blowing up his next-door neighbor."

Einstein urged the government to start working closely with physicists to explore the possibilities of building atomic bombs. The letter ended with one last piece of information: "Germany has actually stopped the sale of uranium from the Czechoslovakian mines, which she has taken over."

This was a chilling clue—the Germans were grabbing all the uranium they could get. Why? Were they already working on a bomb?

Roosevelt thought for a moment. "Alex," he began, "what you are after is to see that the Nazis don't blow us up."

"Precisely."

Roosevelt nodded. He banged his desk, and said, "This requires action!"

# TRADECRAFT

**WITHIN WEEKS** of getting Einstein's letter, President Roosevelt formed the Uranium Committee, a group of military leaders and scientists. Their goal was to figure out the basics of how an atomic bomb might work, and what materials would be needed.

The project got off to a slow start. Sixteen different teams were spread out around the country. They began with a budget of just $6,000. An alarmed Einstein sent a second letter to President Roosevelt.

"Since the outbreak of the war, interest in uranium has intensified in Germany," Einstein warned. "I have now learned that research there is being carried out in great secrecy."

The race to build the atomic bomb was on.

JUST ABOUT THE LAST PERSON anyone would expect to be involved was Harry Gold.

When World War II began, Gold was a twenty-eight-year-old chemist, living with his parents and younger brother in a working-class Philadelphia neighborhood. He stood five foot six, with thick black hair and a soft, round face. Friends described him as shy, smart, and always ready to help anyone who asked. He was the kind of guy who seemed to blend in with the background, who could come and go from a room without being noticed. "You'd never in a million years believe this guy was a spy," one neighbor later said.

And yet Harry Gold was about to become a major player in what FBI director J. Edgar Hoover would call "the crime of the century."

It all began one snowy night in February 1933, in the depths of the Great Depression. Like millions of Americans, Gold had been laid off from his job. His family was way behind on rent and facing eviction from their apartment. One night, after another hopeless job search, Gold was resting at home when a friend came racing through the door. The friend explained that a guy he knew, Tom Black, was leaving his job at a soap factory in Jersey City. Black could arrange to get Gold the job, if Gold was willing to move to New Jersey.

Gold's mother leaped up and started stuffing her son's clothes into a cardboard suitcase. Gold borrowed a few dollars and hurried to the bus station. Arriving in Jersey City after midnight, he walked down slushy sidewalks to Tom Black's apartment.

"Black was waiting for me downstairs," Gold remembered. "I can still see that huge, friendly, freckled face, the grin, and the feel of the bearlike grip of his hand."

The first thing Black said was: "I am a Communist. And I am going to make a Communist out of you."

GOLD EARNED $30 A WEEK at the soap factory, and sent $20 home to his parents. He was proud to be supporting his family and didn't mind the hard work. "I was grateful to Tom Black," he later said, "very much so."

That was exactly what Black was counting on. Black dropped by Gold's rented room often to lecture his new friend about Communism and the Soviet

Union. Gold knew only the basics: Communists had taken over Russia in a recent revolution and renamed the country the Union of Soviet Socialist Republics, or Soviet Union. Black told Gold that the Soviet government had abolished private property and was making all the decisions about what the economy should produce, and how goods should be distributed. In this way, Black said, the Soviets would soon wipe out the greed and poverty plaguing countries like the United States.

Black pressured Gold to officially join the Communist Party. "I just kept stalling," Gold explained. "I had no interest in the matter whatsoever."

Then came some good news. Gold's former employer, a chemical plant called the Pennsylvania Sugar Company, was hiring again. Gold was offered his old job back. He jumped at the chance to move back to Philadelphia.

But Tom Black didn't give up that easily. In early 1934, he came to visit Gold in Philadelphia.

"Harry, you've been stalling me," Black said. "You've been trying to get out of joining the Communist Party. And possibly I don't blame you."

This last line got Gold's attention.

"But, there *is* something you can do," Black continued. "There is something that would be very helpful to the Soviet Union, and something in which you can take pride."

The plant where Gold worked, Black explained, used cutting-edge processes to produce many useful chemicals. "The people of the Soviet Union need these processes," said Black. "If you will obtain as many of them as you can in complete detail and give them to me, I will see to it that those processes are turned over to the Soviet Union."

Gold took a long moment before saying, "I'll think it over."

"But actually," he later explained, "I had already formed my judgment. Yes, I would."

Some spies do it for the money; others are trying to change the world. Gold's reasons were a lot less dramatic. He was thankful to Black for getting him a job and wanted to repay the debt. Also, Gold had what he described as "an almost puppy-like eagerness to please." Here was a chance to do something nice for Black *and* help the Soviet people. The chemical processes Black wanted didn't seem so secret, and if the information could really help the Soviets build a better society, why not share it? Who would it hurt?

"And that," said Gold, "is how I began."

GOLD STARTED SNEAKING DOCUMENTS OUT OF HIS LAB, plans and formulas for making industrial chemicals. Every few weeks he'd travel to New York City to meet with a Soviet contact—Gold knew these men only by fake first names. He'd hand over his stash of stolen documents, then hang around a coffee shop while the papers were copied. He got the papers back, rode back to Philadelphia, and returned the documents before anyone noticed they were missing.

By the time World War II began, Gold had given the Soviets every bit of useful information the Pennsylvania Sugar Company had in its files. He was tired of the long trips to New York, the constant lies to his family. Besides, Gold was starting to realize that the Soviet Union was hardly the workers' paradise Tom Black had described. In fact, it was a police state ruthlessly run by Joseph Stalin, a dictator who arrested and executed his political rivals, just like Hitler. Equally disturbing to Gold was the news that just days before the war started, Stalin and Hitler had signed a special pact, agreeing not to fight each other. *Why would Stalin make a deal with the devil?* Gold wondered. He was convinced—it was time to leave his secret life behind.

The Soviets had different ideas.

Gold's Soviet contact, known to Gold only as "Fred," told Gold to get a job at a weapons factory—someplace with technology worth stealing. And Fred wanted Gold to start recruiting other spies with technical knowledge.

"I'm giving you orders!" Fred shouted.

When Gold hesitated, Fred went further. Should Gold ever get the idea of walking away from the Soviets, Fred assured Gold that his boss would get an anonymous note all about Gold's illegal activities.

"You'll be finished!" Fred shouted. "And don't think we will hesitate to do this!"

LIFE IMPROVED A BIT under Gold's next Soviet contact, a man Gold knew as "Sam." During long walks along New York City streets, Sam gave Gold a basic education in tradecraft—the art and science of spying. Gold was taught never to use his real name when doing secret work, never to share his address. He learned to sit at booths in restaurants, because they kept him more hidden than tables. On the subway he sat right next to the doors. If he was being tailed, he could wait for a stop, let the doors begin to close, then leap up and jump out as the doors shut behind him.

Gold was never to attend Communist meetings, never to read Communist papers, never to express even the slightest interest in the Soviet Union. The main rule was this: "Present the appearance of a normal American."

Gold enjoyed these talks and even felt comfortable enough to bring up his concerns about the Soviet Union, including Stalin's treaty with Adolf Hitler.

"What the hell?" Gold asked.

"Look, you fool," Sam said, laughing, "what the Soviet Union needs more than anything in the world is time, precious time." Stalin had no intention of keeping the agreement, Sam said, but the deal gave the Soviets time to build up their military strength. "And when the proper hour comes, you'll see, we'll sweep over Germany and Hitler like nothing ever imagined."

WHILE GOLD AND SAM STROLLED IN NEW YORK, Adolf Hitler was on the move in Europe. German forces captured Norway and Denmark in April 1940, then turned against France, the Netherlands, and Belgium, forcing all three to surrender within a month. German bombs pounded British cities night after night. Great Britain stood alone in the war against Hitler. The United States rushed weapons to the British, but stayed out of the fighting.

Gold continued bringing Sam documents from his company files, but both knew the stuff was of little value. And in early 1941, Gold got some welcome news from Sam: "They had decided to drop me entirely."

Gold was relieved to have his life back. He even began dreaming of starting a family of his own. It was too good to be true.

Stalin may have intended to break his treaty with Hitler—but Hitler beat Stalin to the punch. In June 1941, the German dictator launched a four-million man invasion force across the Soviet border. The German blitzkrieg drove deep into Soviet territory, capturing millions of soldiers and quickly approaching the Soviet capital of Moscow.

Sam called Gold. The Soviets wanted him back. It was not a request.

The Soviets had spies inside various factories—Americans who were willing to secretly share information with the Russians, in exchange for cash. Gold's new job was to act as a courier. He began taking long bus rides across New York State, picking up files in Syracuse, Rochester, and Buffalo. He was sent to Tennessee to get a sample of a new kind of explosive. He brought everything back to New York City and delivered it to Sam.

SAM'S REAL NAME was Semyon Semyonov. A thirty-year-old engineer with a degree from the Massachusetts Institute of Technology, Semyonov worked for a Soviet trading company based in New York. But that was just a cover for his real work. Semyonov was a secret agent for the Soviet intelligence agency, the KGB.

After picking up materials from Gold, Sam would head for the Soviet consulate, a three-story building in Manhattan. He climbed past the first two floors, where Soviet clerks did normal consulate work, like helping Soviet citizens get travel visas.

Then, making sure no one was in the hall, he would take out a key, unlock a door on the third floor, and enter the secret New York City headquarters of the KGB. It was a large, open room with desks and metal shutters on the windows and a portrait of the Soviet dictator Joseph Stalin gazing down. Semyonov handed his documents to another agent and quickly left the building.

The stolen information was translated into secret code and sent by telegram to KGB headquarters in Moscow.

# RAPID RUPTURE

SEMYON SEMYONOV'S engineering job gave him a legitimate reason to be in the United States. But that didn't make him any less suspect in the eyes of the FBI. American agents had no evidence that Semyonov was a spy, but they knew *some* Soviets living in the United States were spies. They figured Semyonov might be one of them. They followed him on the street, into restaurants, onto the subway.

Semyonov and a KGB colleague named Alexander Feklisov began working together to try to shake the FBI. "We often tailed each other on our way to secret meetings," recalled Feklisov, "to make sure we were not being followed."

If they weren't sure whether they were being watched, they had several strategies ready. "It was a good test to enter a bar or a store," explained Feklisov, "because one of the agents had to run inside to make sure no rendezvous was in progress." You could also hop on a bus, which would force the FBI agent to tip his hand by getting on also.

Years later, Feklisov was asked whether he and Semyonov felt guilty about stealing technology from the Americans. After all, soon after Germany attacked the Soviet Union, the United States began shipping planes, tanks, cannons, and food to the desperate Soviets.

But Feklisov and Semyonov held a view that was common among Russians at the time. Yes, the United States was helping the Soviet Union—but not out of the kindness of its heart. The United States and Soviet Union had never been friendly, and nothing had really changed. America's help to the Soviets was the product of cold logic. The Soviet Union was battling Germany. America badly wanted to see Germany beaten. So Americans were glad to have the Soviets do the bloody work of fighting Hitler.

"When you know you are being taken advantage of," Feklisov said, "you have every right to be clever."

MEANWHILE, THE FBI was watching Americans, too.

One night, early in the war, Robert Oppenheimer drove to the home of a friend and fellow Berkeley professor, Haakon Chevalier. Oppenheimer parked in the street and walked to Chevalier's front door.

Watching from down the block were two agents of the FBI. The agents knew that Chevalier was a member of the Communist Party. They knew he hosted political discussion groups. It wasn't illegal to be a Communist. But it seemed likely that American Communists might feel allegiance to the Soviet Union. Could a citizen be a Communist *and* a loyal American at the same time? The FBI thought not. So agents watched known Communists like Chevalier, paying special attention to their friends and associates.

In 1941, the FBI opened a file on Robert Oppenheimer.

OPPENHEIMER CONTINUED TO TEACH PHYSICS, but he felt restless, like he should be doing something to help stop Hitler. "Many of the men I had known went off to work on radar and other aspects of military research," he later said. "I was not without envy of them."

The war news got worse and worse. Germany formed an alliance with Japan, which had a powerful military of its own, and dreams of building an empire in Asia. While Hitler's forces overran Europe, Japan was on the attack in China and Southeast Asia.

The United States cut off oil exports to Japan. This left Japan—a nation with few natural resources—with barely enough fuel to survive another year. President Roosevelt hoped Japanese leaders would be convinced to stop their armies from advancing further. Instead, Japan became even *more* determined to conquer new territory, new sources of raw materials—even if this meant taking on the United States.

With so many crises competing for Roosevelt's attention, the Uranium Committee continued to just crawl along. Frustrated by the slow pace of progress, physicist and U-Committee member Ernest Lawrence urged the committee to bring in some fresh talent. He suggested starting with a colleague of his at Berkeley, Robert Oppenheimer.

In October 1941, Oppenheimer attended his first meeting of the Uranium Committee. The members discussed the largest man-made explosion in history to that point—in 1917, in Halifax Harbor, Canada, a ship packed with millions of pounds of bombs and ammunition caught fire and blew up. The blast flattened buildings a mile in all directions and killed at least 2,000 people. It sent a 1,000-pound anchor soaring two miles through the air.

One uranium bomb, small enough to fit in a plane, could pack about ten times that power.

The meeting changed Oppenheimer's life. From that moment on, he knew he'd found his role in what was becoming a global showdown. "I spent some time in preliminary calculations about the construction and performance of atomic bombs," he said, "and became increasingly excited about the prospects."

31

TWO MONTHS LATER, at the U.S. military base at Pearl Harbor, Hawaii, an army sergeant named Joseph Pesek woke up early. It was December 7, a Sunday. Pesek was looking forward to a few hours of leave.

"After breakfast, I headed for the bus stop to wait for the 8:05 bus to take me to Honolulu where I was to play golf," he said. "While sitting there on a bench, I noticed a large flight of aircraft approaching from the northwest."

As the planes neared land, Pesek saw them start a sudden dive toward the harbor, where most of the U.S. Navy's Pacific Fleet was docked. *Some kind of training exercise,* he figured.

Standing on the deck of the battleship USS *Arizona*, a sailor named George Phraner had the same thought. First he heard the buzz of airplane engines. Then he saw the planes drop out of the clouds.

"It didn't mean anything to us," he remembered, "until a large group of planes came near the ship and we could see for the first time the rising sun emblem on the plane wings." This red sun was the symbol of Japan—the Japanese were attacking Pearl Harbor.

Bombs began smacking the water, smashing into ships, blasting planes parked on the ground, igniting fires everywhere.

"Air raid! Air raid!" shouted a voice over the ship's loudspeakers. "This is a real attack, real planes, real bombs!"

Phraner dashed below to get ammunition for his gun crew. He was lifting a ninety-pound case when he heard a "deafening roar" and felt the entire ship rock violently.

The lights went out, the cabin filled with smoke. The metal walls were heating up as Phraner felt his way to the ladder leading up to the deck. He started climbing.

"I was nauseated by the smell of burning flesh, which turned out to be my own as I climbed up the hot ladder," he said. "A quick glance around revealed nothing in the darkness—but the moaning and sounds of falling bodies."

When he finally tumbled onto the deck, Phraner saw broken bodies and body parts and pooling blood and flames everywhere. The ship was going down fast. He leaped over the side and struggled toward shore, splashing through water covered with blotches of burning black oil.

THE JAPANESE ATTACK on Pearl Harbor destroyed or damaged 18 warships and nearly 350 planes. More than 1,110 crew members went down with the *Arizona*. A total of 2,390 American soldiers and sailors were killed.

"You gave the right declaration of war!" Adolf Hitler raved to the Japanese ambassador in Berlin. "This method is the only proper one."

Roosevelt was having lunch in the White House when he got the news. "They caught our ships like lame ducks!" Roosevelt shouted, pounding his desk. "They caught our planes on the ground, by God, on the ground!"

As radio and newspapers spread the story, the mood in America shifted quickly from shock to fury to vows of revenge. Roosevelt asked Congress for an immediate declaration of war on Japan, and got it.

"No matter how long it may take us to overcome this premeditated invasion," Roosevelt declared, "the American people in their righteous might will win through to absolute victory."

Hitler responded by declaring war on the United States. The sides were set for the biggest and deadliest war in history—the United States, Great Britain, and the Soviet Union led the Allied Powers against the Axis Powers of Germany, Japan, and Italy.

At stake, the future of the world.


PEARL HARBOR was a turning point for Robert Oppenheimer, too. From that moment on, he decided to forget about politics and discussion groups. He decided to pour all his energy into beating Hitler in the race for the atomic bomb.

"Just a few weeks after Pearl Harbor, I received a phone call from Oppie," recalled a young physicist named Robert Serber. "He said he was in Chicago and wanted to come down and talk with me about something."

A former student of Oppenheimer's, Serber was teaching at the University

33

of Illinois in Urbana. He had no idea why Oppenheimer would want to see him. Oppenheimer drove to the campus and found Serber. They walked out of town and into the cornfields.

When they were alone in the fields, Oppenheimer explained his work with the Uranium Committee. He told Serber he was about to be placed in charge of "fast-neutron research"—the study of speeding neutrons and fission. His ominous official title would be "Coordinator of Rapid Rupture." He wanted Serber in Berkeley as his assistant.

Serber and his wife packed up their car, drove west, and moved into the apartment above Oppenheimer's garage. At Oppenheimer's office on the Berkeley campus, they began designing the atomic bomb.

The work was thrilling—and frightening. There was no way to know what German scientists were up to, or how far ahead they might already be. Oppenheimer knew that this was a duel the United States could not afford to lose.

"We were aware," he said of the Germans, "of what it might mean if they beat us to the draw."

# NORWAY CONNECTION

**LUCKILY FOR OPPENHEIMER**, he was not in the fight alone. One of his most valuable allies would be a man he didn't know, and would never meet—a twenty-nine-year-old Norwegian named Knut Haukelid.

Haukelid had dark wavy hair and a broad, muscular body toughened by years of hiking and skiing. When the Germans conquered Norway in 1940, Haukelid and a few friends had refused to admit defeat. They strapped guns to their backs and skied deep into the roadless forests and mountains. "There was only one thought in our heads," he later said. "Hitler and his gang should be thrown back into the sea."

While crossing a lake on a ferry boat, they found an outlet for their rage. Standing on deck, leaning casually on the rail, was a Norwegian man in a Nazi uniform—some Norwegians were Nazi sympathizers who aided the invading army.

After waiting until the boat was about 300 yards from shore, Haukelid gestured for his friends to follow. He walked up to the Nazi.

"Heil Hitler!" Haukelid said, using the typical Nazi greeting.

"Heil Hitler!" the man said, reaching out to shake hands.

As Haukelid grasped the man's hand, his friends grabbed the Nazi, lifted him over the rail, and dropped him into the lake.

The only thing that floated was his hat.

OVER THE FOLLOWING YEAR, Knut Haukelid found a more organized and effective way to fight the Germans. He joined one of the secret resistance groups that were forming all over Norway. He began working as a radio operator and spy.

"No one—not even those nearest to us—could know what was going on," he said. Anyone caught resisting the German occupation was instantly shot. "In the daytime we had to do our ordinary work," he explained. "We were dropping with fatigue. What kept us going was a growing pride in doing *something*, little as it was, against the hated invaders."

By day, Haukelid worked at a German-controlled submarine base. After dark, he gathered his radio equipment, snuck out of town on a bicycle, and searched for a remote electrical pole. He climbed the wooden pole, tapped into the electrical wires, powered up his radio, and sent information on German military movements to British intelligence officers in London.

"We had many wild plans in those days," Haukelid remembered. Hoping to deal the Nazis a more direct blow, he and his friends concocted a plot to kidnap Vidkun Quisling, leader of the Norwegian Nazis. The plan was to knock Quisling unconscious, drive him into the mountains, call Britain for a plane, fly him to London, and put him on display in a cage.

Haukelid found out where Quisling was staying in Oslo. He rented a room across the hall, contacted a fellow resistance fighter who worked for the telephone company, and arranged to listen in on Quisling's phone line. "The plan was to find out when he ordered a car," Haukelid said, "so that we could pick him up in one of ours." Haukelid's men dressed in stolen Nazi uniforms, so Quisling wouldn't be suspicious until it was too late.

But before they could pull the trigger on the operation, German intelligence uncovered Haukelid's crew of radio operators. Some of the men were thrown into concentration camps. Haukelid escaped into the mountains. He managed to get across the border to Sweden by bicycle and traveled from there, by plane, to Great Britain.

Haukelid was safe, but all he could think about was getting back home to continue the fight. He would get his wish, and more. What Haukelid did not yet know was that a remote factory perched on the side of a cliff in Norway was the key to Germany's top-secret atomic bomb project. Someone had to put that factory out of operation. And he was about to get the job.

BACK IN NORWAY, Hitler's secret police force, the Gestapo, got Haukelid's name and stormed his family's house. They ransacked the place for evidence of his undercover work. A Gestapo officer cornered his mother, demanding information.

She wouldn't talk.

A furious S. W. Fehmer, chief of Gestapo intelligence in Norway, stepped forward and ordered her to tell him where Haukelid had gone.

"He is in the mountains," she responded.

"No!" shouted Fehmer. "He is in Britain. Our contact in Sweden tells us that he has been taken across the North Sea in a fighter plane. And what do you think he is doing there?"

Haukelid's mother had no idea. But she knew her son. She suspected it would be something big.

Staring Fehmer straight in the eyes, she said. "You will find out when he comes back."

# ENORMOZ

EARLY IN 1942, a young Soviet physicist named Georgi Flerov sat in the library of a military base in southwestern Russia, flipping through a tall stack of physics journals from the United States. When the Germans invaded, Flerov had put his studies aside to serve in the Soviet air force. But he couldn't stop thinking about fission. So when he had a free moment, he snuck off to the library to read of the newest discoveries.

"I hoped to look through the latest papers on the fission of uranium," he said. Up until that point, American physics magazines had been filled with articles on new experiments and theories about fission.

Suddenly there was nothing.

"This silence is not the result of an absence of research," Flerov warned his government. "In a word, the seal of silence has been imposed, and this is the best proof of the vigorous work that is going on now abroad."

Flerov guessed right. The work being done by Oppenheimer and others on the Uranium Committee was top secret. The Soviet Union and the United

States were allies in World War II. But that's because they were fighting common enemies—not because they liked each other.

Even more distressing to Flerov was the idea of a German atomic bomb. Germany had "first-class scientists," he said, "and significant supplies of uranium ore." If Hitler got his hands on atomic bombs, that would be the end of the Soviet Union.

To Soviet physicists like Flerov, this made it vitally important that the Soviet Union develop its own atomic bomb. But the war was making this impossible. Russian forces stopped the German advance just short of Moscow, but the two massive armies were still slugging it out along a battlefront stretching 1,500 miles from north to south. Soviet scientists had to abandon fission experiments to work instead on weapons that could be used right away.

The message to Soviet leaders was clear. If the Soviets were going to get an atomic bomb any time in the near future, they were going to have to steal it.

THIS WAS A JOB FOR THE KGB.

In March 1942, Semyon Semyonov and his fellow KGB agents in New York got a coded telegram from Moscow headquarters explaining the task. "Germany and the USA are frantically working to obtain uranium," Moscow warned, "and use it as an explosive to make bombs of enormous destructive power, and to all appearances, this problem is quite close to practical solution. It is essential that we take up this problem in all seriousness."

Soviet spies in American cities began working on what they called "agent cultivation." In tradecraft, "cultivation" means gathering information on a potential source, feeling him out to see if he might be convinced to cooperate. This was a tough task, since Soviet agents didn't know which American scientists were working on the atomic bomb.

Suddenly, in late March, the KGB got a break. One night, on the New

York City subway, a KGB courier named Zalmond Franklin ran into an old friend, Clarence Hiskey. Hiskey was a chemist and professor at Columbia University. The two had gone to college together in the 1930s. Both had been sympathetic to the Soviet Union, and members of the Communist Party.

The friends went to dinner and talked over old times. "He decided to walk me to the subway," Franklin reported to his KGB contact. "Our conversation on the way is what leads to the reason for this report."

As they strolled, Hiskey shocked Franklin by saying: "Imagine a bomb dropped in the center of this city, which would destroy the entire city."

Franklin laughed.

"There is such a bomb," Hiskey blurted out. "I'm working on it."

Trying to appear only casually interested, Franklin asked for a few more details.

Hiskey explained that he and other scientists were "working with desperate haste" to build an atomic bomb. It would be the most powerful weapon ever produced. The Germans, he added, were probably "far ahead on the bomb."

Then, after this burst of top-secret information, Hiskey went silent.

"Hiskey was sorry he told me about this," Franklin reported, "and swore me to silence."

Vasily Zarubin, the top KGB agent in New York City, telegraphed Franklin's report to headquarters in Moscow. Moscow responded quickly, telling Zarubin the information "is of great interest to us," and attaching a long list of technical questions about fission and bomb making. Zarubin gave the list to Franklin, ordering Franklin to get answers from his friend.

Franklin went to Hiskey's apartment but faced a major obstacle: Hiskey's wife was there. Franklin was under strict KGB orders not to discuss the subject of atomic bombs in front of anyone but Hiskey.

The three sat down to dinner. "At no time did Clarence bring up the subject of his work," Franklin reported, "and following instructions, I did not mention the subject." After the meal, Franklin tried to get Hiskey alone, with no success. "His wife was present the entire evening," explained Franklin.

That proved to be Franklin's one and only chance. Hiskey was soon transferred to the University of Chicago. When a Soviet agent in Chicago made contact with Hiskey, the meeting was observed by FBI agents. The FBI informed the U.S. Army that Hiskey had been spotted with a suspected Soviet agent. Hiskey suddenly found himself drafted into the army and shipped to a remote military base in the Northwest Territories of Canada—far from atomic bomb secrets.

Hiskey was never given an explanation. He knew better than to ask for one.

HISKEY'S STORY illustrates just how hard it was for Soviet spies to get at American secrets. "It was difficult because we always felt we were under FBI surveillance," said KGB agent Alexander Feklisov. "From the moment I arrived in New York, I was always shadowed as soon as I stepped outside."

Still, the Soviets were absolutely determined to steal the bomb. It was such a high priority, they code named the project "Enormoz"—Russian for "enormous."

But Enormoz could go nowhere until the KGB got a reliable source *inside* the American bomb project. With this goal in mind, Moscow headquarters made up a list of top American scientists to target for cultivation. "Of the leads we have," Moscow informed its agents in the United States, "we should consider it essential to cultivate the following people."

Then came the names. The people on the list were all top scientists the Soviets suspected might be in on the bomb work. They were all known to have been sympathetic to communism before the war.

The first name on the list was Robert Oppenheimer.

THE CHICAGO
PILE TEAM

KLAUS FUCHS
Manhattan
Project
physicist; spy

CARL EIFLER
U.S. Army
officer;
OSS operative

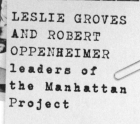

LESLIE GROVES
AND ROBERT
OPPENHEIMER
leaders of
the Manhattan
Project

JENS POULSSON
Norwegian
resistance
fighter

# PART 2: CHAIN REACTIONS

# ON THE CLIFF

**ON THE MORNING OF JUNE 19, 1942,** President Franklin Roosevelt sat in the driver's seat of his Ford convertible, parked beside an airstrip in Hyde Park, New York. He watched a small U.S. Army plane descend toward the runway. The plane hit the ground hard, bounced several times, and rattled to a stop.

The plane door opened, and out hopped Winston Churchill, prime minister of Great Britain, a fat cigar in his hand. Roosevelt smiled and waved. Churchill walked over to the car and got into the passenger seat. The two leaders shook hands warmly. Then Roosevelt gunned his car engine and sped off.

"He took me to the majestic bluffs over the Hudson River on which Hyde Park, his family home, stands," Churchill remembered. But as the car raced along the edge of the cliff, the prime minister had a tough time keeping his mind on the gorgeous view. He kept glancing over at the American,

*President Franklin Delano Roosevelt takes Prime Minister Winston Churchill for a drive in Hyde Park, New York, during a later visit by the prime minister, September 3, 1943.*

wondering how exactly the man was controlling the vehicle. Roosevelt had had polio as a young man and had lost the use of his legs.

Roosevelt saw the worry on his friend's face. He explained that he'd had this car specially rigged, allowing him to work the gas, clutch, and brakes with his hands—while also steering, of course. Churchill was impressed, but still terrified. Smiling, Roosevelt assured Churchill his arms were more than strong enough to do the job.

"He invited me to feel his biceps," Churchill recalled, "saying that a famous prize-fighter had envied them. This was reassuring."

As Roosevelt drove, the two men began talking over the state of the war. "And though I was careful not to take his attention off the driving," Churchill said, "we made more progress than we might have done in a formal conference."

LATER THAT DAY the conversation continued in a small office inside Roosevelt's family mansion. They focused on the subject Churchill called "overwhelmingly the most important"—the race to build an atomic bomb. British and American scientists were both exploring the science. Both had come to the conclusion that a fission bomb was technically possible.

"I strongly urged that we should at once pool all our information, work together on equal terms, and share the results, if any, equally between us," Churchill said of the meeting.

Roosevelt agreed. The project would be enormously expensive, they knew, and it would mean pulling top scientists off other high-priority weapons projects. It was worth the risk, they decided. With Britain still under attack from German bombers, they agreed the actual work of building a bomb would be done in America.

There had been a lot of talk so far, and some research. Now it was time for action. "We both felt painfully the dangers of doing nothing," Churchill recalled. "What if the enemy should get an atomic bomb before we did!"

• • •

Three months later, a six foot, two-hundred-fifty-pound army colonel named Leslie Groves was walking down the hallway of a congressional office building on Capitol Hill, in Washington, D.C. Groves had one thing on his mind: getting out of Washington. "I was," he later said, "like every other regular officer, extremely eager for service abroad as a commander of combat troops."

When he saw General Brehon Somervell walking toward him, Groves stopped. The men were alone in the hall.

"The secretary of war has selected you for a very important assignment," Somervell told Groves. "The president has approved the selection."

"Where?" asked Groves.

"Washington."

"I don't want to stay in Washington."

"If you do the job right, it will win the war."

Groves felt his heart sink. He'd heard rumors about a project to build some kind of super-bomb. He was not impressed.

"Oh," he sighed. "*That* thing."

"You can do it," Somervell assured him. "If it can be done."

Forty-six-year-old Leslie Groves was an engineer by training. He'd just finished managing the construction of the Pentagon, the biggest office building in the world. Groves brought the job in on time and on budget. As a reward he was put in charge of the atomic bomb project.

"My initial reaction was one of extreme disappointment," he confessed.

Groves was a big man, with a big personality—loud, bossy, demanding, quick to criticize. "He had no hesitation in letting others know of his own high opinion of himself," said one former staff member.

Another put it simply: "Groves is the biggest S.O.B. I have ever worked for."

And yet everyone agreed that to lead a huge project, involving the juggling of dozens of complex tasks, Groves was the right choice.

47

"If I can't do the job," said Groves, "no one man can."

In meetings over the next few days, Groves was given the complete picture. Roosevelt wanted the U.S. Army to take over the atomic bomb project—code named the Manhattan Project, because its first offices were located in Manhattan. It was Groves's job to make sure the bomb got built quickly, and in complete secrecy. Groves was promoted to general and took command of the Manhattan Project on September 18, 1942.

"I was not happy with the information," Groves grumbled about what he'd learned so far. "In fact, I was horrified. It seemed as if the whole endeavor was founded on possibilities rather than probabilities. Of theory there was a great deal, of proven knowledge not much."

When Groves met with Uranium Committee members in Chicago, they told him it would take somewhere between ten and one thousand pounds of uranium to make an atomic bomb. The wide range infuriated Groves. It would be like trying to plan a wedding, he shouted, and telling the caterer, "We don't know how many guests are coming—maybe somewhere between ten and a thousand—but see to it that you have the right amount of food for them!"

Groves knew he could handle the planning and logistics. The problem was, he was going to have to rely on physicists to figure out how to build the bomb. Groves needed to quickly gather a team of the best scientists in the country— and he needed to pick someone to lead it.

ROBERT OPPENHEIMER WANTED THE JOB.

Oppenheimer first met Groves on October 8, on the Berkeley campus. Groves was traveling around the country, meeting people who'd been working on the Uranium Committee. He and Oppenheimer chatted at lunch, then Oppenheimer invited Groves back to his office for a longer talk.

Oppenheimer laid out his vision for getting the bomb built. Work was being done at universities all over the country, he told Groves. Scientists were wasting time doing the same things on different campuses. And, because of security worries, they weren't allowed to share information over the phone or by mail. That had to end.

"A major change was called for in the work on the bomb itself," Oppenheimer later explained. "We needed a central laboratory devoted wholly to this purpose, where people could talk freely with each other."

Groves was impressed. "He's a genius, a real genius," Groves told a reporter years later. "Why, Oppenheimer knows about everything. He can talk to you about anything you bring up. Well, not exactly, I guess there are a few things he doesn't know about. He doesn't know anything about sports."

Groves also liked the fact that Oppenheimer had been born in the United States. Most of the top physicists in the country were from Europe. That made it nearly impossible to carefully check their backgrounds, to make sure they could be trusted with American secrets.

But Oppenheimer presented problems, too. "No one with whom I talked showed any great enthusiasm about Oppenheimer as a possible director of the project," Groves lamented. First of all, he was a famously absent-minded scientist, living in an abstract world of ideas and numbers. Could he really be a disciplined, focused team leader? Probably not, said most who knew him.

"He had, after all, no experience in directing a large group of people," said the German-born physicist Hans Bethe. A Berkeley colleague put it more bluntly: "He couldn't run a hamburger stand."

Groves had a gut feeling Oppenheimer could rise to the challenge. The more he thought about it—and the more potential candidates he met—the more convinced he became that he wanted Oppenheimer. But there was a bigger problem.

Oppenheimer couldn't work on the Manhattan Project until he got security clearance from the army. Thanks to a report from the FBI, army intelligence officers knew all about Oppenheimer's past associations with Communists. Oppenheimer shouldn't be allowed anywhere near the most dangerous secret in the world, argued the FBI, because he might leak the information to his Communist friends, and from there, to the Soviet Union.

Oppenheimer insisted he was a loyal American. He swore he'd never actually joined the Communist Party and that, in any case, his interest in Communism was a thing of the past.

Groves believed him. FBI agents and army intelligence officers did not.

Groves made the call. "It is desired that clearance be issued for the employment of Robert Oppenheimer without delay," ordered Groves. "He is absolutely essential to the project."

Oppenheimer was given an army physical—and failed. Nearly six feet tall, he weighed just 128 pounds. His chain smoking gave him a chronic cough, causing army doctors to declare him "permanently incapacitated for active service." Again, Groves pulled rank. He ordered the doctors to make Oppenheimer eligible for active duty.

Oppenheimer wasn't fit to be a soldier, Groves acknowledged. But he just might be able to win the war.

# INTERNATIONAL
# GANGSTER SCHOOL

**WHEN KNUT HAUKELID** stepped off the train in London, he was met immediately by two British officers. They knew Haukelid had been battling the Germans in Norway and had barely gotten out alive. They had special orders for him.

Haukelid climbed into a car with the British officers, and they drove though a city battered by German bombs. "Ruined houses and bombed blocks of flats made gaps in the vista," remembered Haukelid. "One area in the heart of the city was just a desert of ruins. Only the street remained, running empty and purposeless between heaps of fallen masonry."

Haukelid was taken to meet with an officer of the Special Operations Executive. The S.O.E. was a secret British organization tasked with carrying out acts of sabotage behind enemy lines all over Europe.

The S.O.E. officer suggested that perhaps Haukelid would be interested in returning to Norway on a secret mission.

"Can I have more instruction in the use of weapons?" Haukelid asked.

"Yes," said the officer. "There's a section which is just the thing for you."

Haukelid was sent to a remote spot in the south of England and enrolled in Special Training School No. 3. The Germans, who'd heard rumors about the place, called it "International Gangster School."

"From a purely practical standpoint," Haukelid conceded, "they were undoubtedly right."

"HERE I FOUND nearly thirty Norwegian boys from all parts of the country," Haukelid said of Special Training School No. 3. The men all had one goal in mind: to get back home and liberate their country from the Germans.

"This is the only friend you can rely on," said their instructor, holding up a pistol. "Treat him properly, and he'll take care of you."

The men were taught to pick locks, crack safes, set booby traps, and use poison. They were taught to kill with their hands and feet.

"Never give a man a chance," the instructor told them. "If you've got him down, kick him to death."

Haukelid and his class were then transferred to Scotland, where they began parachute school. To get back into Norway, they'd have to be dropped by plane—in the dark. They practiced by jumping out of hot air balloons at night.

"It was not at all like jumping from a plane," explained Claus Helberg, one of Haukelid's fellow students. "It takes about five seconds for the chute to open, and since you can't see how close you are to earth, you keep wondering, 'Will I hit before it opens?' Everything is quiet, it's dark, and as you fall you get this terrifying sense of the increasing velocity of your descent from the sound of the air rushing through your clothing."

When the parachutes finally opened, the men floated toward the ground, still unable to see anything around them. But they could hear the instructors below, joking about which of the "poor bastards" would be the first to break his legs.

The S.O.E. picked five of the best men for a special mission. Haukelid was part of the team, until an accident put him out of action. "During a field exercise," he remembered, "I stumbled with a loaded pistol in my hand, and put a bullet through the sole of my foot."

Haukelid lay in the hospital, cursing his stupid mistake. The other four men were taken to London to prepare for the job.

ONLY JENS POULSSON, the leader of this small Norwegian team, was given a full briefing. At S.O.E. offices in London, the twenty-four-year-old Poulsson puffed on his pipe while a British colonel named John Wilson announced the target of the secret mission: the Vemork power plant, built into the side of a mountain near the town of Rjukan, Norway.

Poulsson tapped ashes from his pipe into the palm of his hand. "Interesting," he said.

Rjukan was Poulsson's hometown. He'd spent his childhood climbing and skiing in the nearby mountains.

Vemork was a vital target, Wilson explained, because it was the only plant in the world capable of producing large quantities of "heavy water." He gave Poulsson the basic chemistry: a molecule of water is made up of two atoms of hydrogen and one atom of oxygen. A normal hydrogen atom has a nucleus with just one proton and no neutrons. But some hydrogen atoms have one proton *and* one neutron. The neutron makes the hydrogen atom heavier. When these heavier hydrogen atoms join with oxygen to form water, the result is heavy water—it's about 10 percent heavier than regular water. Heavy water occurs naturally in very small quantities, and it's perfectly harmless.

Except for one thing: It was a key ingredient in the German atomic bomb program.

Wilson didn't explain to Poulsson *why* German physicists needed heavy water. All Poulsson needed to know was that the Germans had rapidly increased production of heavy water at Vemork since taking over Norway. This had to be stopped.

"The Germans could destroy all of London if they succeed," Wilson said.

"I didn't really believe him," Poulsson later admitted. "In those days, no one thought in terms of one bomb destroying a whole city."

But the young Norwegian had his orders.

THE PLAN WAS FOR POULSSON'S TEAM to parachute onto Norway's Hardanger Plateau, a 3,500-square-mile wilderness of mountains, marshes, and lakes. On the plateau, the team would set up camp, scout routes to the target, radio weather reports back to Britain, and light up a landing strip on the edge of a frozen lake. When everything was ready, thirty-four British commandos would fly in on gliders, land, and set out for the plant. The Norwegians would lead the way and do everything possible to help the British soldiers demolish key parts of Vemork.

The S.O.E. gave Poulsson's team cash, and the men went from store to store in London buying winter clothing, warm sleeping bags, tents, and compasses. Unable to find Norwegian-made skis and boots, they special-ordered them from Iceland.

On a clear, cold night in late October 1942, the men climbed into a British bomber. The plane flew over the North Sea to Norway. When the pilot reached the Hardanger Plateau, the Norwegians heard the engines slowing as the plane's altitude dropped quickly from 10,000 to 1,000 feet. In the bright moonlight, Poulsson and his men could just make out the shapes of dark rocks sticking up from the snowy ground.

"Action stations!" the British dispatcher shouted.

The Norwegians lined up near the hatch in the bottom of the plane. They'd been taught to jump in quick succession, no more than one second between men—any longer than that and they'd land too far apart to find each other in the dark.

Poulsson sat over the hole, his legs dangling in the icy air.

The dispatcher shouted, "Number one, go!"

# GLIDERS DOWN

**POULSSON JUMPED,** followed quickly by Knut Haugland, Arne Kjelstrup, and Claus Helberg.

"The wind tore and pulled at me as I fell," remembered Helberg. "Suddenly the parachute filled with air and stiffened; there was a violent jerk as it opened wide above me."

In the sky around him, Helberg could see the other men, along with the supply crates the British crew had tossed out of the plane behind them. "I found myself floating slowly down toward the ground," Helberg recalled, "with all our equipment, twelve huge containers, floating down through the moonlight behind us, and the plane disappearing westwards."

Helberg hit the ground hard, but safely. He sat in the deep snow, thinking, "And here we are, in Norway, cold and inhospitable, but marvelous all the same."

The men gathered and unrolled their sleeping bags. At sunrise they could begin looking for the supply crates. For now, nothing more could be done.

Poulsson took out his pipe and filled it with tobacco. "It's time I told you the truth," he said.

He lit a match and looked at the men. To prevent word of the secret mission from leaking out, he explained, they'd been told they were coming to Norway to train other resistance fighters.

"That was just a cover story," Poulsson now informed them, touching the match flame to his pipe. "We're here on a far more vital assignment—to help destroy the heavy water factory at Vemork."

He gave them the details and told them about the British commandos who'd be coming in by plane. The operation would take place during the next full moon. "We have four weeks to reconnoiter the plant, get information on the German guards, and check on the landing site."

None of the team members made any objection to what—for them—was a radical change in plans.

"Goodnight," Poulsson said.

IN THE MORNING the men took out their maps and compasses, checked nearby landmarks . . . and realized the British plane had badly missed the intended drop target. They were at least 65 mountainous miles from the glider landing site. All expert skiers, they weren't worried about the distance. But they would be carrying more than six hundred pounds of weapons and supplies, and they could expect no help along the way. "We had been told to make no outside contacts except in the gravest emergency," Poulsson said. "It was important that we avoid being seen by anyone."

The twelve equipment crates were scattered in the deep snow, and it took the men two days to find them. They divided the stuff into eight loads of about seventy pounds each, figuring it would be foolish to try to carry more over the rough terrain ahead. Finally, they put on their boots and skis and set off.

Progress was slow, since they each had to handle two seventy-pound loads. They would ski a set distance with one load, put it down, return to the starting point, pick up the second load, and make the trip again. Making things worse, it had been a relatively mild autumn on the Hardanger Plateau. The snow was wet and sticky, the ice on the lakes still thin—forcing them to take the long way around the water. The men reminded each other of an old Norwegian saying: "A man who is a man goes on until he can go no further—and then goes twice as far."

The team had enough food for thirty days, but they were burning calories so quickly, they were constantly ravenous. What saved them was that along the way they found several summer cabins, abandoned for the winter. Inside they scrounged a few cans of food, a few handfuls of flour. In one cabin they found, sitting on the table, a frozen lump of unidentified meat. They chopped it up with an axe, dropped the pieces into a pot with snow, and set the pot over a fire.

"We ate our fill for the first time since our arrival," Poulsson said.

On November 9, after three grueling weeks on the plateau, Poulsson and the team finally reached their assigned base near the glider landing site. The men found a thin-walled cabin nearby, stumbled inside, built a fire, and felt lucky to find some food. "We made fish soup," Poulsson said, "good soup, too—out of dog's food."

The next step was to contact London. With wind whipping snow crystals into his face, Knut Haugland set up his radio antenna on the roof of the cabin. He climbed down, slammed the door behind him, dove into his sleeping bag on the floor, and pulled the radio close. As snow blew in through cracks in the wall, Haugland tapped out a coded message: the team was intact and healthy, and would now begin scouting the target area and preparing the landing site.

The message was received in London, but it didn't sound right. Telegraph messages were sent using Morse code, in which each letter of the alphabet is represented by a certain combination of long and short sounds. Every telegraph operator has what's known as an "operator's fingerprint"—each person taps out the sounds slightly differently. British intelligence had Haugland's fingerprints on file. This new message was not a match. What they didn't

57

take into account was that Haugland's fingers were frozen stiff when he sent the most recent message.

Concerned they might actually be in contact with German agents, the British sent Haugland a prearranged security question—something only he could answer: "What did you see walking down the Strand in the early hours of January 1, 1941?"

Haugland's blue fingers tapped back, "Three pink elephants."

Poulsson's team was all right, the British knew. The plan could proceed.

ON A DRIZZLY AFTERNOON TEN DAYS LATER, thirty-four British commandos gathered on an airfield in Scotland. They divided into groups of seventeen, and each group climbed into a glider. These were super-light wooden planes, specially made for Britain's Royal Air Force. They had no engines, which meant they could fly silently. Perfect for making an unnoticed approach into enemy territory.

Of course, the gliders couldn't take off by themselves. Each was attached by a rope to a Halifax bomber—the bombers took off, towing the gliders behind them. The planes headed east across the water as the sun set.

On the ground in Norway, Poulsson and his team found the best possible landing spot and set up lights along a strip of land. "It was overcast," Poulsson said, "but the moon was full."

At 11:00 p.m., the Norwegians heard the hum of engines in the thick clouds above. But they couldn't see the planes, and the pilots couldn't see the landing lights.

As one of the bomber pilots was turning around to make another run over the target area, the rope pulling the glider snapped. The glider pilot felt his plane descending. He couldn't see even a few feet in any direction, and—with no engines—had no way to keep the plane in the air for long. The glider slammed into a snowy hillside. Eight men were killed instantly. Of the survivors, four had broken bones; the other five just minor injuries.

Two of the men who were able to walk made it to a nearby farmhouse and convinced the owner to call a doctor. The doctor agreed to come, but, before leaving, alerted the Gestapo of the crash. The Germans arrived to search the plane and crash site. They found weapons, snowshoes, Norwegian currency, radio transmitters, and a map with Vemork circled in blue ink.

The Germans loaded the four badly injured men into a truck. By the accepted rules of war, the British soldiers should have been treated as prisoners of war. Instead, the Germans poisoned them and dropped their bodies into the sea. The other five were taken to a concentration camp and interrogated by the Gestapo. They refused to give more than their name, rank, and service number. German soldiers blindfolded and handcuffed the prisoners and shot them in the head.

The second glider's story was similar. It lost its way in the fog and crash-landed, killing several of the crew. The Germans quickly found the wreck, questioned survivors, then shot them and dumped them in a ditch.

The next night Poulsson's team got the news from London. "The glider disaster was a hard blow," he later said. "It was sad and bitter."

Thirty-four British soldiers were dead, and nothing had been accomplished. Worse than nothing, because now the Germans knew that the Allies considered Vemork a high-priority target. British intelligence soon learned that German commanders had assigned extra soldiers to guard Vemork, night and day. They had begun placing land mines around the plant.

Meanwhile, the plant continued pumping out heavy water, which was piped into barrels and shipped to Germany. This had to be stopped, no matter the risks. Colonel Wilson contacted the Norwegian volunteers who were still training in Scotland.

He told them: "Stand by for a particularly dangerous enterprise."

59

# QUIET FELLOW

ONE AFTERNOON IN LATE 1942, a dark-haired woman in her mid-thirties rode a bicycle along a country lane near the English town of Banbury. She pulled to the side of the path, got off the bicycle, and leaned it against a tree.

She had not been waiting long when she saw a tall man in a suit approaching. He was about thirty, pale and thin, with glasses. The man and woman exchanged a few words and began walking arm in arm down the lane. "It was pleasant just to have a conversation with so sensitive and intelligent a comrade and scientist," the woman later said. "We spoke of books, films, and current affairs."

To any viewer, they looked like close friends out for a little stroll. Actually, it was the first time they'd ever met.

After about half an hour, the man handed the woman an envelope. She climbed back on her bicycle and peddled toward her small cottage in the nearby town of Oxford, where she was known as "Mrs. Brewer," a refugee from Germany and mother of two.

In fact, her name was Ruth Werner, and she was a spy for the KGB. A

German-born Communist trained in tradecraft in Moscow, Werner had spent the 1930s working as a Soviet secret agent in China and Switzerland. She'd been sent to Britain in 1941, charged with setting up a network of informants and sending useful intelligence to the Soviet Union.

It was illegal in wartime Britain for private citizens to use radio transmitters, so Werner smuggled in transmitter parts by hiding them in her children's stuffed animals and assembled the machine at home. She asked her landlord if she could put an antenna on the roof. It looked just like a regular radio antenna. The landlord had no objection. With this setup, she was able to communicate by radio with her KGB bosses in Moscow.

Moscow was particularly interested in reports from Werner's new contact, the thin man with glasses. And with good reason—he was helping British scientists figure out how to build an atomic bomb.

THE MAN WAS a German-born physicist named Klaus Fuchs.

"The spelling," a fellow German said of Fuchs's name, "sometimes caused people to pronounce it in a somewhat embarrassing way." The solution for English speakers: pronounce it to rhyme with "books."

As a college student in Germany, Fuchs had watched the rise of the Nazis with disgust. He joined the Communist Party, impressed by the party's willingness to speak out against Hitler. When Hitler took power in Germany in 1933, Nazi thugs beat Fuchs nearly to death and tossed him in a river. That only strengthened Fuchs's commitment to communism.

Fuchs escaped to England, where he earned his PhD in physics. When the war began, British scientists recruited him to help with a secret war-related project—the atomic bomb. "I accepted," recalled Fuchs, "and I started work without knowing at first what the work was."

61

A gifted physicist, Fuchs was well liked by his fellow scientists, though they found him difficult to get to know. He was always inside, hunched over his desk. He spoke very little, and never about politics.

"A very nice, quiet fellow, with sad eyes," commented one.

"He seems like a chap who's never breathed any fresh air," said another.

The British knew he'd been a Communist in Germany, but they figured he'd put that behind him. And in any case, they wanted his brain. No one guessed that their shy, pale coworker was capable of leading a double life.

"When I learned about the purpose of the work," Fuchs later said, "I decided to inform Russia and I established contact through another member of the Communist Party."

That led to Fuchs's contact with Ruth Werner. He and Werner met every couple of months on quiet rural roads. He passed her envelopes containing reports on everything British scientists knew about atomic bomb physics, and she radioed the material to Moscow.

"Once," Werner recalled, "Klaus gave me a thick book of blueprints, more than a hundred pages long, asking me to forward it quickly." This obviously couldn't be done by radio. Like all experienced spies, Werner had backup plans in place.

"I had to travel to London and, at a certain time in a certain place, drop a small piece of chalk and tread on it," she explained. This was a signal to her Soviet contact—it meant that a drop-off would be made at a prearranged time and place.

Two days later she got on her bicycle, with Fuchs's report hidden under her clothes. "After about six or seven miles, I turned onto a side road," she said. There, parked under a tree, was a car. Behind the wheel sat a Soviet agent.

"I cycled on, hid my bike, and went to sit in the car beside him for a moment," Werner said. She handed over the papers, got back on her bike, and rode home.

"IMPORTANT," officials in Moscow said of Fuchs's information, "very valuable."

But it was of limited worth. Fuchs was doing interesting calculations, but the real action was taking place in the United States. And the Soviets were getting nothing at all from their agents in America.

By the fall of 1942, this was making KGB officials in Moscow very angry. "The organizational pace is entirely unsatisfactory," Moscow scolded its American spies. "The project is taking a very long time to get going."

In New York, Semyon Semyonov got the message. As part of his search for a way into the America bomb project, he turned to his best courier, Harry Gold.

"One evening in New York City," Gold remembered, "about October-November 1942, Semyonov asked me if I had heard anything of a military weapon." It was a bomb, Semyonov said, a weapon of almost unimaginable power.

"I was puzzled," Gold said. "I had no idea that anything was going on in regard to atomic energy in the United States."

Semyonov knew it was a long shot, but he was desperate. He asked Gold to keep his eyes and ears open.

MEANWHILE, Moscow officials reminded their West Coast agents that they'd been sent a list of scientists to cultivate. Moscow was particularly annoyed that no contact had been made with Robert Oppenheimer. The Soviets had no way of knowing that Oppenheimer had just been named the scientific director of the American atomic bomb project, but they knew he was a top American physicist. They knew it was *probable* he was involved.

Peter Ivanov, a KGB agent in San Francisco, thought about how he could get close to Oppenheimer. As a Soviet agent, watched closely by the FBI, it would be too risky for him to make a direct approach.

Ivanov went to see George Eltenton, a chemical engineer known to be sympathetic to the Soviet Union. Ivanov pointed out to Eltenton that the Americans and Soviets were allies in World War II, but the Soviets were the ones doing the fighting against Hitler. Why, Ivanov asked, was America keeping secrets from its ally?

Eltenton agreed; the Soviets deserved better.

Ivanov then asked Eltenton what he knew about atomic bomb research being done at the University of California, Berkeley.

"I, personally," said Eltenton, "know very little of what's going on."

"Do you know any of the guys?" asked Ivanov. "Any others connected with it?"

"Not very well," Eltenton said.

Ivanov tossed out names of well-known Berkeley physicists: "Ernest Lawrence? Luis Alvarez? Robert Oppenheimer?"

Eltenton said he knew Oppenheimer casually. They'd been at a few political meetings together over the years.

Ivanov asked Eltenton to talk with Oppenheimer, to subtly feel out his interest in sharing information with the Soviets. Eltenton said he didn't know Oppenheimer well enough to do it. Ivanov wouldn't give up—wasn't there anyone Eltenton knew who could be trusted to approach Oppenheimer?

"On thinking the matter over," Eltenton remembered, "I said that the only mutual acquaintance whom I could think of was Haakon Chevalier."

Chevalier was a professor of French literature at Berkeley and the host of the Communist discussion group at which Oppenheimer had been spotted by the FBI about two years earlier. Chevalier and Oppenheimer were good friends. Eltenton asked Chevalier to approach his friend on behalf of the Soviets. Chevalier agreed.

THE PERFECT OPPORTUNITY arose a few weeks later, when Robert and his wife, Kitty, invited Haakon and his wife, Barbara, over for dinner.

"Haakon was one hundred percent in favor of finding out what Oppie was doing and reporting it back to Eltenton," Barbara remembered. "Haakon also believed that Oppie would be in favor of cooperating with the Russians." Barbara strongly disagreed. They fought about it in the car on the way to dinner.

As soon as the guests arrived, Oppenheimer announced it was time to mix a batch of his famous martinis. He walked toward the kitchen. Chevalier followed.

As Oppenheimer began carefully pouring the liquor, a nervous-seeming Chevalier announced, "I saw George Eltenton recently."

Oppenheimer looked up from his work.

Chevalier continued, saying that Eltenton had a contact with Soviet intelligence. If Oppenheimer ever wanted to share any scientific information with the Soviets, he could use this connection.

Oppenheimer was visibly disturbed by the suggestion. "That would be a frightful thing to do," he said. "That would be treason."

Chevalier said nothing more.

Oppenheimer went back to his martinis. "That was the end of it," he later said. "It was a very brief conversation."

Chevalier reported the results to Eltenton. A disappointed Eltenton told Peter Ivanov, the KGB agent, that there was "no chance whatsoever of obtaining any data—Dr. Oppenheimer does not approve." Ivanov relayed the news to Moscow.

Oppenheimer chose not tell General Groves that he'd been approached by the Soviets. It was a decision that would haunt him for the rest of his life.

# DISAPPEARING SCIENTISTS

**ON THE AFTERNOON OF NOVEMBER 16, 1942,** Robert Oppenheimer and Leslie Groves stood together in a deep canyon in northern New Mexico. Steep red-rock cliffs rose on both sides of the canyon. A clear mountain stream trickled down the center. It was a gorgeous spot.

"This will never do," Groves grunted.

The two men walked back toward their car.

"If you go on up the canyon," Oppenheimer suggested, pointing east, "you come out on top of the mesa, and there's a boys' school there which might be a usable site."

The men climbed into the car and continued their search for the perfect place to build an atomic bomb lab. The site had to be remote, so work could be kept secret. But it also had to be fairly close to railroad lines, so people and equipment could quickly move in and out. And, ideally, it would have some buildings already in place, so scientists could move right in and get to work.

A light snow began falling as the car wound its way up a narrow dirt road carved into the side of a mesa. The car reached the top and pulled up to a gate with a sign reading Los Alamos Ranch School.

From their car seats, Groves and Oppenheimer peered through the gate. "We didn't want to get out," Groves remembered, "as we should have had to give some reason why we were inspecting the place."

Inside the gate, boys ran around playing sports in the snow—in shorts. "It was bitterly cold," recalled Groves. "I thought they must be freezing."

Beyond the playing fields were a few school buildings, a dining lodge, log dormitories, and several small houses for teachers. Oppenheimer loved the mountain and desert views. Groves loved the isolation.

"This is the place," Groves said.

A few weeks later, the school director opened an official-looking letter and saw that it was signed by Secretary of War Henry Stimson. "You are advised," declared Stimson, "that it has been determined necessary to the interests of the United States in the prosecution of the war that the property of Los Alamos Ranch School be acquired for military purposes."

The school was closed, the students sent home.

While construction crews began expanding roads and nailing together new buildings at Los Alamos, Oppenheimer turned to his next task: "a policy of absolutely unscrupulous recruiting of anyone we can lay hands on."

A SHORT WHILE LATER, a Harvard University chemistry student named Donald Hornig was doing research in an explosives lab when the lab director walked in. Hornig's boss took him to the attic and locked the door.

"How would you like another job?" asked the lab director.

"What have I done wrong?" Hornig asked.

"Nothing," said his boss.

"What kind of job?" Hornig wanted to know.

"Can't say."

"Well, where is it?"

"Can't say."

"East or west?"

"Sorry, my lips are sealed," said the director. "Think it over and let me know in the morning."

Hornig decided to turn the offer down. It just sounded too strange. Then he started getting phone calls from former professors, and the president of Harvard. They all wanted to know what his problem was—didn't he realize his country needed him?

He took the job.

SIMILAR SCENES were taking place at top universities all over the country.

"People I knew well began to vanish, one after the other," Stanislaw Ulam, a mathematician at the University of Wisconsin, recalled. Then Ulam got a letter inviting him to join a project doing important war work in New Mexico. Suddenly he knew where everyone had gone.

"I accepted immediately with excitement and eagerness," he said.

When the physicist Robert Marshank got a similar letter, he announced to his wife that they were leaving immediately.

"What's it all about?" she asked.

"I can tell you nothing about it," he replied. "We're going away, that's all."

"At least tell me why we are going away," she demanded.

He refused. Only when they were halfway across the country did she find out they were headed for the Southwest.

Oppenheimer did a lot of the recruiting personally. "I traveled all over the country," he said, "talking with people who had been working on one or another aspect of the atomic energy enterprise." It wasn't always easy to get them to sign up. "The notion of disappearing into the New Mexico desert for an indeterminate period," he recalled, "disturbed a good many scientists."

And yet Oppenheimer's offer did have appeal. "Almost everyone knew that if it were completed successfully and rapidly enough, it might determine the outcome of the war," he said. "Almost everyone knew that this job would be part of history. This sense of excitement, of devotion and of patriotism prevailed. Most of those with whom I talked came to Los Alamos."

AMONG THOSE WON over was a twenty-four-year-old physics grad student named Richard Feynman. He was working in his room at Princeton University when in burst a young physics teacher named Bob Wilson.

Wilson announced that he'd just been given a top-secret job. "He wasn't supposed to tell anybody," Feynman remembered, "but he was going to tell me because he knew that as soon as I knew what he was going to do, I'd see that I had to go along with it."

The work, Wilson explained, had to do with uranium and fission and a whole new kind of bomb. "There's a meeting at—"

"I don't want to do it," Feynman cut in.

"All right," said Wilson. "There's a meeting at three o'clock. I'll see you there."

Wilson turned and left.

"I went back to work," Feynman said, "for about three minutes."

Then he got up and started pacing, thinking about what little he knew about fission and the possibility of building atomic bombs. "This would be a very, very powerful weapon," he said, "which in the hands of Hitler and his crew would let them completely control the rest of the world."

He decided to go to the meeting. Soon after, Richard Feynman disappeared from the Princeton campus.

# CHICAGO PILE

**EARLY ON THE MORNING OF DECEMBER 2, 1942,** two figures crunched over the frozen snow covering the campus of the University of Chicago.

"It was terribly cold—below zero," remembered Leona Woods, a twenty-three-year-old physics grad student. Walking alongside Woods, hunched against the cold, was the world-famous Italian physicist Enrico Fermi.

Woods and Fermi ducked through a gate leading into the football stadium. They nodded to security guards and hurried down a dark hallway beneath the stands, their breath forming frost clouds in the air. It was just as cold inside as out.

Under the football stands were a series of unheated squash courts. They opened the door to one of the courts and stepped inside.

"The scene of this test at the University of Chicago would have been confusing to an outsider," Fermi later said. "He would have seen only what appeared to be a crude pile of black bricks." Shaped like an oval, the black pile was about twenty-five feet wide in the middle and twenty feet high.

Woods and Fermi climbed up to a balcony high above the court. "The balcony was originally meant for people to watch squash players," said Woods, "but now it was filled with control equipment and read-out circuits glowing and winking."

A young physicist named Herb Anderson walked in, yawning, and helped do a few last-minute checks. Everything was set for one of the most important experiments in the history of science.

But first, breakfast.

"Herb, Fermi and I went over to the apartment I shared with my sister," Woods said. "I made pancakes, mixing the batter so fast that there were bubbles of dry flour in it. When fried, these were somewhat crunchy between the teeth, and Herb thought I had put nuts in the batter."

After the quick meal, the three set out across campus to the football stadium. "Back we mushed," said Woods, "through the cold, creaking snow."

OPPENHEIMER WAS BUSY recruiting scientists for Los Alamos—but that didn't mean he knew for sure an atomic bomb was technically possible. He and other physicists had spent a few years studying fission. They knew they could bombard a uranium atom with neutrons and cause its nucleus to split. They knew the splitting nucleus would release energy. But what happened next?

Theoretically, as the uranium nucleus split in two, more neutrons would break free and fly off on their own. The speeding neutrons would collide with other uranium atoms, causing them to fission also. As these uranium atoms split, they would release more neutrons, which would hit more uranium atoms. These atoms would also split, releasing still more neutrons, which would hit more uranium atoms, causing more fission, more free-flying neutrons, more fission, more neutrons, and so on. Though they didn't know if it would actually happen, physicists had a name ready for this process: *chain reaction*.

Each splitting atom would release a small amount of energy. So scientists knew that if they could cause a fast enough chain reaction, they might be able to build atomic bombs. But first they had to prove a chain reaction was even possible.

That's what Enrico Fermi and his team were trying to do in the squash court under the football stands in Chicago. The black blocks were graphite, the mineral used to make pencil leads. Slid into holes in some of the blocks were small pieces of uranium. Fermi used graphite to slow down the speeding neutrons—he knew that neutrons would bounce off the carbon atoms that make up graphite and lose speed. Traveling a bit more slowly, they'd be more likely to hit the uranium atoms and cause fission.

Stuck through the pile at various points were long wooden poles wrapped with a bluish-white metal called cadmium. Cadmium was chosen for its ability to absorb huge numbers of neutrons. As long as the cadmium poles were in place, they would absorb the neutrons shooting out of the uranium. This, Fermi told Leslie Groves, would prevent a chain reaction from starting.

Still, the idea of attempting to release nuclear energy in the middle of a city of three million made Groves very nervous. "If the pile should explode, no one knew just how far the danger would extend," Groves fretted. "Because of this I had serious misgivings about the wisdom of doing the experiment there."

Fermi assured Groves he knew exactly what he was doing.

A LITTLE BEFORE 10:00 A.M., Fermi and his team of about fifteen students and scientists assembled in the freezing squash court. Most climbed to the balcony, but three stood on an elevated platform near the ceiling, holding buckets full of cadmium. If the reaction got out of control, they were to dump the cadmium on the pile—then get out fast.

Fermi sat in a chair on the balcony. He looked over his blinking monitors, then ordered the first cadmium rod to be lifted out of the pile.

As the rod went up, specially built machines measured the flying neutrons, clicking loudly as more and more neutrons were released inside the pile. Fermi did some quick calculations in his notebook. Then he ordered another rod up. The clicking sounds increased again. Fermi did a new set of calculations and called for another rod to be lifted.

As the experiment continued, more and more curious scientists crammed onto the balcony. Leo Szilard and Eugene Wigner—the ones who'd triggered the Manhattan Project by convincing Albert Einstein to warn President Roosevelt of the danger of atomic bombs—came to watch. Everyone was shivering and covered with black graphite dust. No one spoke but Fermi.

Only one cadmium rod remained in the pile; Fermi's team called it the "zip" rod. A physicist named George Weil stood on the floor, holding the rope that lifted it.

Fermi called, "Go ahead, George!"

The rod went up a foot. The clicking increased.

"Another foot, George."

Weil pulled the rod a bit higher.

"You could hear the sound of the neutron counter, clickety-clack, clickety-clack," said Herb Anderson. Leona Woods kept her eyes on the monitors, calling out measurements to Fermi.

"Another foot, George."

The rod went up again. The tension in the room rose with the clicking. Only Fermi seemed to be enjoying himself. "This will do it," he announced, a confident grin spreading across his face. "Now the pile will chain-react."

Weil pulled the rod completely out of the pile. "Then the clicks came more and more rapidly," said Anderson, "and after a while they began to merge into a roar."

Fermi's smile got bigger. "The pile has gone critical," he said. The chain reaction was going and would continue doubling in power every two minutes until he shut it down.

Two minutes passed. Fermi watched the monitors, but said nothing.

"Everyone began to wonder why he didn't shut the pile off," Anderson said.

The machines continued to roar. Fermi calmly took a few notes.

"He waited another minute, then another," said Anderson. "The anxiety was too much to bear."

Finally Fermi said, "Zip in!"

The cadmium rod dropped back into the pile, followed by the other rods. The clicking machines went quiet. There was a long silence in the squash court. Then, unsure what else to do, everyone began to clap.

"THE CONTROLLED RELEASE of atomic power has been demonstrated for the first time in history," Fermi said of his experiment. The pile had generated only enough energy to power a small light bulb. But the chain reaction had been proved—humans now knew they could release the enormous power locked inside atoms.

"For some time, we had known that we were about to unlock a giant," remembered Eugene Wigner. "Still, we could not escape an eerie feeling when we knew we had actually done it."

Wigner pulled out a bottle of red wine and a stack of paper cups. He filled the cups, and the scientists and students silently passed them around.

No one offered a toast, Leona Woods recalled. "There was a greater drama in the silence than if words had been spoken."

Woods couldn't be sure what the others were thinking. She had a feeling their thoughts were similar to her own. "Of course, the Germans have already made a chain reaction," she said to herself. "We have, and they have been ahead until now."

Then she thought, *When do we get as scared as we ought to?*

# OPERATION GUNNERSIDE

**KNUT HAUKELID LAY** in his hospital bed in Britain, recovering from the accidental bullet wound in his foot. He was furious with himself for missing the chance to parachute into Norway. But he was about to get a second chance.

In spite of the glider disaster, the British and Americans were still determined to destroy the Vemork heavy water plant in Norway. Like the graphite Enrico Fermi used in his Chicago pile, heavy water can be used to slow down neutrons and create a chain reaction in uranium. In fact, heavy water is more efficient than graphite—Fermi would have used heavy water if he could have gotten his hands on enough. But Adolf Hitler held tight to the world's only supply. Breaking that grip was the key to stopping the German bomb. The Allies could try bombing Vemork from the air, but the cliffside target would be difficult for planes to hit. They'd be more likely to kill civilians living nearby than to seriously damage the plant.

As soon as Haukelid got out of the hospital, he was brought to London with five other Norwegian volunteers for a talk with Colonel John Wilson of the S.O.E. Wilson explained the new mission, code-named Gunnerside. The Norwegians would parachute onto the Hardanger Plateau and find Jens Poulsson and his team—they were still camped somewhere on the plateau. Together, they'd ski to Vemork, bust into the building, and blow up vital equipment in the plant basement.

Wilson told them about the glider operation. He told them the Nazis had executed every one of the British soldiers. "You must reckon," he said, "that the Germans will in no circumstances take any prisoners." It was not normal procedure to give commandos this kind of information, but Wilson wanted the men going in with no illusions.

"You have a fifty-fifty chance of doing the job," Wilson said, "and only a fair chance of escaping."

ON THE NIGHT OF FEBRUARY 17, 1943, Knut Haukelid and the other Gunnerside men hunched inside a British plane, cruising 10,000 feet above the North Sea.

"It was a tight fit inside the aircraft," remembered Haukelid. "With our heavy equipment, weapons, and thick clothes, we could hardly move."

The team had spent weeks preparing for their mission. They studied photographs and technical drawings of the Vemork plant. They planned routes in and out of the factory and practiced wrapping explosives around the type of equipment they expected to find inside. They were given cross-country skis, with which they needed no training. And there was one final tool.

"We were all issued the death pill," Haukelid recalled.

Rather than allow themselves to be taken prisoner and tortured for information, the men were instructed to bite this pill. "It was cyanide enclosed in a rubber cover," said Haukelid. "It could be kept in the mouth. Once bitten through it would ensure death within three seconds."

At one in the morning, the British pilot announced they were ten minutes from the jump site. The team leader, twenty-two-year-old Joachim Ronneberg, stood over the open hatch in the plane's floor, looking down. The drop target was a frozen lake deep in the wilderness—hopefully, far from any German patrols.

"No doubt the hearts of most of us beat a little faster at the thought that we were about to jump into the moonlight over heaven knew what," Haukelid later said. "The warning lamp in the roof burned green. All clear!"

Ronneberg tumbled out first, then the others, and then crates of equipment.

"I felt the marvelous jerk, which told me that the parachute had opened," said Haukelid. "Beneath me there was nothing but snow and ice. Here lay the Hardanger Plateau, the largest, loneliest, and wildest mountain area in northern Europe."

Haukelid landed in the snow. The other men and the equipment glided down all around him. He got up and looked around at the low, snow-covered hills dotted with bare bushes. Clearly they were not on the frozen lake they'd been aiming for.

"Do you know where we are?" asked Ronneberg.

Haukelid shook his head. "We may be in China, for all I know."

"IT WAS OBVIOUS that we had not landed on the lake," Ronneberg recalled. "But we didn't have time to worry about that. We had to gather our equipment and stow it away before daylight."

The men dragged the equipment crates to a nearby hunting cabin, chopped open the locked door with an axe, and slept in their clothes on the floor.

The next day they set out on skis to find Poulsson's team. As snow began falling and the temperature dropped, the men labored up and down icy slopes. After months in the comparatively warm and flat English countryside, they just weren't in shape for this kind of work. "We felt disoriented and feverish," said Ronneberg. "Meanwhile the snowfall was thickening and the wind increasing." After covering just four miles, the growing storm forced them to turn back toward the cabin.

They dove inside, lit a fire, and started scraping the ice off their faces. Then they searched the cabin and got lucky—in a drawer they found a log-book with the location of the cabin written inside. Now, at least, they knew where they were. They could set out with confidence when the blizzard let up.

It lasted five days. The temperature fell to ten below zero, and fifty-mile-per-hour winds rocked the thin walls. "The cabin seemed about to be lifted," said Ronneberg. Then, suddenly, the wind fell and sky turned bright blue. The men stepped out into a world of blinding white.

THEY QUICKLY GATHERED their supplies and set out in the direction Poulsson and his team should be. That afternoon they spotted, in the distance, two men on skis.

The Gunnerside men ducked behind boulders and drew their guns. Ronneberg peered through his binoculars. Then he handed them to Haukelid, saying, "Do you recognize them?"

Haukelid took a look. The two figures were 300 yards away and bundled in thick winter coats. The men could be their Norwegian comrades—or they could be Germans on patrol.

Deciding he needed to get closer, Haukelid tucked his pistol into his belt. He let the two men pass by his hiding spot, then skied toward them from behind. The wind blew the sound of his skis away from the men ahead of him.

Haukelid got within fifteen yards, still unnoticed. At this distance there was no doubt—they were skinny from a hungry winter, but these were Claus Helberg and Arne Kjelstrup, two of Poulsson's team.

Haukelid stopped. He coughed loudly. Helberg and Kjelstrup spun around, pulling out pistols, and were about to fire when they recognized their old International Gangster School mate. All three men shouted with joy.

"There was back-slapping," Haukelid said of the happy moment, "and much strong hearty cursing."

THE TEN YOUNG Norwegians gathered in a nearby cabin to review the job ahead. Their target was the Vemork plant, built into the side of a steep, 3,000-foot gorge. At the bottom of the gorge was the now-frozen Mann River.

"As you all know," Ronneberg said, "our main problem is the approach itself. We have all the necessary equipment and explosives to do the job, but we must reach the target to get the job done."

Claus Helberg had grown up in Rjukan, right near the plant, and knew the area as only a native could. There were two ways to get at the place, he said. First, the way everyone went: across a suspension bridge over the gorge. The bridge led right to the plant, but it was patrolled by German soldiers. "Shooting the guards will create too much noise before we get inside the building," said Helberg.

Option two was to climb down the gorge, cross the river, and come up at the plant from below. "We know the Germans don't expect anyone to try that route," Helberg said, "because the gorge itself is not patrolled."

"It's the one weak point in the defense system around the plant," Ronneberg agreed.

He divided the men into a five-man demolition party, led by himself, and a five-man covering party, led by Haukelid. Drawing diagrams of the plant buildings, he showed each man where to position himself during the attack. If the factory doors were bolted, he explained, rather than make noise blasting them open, they'd go in through an air duct that led into the main building. "There is just enough space for one man at a time to crawl through," he said.

"If anything should happen to me, or anything should upset the plan, everyone must act on his own with the goal in mind to complete the operation,"

Ronneberg insisted. "In short, if fighting breaks out, everyone must act on his own initiative in order to complete the operation."

All were in agreement.

"Finally, to repeat what we were all told in Britain," added Ronneberg, "if any man is wounded, or about to be taken prisoner, he ends his own life."

All agreed.

# HIGH CONCENTRATION

**AT ABOUT EIGHT** on the night of February 27, 1943, the Norwegians pulled on white camouflage suits, shouldered their fifty-pound packs, put on skis, and started for Vemork. "The weather was overcast," Ronneberg later reported, "mild, with much wind."

They glided down a mountain and into a forest, thick with bushes and low branches. They had to take off their skis and trudge on foot through the wet snow. "We sank in the snow up to our waists," Ronneberg said.

Claus Helberg led the way out of the trees and back into the faint moonlight. They put their skis back on and continued. Soon they could hear the low, steady hum of machinery—the Vemork plant. When they came near the edge of the gorge, they could see it.

"The great seven-story factory building bulked large on the landscape," Haukelid later said. "The colossus lay like a medieval castle, built in the most inaccessible place, protected by precipices and rivers."

They slid downhill toward a road running along the top of the gorge.

They were about to cross, when the flash of headlights suddenly lit the snow at their feet. The men dove away from the road as two buses rounded a curve and sped past, carrying night-shift workers to Vemork.

At about ten o'clock they reached the spot from which they would descend into the gorge. In silence, they took off their skis and hid them under pine trees. They removed their white camouflage suits, revealing British military uniforms. They wanted the Germans to know they were soldiers on an official Allied mission—that way, hopefully, the Germans wouldn't retaliate against Norwegian civilians in nearby towns.

Then they started down the gorge.

HANGING FROM THE BRANCHES of trees growing out of the rocky gorge face, the men slid and tumbled down toward the river. As they got closer they saw big cracks in the melting river ice and areas of free-flowing water. They stepped lightly across, splashing through three inches of water sitting atop the slushy surface.

When they reached the far side, each man lifted an arm and grabbed a rock on the steep gorge wall. With his hand, Ronneberg gave the "Go" signal.

The men pulled themselves up the 600-foot rock face, inch by inch. With hands and feet, they felt for tree branches or cracks in the rock. When the fiery pain in their muscles became unbearable, they clung to the side of the cliff and rested, thinking of what their trainers in Britain had taught them: Never look down.

A few minutes before midnight, all ten men reached a ledge just below the plant. They gathered, panting and sweating, and waited a few minutes for their hearts to stop pounding.

"All right, men," said Ronneberg. "Let's get closer."

THE COVERING PARTY, commanded by Knut Haukelid, led the way to a storage shed 500 yards from the plant. The roar of machines covered the slap of their boots on the wet snow.

From behind the shed, the men looked out at the suspension bridge leading across the gorge. Two German guards, holding rifles, paced the narrow bridge. They never looked toward the gorge, assuming no one could come in that way.

The team dashed toward an iron fence surrounding the plant. There was a gate, locked with a chain and padlock. Haukelid and Arne Kjelstrup ran ahead with heavy wire cutters, cut through the chain, and swung the gate open. Haukelid, Kjelstrup, and the rest of the covering party went in first, taking assigned positions around the outside of the plant. Then the demolition team raced in.

"The hum of the machinery was steady and normal," said Ronneberg. "There was a good light from the moon, with no one in sight except our own men."

RONNEBERG LED THE TEAM to the door of the plant nearest to their target—the "high concentration room," in which the heavy water equipment did its work. He tried the door. "Locked," he whispered.

The plant's windows were covered with black paint, blocking light from escaping and making the building nearly invisible to enemy bombers. Ronneberg put his face to the glass. Through thin scratches in the paint, he could see down to the high concentration room. A single Norwegian worker sat at a desk, writing in a book.

Ronneberg sent three team members to try other doors while he and Fredrik Kayser started looking for the air duct.

"Here it is," he whispered.

Ronneberg climbed in first. The space was too narrow for him to turn and look back, but he knew Kayser was behind him—he could hear the man's breathing.

Flashlight in hand, Ronneberg crawled through the duct. From studying technical drawings of the plant, he knew he had about thirty yards to go. Suddenly he was startled by a loud metallic crack—a pistol had dropped from Kayser's belt and smacked the duct floor. Both men froze.

Through seams in the duct they could see the Norwegian worker at his desk. He never looked up from his book.

Reaching an inner hallway, Ronneberg removed a grate covering an opening in the duct. He and Kayser lowered themselves to the floor. Drawing their pistols, they tiptoed to the door of the high concentration room.

A sign on the door read NO ADMITTANCE EXCEPT ON BUSINESS.

Ronneberg smiled. He reached for the doorknob. The door was unlocked.

THE NORWEGIAN WORKMAN LOOKED up from his notebook as Ronneberg and Kayser opened the door.

"On your feet. Hands up!" shouted Kayser, pointing his gun. "Nothing will happen to you if you do as you are told."

Ronneberg set down his pack and began pulling out snake-shaped explosive charges, each about a foot long. He put on rubber gloves, to prevent static electricity from jumping from his skin to the fuses. Then he looked over the eighteen heavy water machines—they looked exactly like the ones he'd trained on back in Britain.

Ronneberg had wrapped charges around half the machines when the sound of shattering glass broke his focus. He turned toward a window high up on the wall.

Peering down through the window frame was the face of Birger Stromsheim, part of the demolition party. Stromsheim had been unable to find the air duct.

Knowing the smashing sound could have alerted the German guards, Ronneberg quickly pulled pieces of broken glass from the frame, slicing open his hand. He wrapped a handkerchief around the gash as Stromsheim climbed down into the room. Together, the two set the remaining charges and connected them to a single 30-second fuse.

"All right," Ronneberg said, blood dripping from his hand as he pointed to the night worker, "let's get that door to the yard unlocked."

The night worker put a key in the lock and turned it. Kayser reached forward and opened the door a crack, just to make sure.

"It's not that I don't trust you," he said. "I'm just not allowed to trust any-body."

"I understand," said the worker.

Ronneberg struck a match and held it to the fuse.

"Wait, please!" cried the night worker. "My eyeglasses. They're on the table. I need them for my job. They're almost impossible to replace these days."

Cringing, Ronneberg blew out the match. He hurried to the desk, picked up the man's glasses case, and threw it to him.

He lit another match and bent toward the fuse.

"I beg you, wait!" shouted the worker. "My glasses! They are not in the case."

Biting back fury, Ronneberg blew out the second match. "Where *are* your damn glasses?"

The worker pointed to the desk. Ronneberg ran back over, shuffled through the papers, found them, and handed them to the man.

"A thousand thanks," said the worker.

Ronneberg lit a third match and held it to the fuse.

"Go!" he shouted, "Run! Run as fast as you can!"


"THE TIME SEEMED LONG to us who stood waiting outside," remembered Knut Haukelid. "We knew that the blowing-up party was inside to carry out its part of the task, but we did not know how things were going."

Haukelid held a pistol and grenades. Next to him stood Jens Poulsson with his finger on the trigger of a machine gun.

"What could be holding them up?" Poulsson whispered.

"I wish I knew."

Then it came: the sound of an explosion. The windows around the high concentration room blew out. They felt a rush of air race past them.

The door of the German soldiers' barracks opened and a soldier stepped out with a rifle in one hand a flashlight in the other.

"Shall I fire?" asked Poulsson.

"Not yet," said Haukelid.

The soldier swung his light across the snowy ground around the plant. Haukelid and Poulsson stood with their backs flat against a shed, just out of view.

The soldier turned back toward the barracks.

Ronneberg and the demolition team came racing toward Haukelid. Together, they ran out the open gate, and gathered about 300 yards from the fence.

"The Germans still don't seem to know what's happened," Haukelid said.

ALL TEN MEN scrambled down the gorge. They slid from one wet icy rock to another, resting briefly on thin ledges, then continuing the slippery descent.

At the bottom of the gorge, the ice on the river had continued melting. Big chunks were now spinning in the rushing black water. The men were leaping from chunk to chunk when the scream of Vemork's sirens ripped through the air.

"It was as if we were being pursued across the river by the shrieking sound itself," Ronneberg reported. "We slipped and fell, grabbing on to rocks and blocks of ice."

They made it across and immediately started up the far side of the gorge. They reached the top and ducked back down just as a car raced past on the road in front of them. Then they crossed the road, found their skis and poles, jumped into their white camouflage suits, and sped across the snow away from the road.

"German cars and trucks kept zipping past us," remembered Jens Poulsson. "That was all to the good. Those Nazis were in too much of a hurry to get to Vemork to look right or left as they raced along."

THE GUNNERSIDE TEAM SPLIT UP, most heading on skis to the Swedish border, 250 miles to the northeast. Knut Haukelid and Arne Kjelstrup stayed behind in Norway to help organize the anti-German resistance. They skied to a mountain hut, found radio equipment that had been stashed by other resistance fighters, and wrote out a short, coded message for London: "High concentration installation at Vemork completely destroyed on night of 27–28—Gunnerside has gone to Sweden."

Then they headed deeper into the wilderness. "You can bet the Germans are in a fury," Haukelid told Kjelstrup. "And you can be sure that they'll search every corner of the mountains."

Only later did Haukelid learn how right he was. Enraged German commanders were already sending out a ten-thousand-man German force to track down the saboteurs.

Not a single one of the Norwegians was ever caught.

DOROTHY
MCKIBBEN
AND ROBERT
OPPENHEIMER

HARRY
TRUMAN
Democratic
senator from
Missouri

THEODORE
(TED) HALL
Manhattan
Project
physicist and
spy

WERNER
HEISENBERG
leader of the
German atomic
bomb program

RICHARD
FEYNMAN
Manhattan
Project
physicist

# PART 3: HOW TO BUILD AN ATOMIC BOMB

THE HYDRO

ROBERT SERBER
physicist;
righthand
man to
Oppenheimer

IGOR
KURCHATOV
head of the
Soviet atomic
bomb program

# THE GATEKEEPER

ONE AFTERNOON IN LATE MARCH 1943, Dorothy Mc-Kibben, a forty-five-year-old single mother, was crossing the street in Santa Fe, New Mexico. Halfway across she ran into Joe Stevenson, a local businessman she knew casually. There were no cars coming, so they talked in the street.

"How would you like a job as a secretary?" asked Stevenson, who'd heard McKibben was looking for work.

"Secretary to what?" she wanted to know.

He smiled. "Secretary," he said.

She knew he was doing something for the government, something to do with the war.

"Well, what would I do?" she asked.

"You would be a secretary," he said. "Don't you know what a secretary does?"

*The Main Gate of the Los Alamos campus in the early 1940s.*

"Not always."

"Well, think it over. I'll give you twenty-four hours."

Intrigued, McKibben agreed to meet her potential employer the next day in the lobby of La Fonda, the nicest hotel in town. She was standing there, waiting, when she saw a man enter. He wore a trench coat. He had wiry black hair and bright blue eyes. He strode directly to her and introduced himself as "Mr. Bradley."

Then he fired quick questions about her background, her skills, her knowledge of Santa Fe. As she answered he leaned forward and stared intensely at her.

"I never met a person with a magnetism that hit you so fast and so completely," she said later. She had no idea who this man was, or what he was doing in town. She didn't care. "I knew anything he was connected with would be alive," she said. "I thought to be associated with that person, whoever he was, would be simply great!"

She took the job. When she reported for work the next day, the man was waiting for her. Only when they got inside and closed the door did he tell her that his real name was Robert Oppenheimer.

A WEEK LATER, CONFUSED scientists began showing up in Santa Fe, wandering the streets holding a letter that read: "Go to 109 East Palace Avenue, Santa Fe, New Mexico. There you will find out how to complete your trip."

Friendly locals directed the strangers to an ancient wrought-iron gate that opened onto a courtyard built by Spanish settlers in the 1600s. In one of the buildings surrounding the courtyard was a door marked with the number 109. When newcomers knocked they were greeted by Dorothy McKibben—"the Gatekeeper," as she quickly became known.

"They arrived, breathless and sleepless and haggard, tired from riding on trains that were slow," she remembered. "The new members were tense with expectancy and curiosity."

Those were the ones who found the address. McKibben often got calls from nearby drugstores that began, "There is a party here who is lost."

She'd say, "Send him over right away."

In a small office crammed with desks and boxes, McKibben wrote out security passes for the scientists. She told them that from now on their mailing address was Post Office Box 1663, Santa Fe, New Mexico. To avoid drawing attention to the arrival of so many scientists, she cautioned them never to refer to each other as "doctor" or "professor" while in town. Then she gave them directions to Los Alamos.

Scientists continued arriving throughout April. "The office was a madhouse," said McKibben. Famous physicists were given code names—Enrico Fermi, for example, was supposed to tell people his name was Henry Farmer. But Fermi had a hard time remembering his new name and felt absurd pronouncing it with his thick Italian accent. Like Fermi, much of Oppenheimer's scientific dream team was European, many of them Jews who had escaped from Hitler. This gave America a huge advantage in its race with Germany, but it also presented a security problem. The people of Santa Fe, a city of just twenty thousand, began to wonder why so many men with European accents were suddenly walking the streets.

And there were other clues that something was going on. Long lines of army trucks were seen driving up the narrow road to Los Alamos. They always went up the hill loaded. They always came back empty.

"Some amazing rumors began to circulate through Santa Fe," remembered Leslie Groves. Some guessed that Los Alamos housed a secret military project. They were making submarines according to one rumor, death rays according to another. Others claimed Los Alamos was home for pregnant military personnel—or possibly a nudist colony.

The crazier the rumors got, the more they worried Groves and Oppenheimer.

• • •

Up on "the Hill," as Los Alamos became known to its residents, Oppenheimer asked Charlotte Serber to step into his office. He needed her help, he told her.

Charlotte was married to Robert Serber, the physicist and former student who'd become Oppenheimer's right-hand man the year before. Oppenheimer knew Robert and Charlotte well. He trusted them completely.

The rumors in Santa Fe were getting wilder and wilder, Oppenheimer told Serber. The danger was that sooner or later someone might stumble onto the truth, and the story could spread. And if the Germans learned how seriously the Americans were working on an atomic bomb, they'd surely double their own efforts.

Oppenheimer's solution was to plant a false, but believable, story about what was happening at Los Alamos. "Therefore," he told Serber, "for Santa Fe purposes, we are making an electric rocket."

Charlotte Serber was unsure what this had to do with her.

"Go to Santa Fe," Oppenheimer continued. "Talk. Talk too much. Talk as if you had too many drinks. Get people to eavesdrop. Say a number of things about us that you are not supposed to. Finally, I don't care how you manage it, say we are building an electric rocket."

Charlotte explained the mission to her husband, and they drove from Los Alamos to Santa Fe. They walked into the bar at La Fonda at about 9:00 p.m., sat at a table, and ordered drinks.

"Our conversation was singularly dull as we each wondered how to bring electric rockets into it," Charlotte recalled. "We told little stories about Los Alamos, mentioning the forbidden name boldly and loudly. But no ears cocked in our direction."

Unable to attract attention, they walked down the street to Joe King's Blue Ribbon Bar, which, Robert described as "jumping, jammed, and crowded."

A young man immediately approached Charlotte, bowed, and asked her to dance. She agreed.

While they danced, she got the conversation started by asking if he lived in Santa Fe.

"Yes," he said.

"What do you do?" she asked.

"Nothing."

"How come you're not in the service?"

"Four F," he said—a military classification for those physically unfit for service. "Want to get a job on a ranch."

"We're up at Los Alamos," she said, steering toward the target.

"Uh-huh."

"It's quite a place, don't you think?" she asked. "So mysterious and secret."

"Yeah," he shrugged. "You know, I sure want to run a ranch someday."

"But what do you suppose they're doing at Los Alamos?"

"I dunno," he said. "Come to town often? You sure dance fine."

"We come to town as often as we can, but they don't like to let us out much. What's your guess about what cooks up there?"

"Beats me. Don't care. May I have another dance later?"

Robert Serber watched it all from a booth near the dance floor. Seeing that things were going badly for his wife, he walked up to the tightly packed bar, turned toward the man next to him, grabbed the lapels of his jacket, and shouted: "Do you know what we're doing at Los Alamos? We're building an electric rocket!"

The man grunted and sipped his drink.

DRIVING BACK to Los Alamos that night, the Serbers knew their mission had failed.

"The FBI and Army Intelligence never reported picking up any rumors about electric rockets," Robert said. "The spy business isn't as easy as it appears in the movies."

And so the rumors in Santa Fe kept flying. Something big was obviously going on, and locals wondered if jobs might be available. Almost every day someone knocked on the door at 109 East Palace and asked Dorothy Mc-Kibben for work on the new government project in town.

"I can't understand wherever you got that idea," said the smiling Gate-keeper. "There's nothing of that sort in Santa Fe that we know of."

# THE GADGET

ON THE EVENING OF APRIL 15, 1943, about forty physicists gathered in what used to be the library reading room of the Los Alamos Ranch School. A small blackboard on wheels stood at one end of the room. In front of the blackboard were several rows of folding chairs. Everyone took seats, except for Robert Oppenheimer and his assistant, Robert Serber.

"Buildings were still under construction," remembered Serber. "There was a hammering off in the background, carpenters and electricians working out of sight but all over the place."

Oppenheimer introduced Serber and sat down. Serber looked down at his notes and began reading quietly, with a slight stutter. But he opened with a bang: "The object of the project is to produce a practical military weapon in the form of a bomb in which the energy is released by a fast-neutron chain reaction."

There was a second of stunned silence. Until that moment, many men in the room had not known exactly why they'd been dragged to this remote mountaintop.

Scribbling graphs and formulas on the blackboard as he spoke, Serber began to explain the physics of an atomic bomb. "He wasn't much of a speaker," the physicist Isidor Rabi recalled, "but for ammunition he had everything Oppenheimer's theoretical group had uncovered during the last year. He knew it all cold and that was all he cared about."

Serber had the room's attention—until a sharp *crack* interrupted the talk. Startled, everyone looked up. They saw a jagged hole in the thin ceiling above, and, dangling through the hole, the wiggling leg of an electrician. The scientists heard the man call for help. They heard men running on the floor above, then saw the leg slowly slide up through the hole and disappear.

Serber returned to his lecture. Almost every sentence included the word *bomb*, which began to worry Oppenheimer. He leaned to the physicist beside him, John Manley, and whispered something. Manley walked up to Serber and told him to stop saying "bomb"—there were too many workers around.

When Serber resumed his talk, he referred instead to the "gadget." The name stuck. "Around Los Alamos after that," explained Serber, "we called the bomb we were building 'the gadget.'"

IN FOUR MORE LECTURES over the next two weeks, Serber described the physics of how the gadget might work. Enrico Fermi's Chicago experiment had proved that it was possible to spark a chain reaction in uranium. Fermi's uranium and graphite pile had released energy, but only a tiny amount, and slowly. The problem facing Oppenheimer's team was to figure out how to create a much faster chain reaction that would release so much energy it would cause a massive explosion—and the whole thing had to be light enough to travel by airplane.

In theory, Serber explained, the design of the bomb could be very simple. They could load two pieces of very pure uranium into a specially adapted artillery gun. Inside the gun barrel, they would fire one piece of uranium at the other. When the two pieces met, they would form a critical mass, the amount of material needed to get a chain reaction going. The reaction would begin—speeding neutrons would hit uranium atoms, which would split, releasing energy and more neutrons. Each fission would release just enough energy to move a grain of sand. But within less than one millionth of a second, so many atoms would fission that the lump of uranium would blow itself apart with the force of millions of pounds of regular explosive.

Serber drew a rough sketch of what became known as the "gun assembly" method. Surrounding the uranium would be a tamper—a shield of very dense metal. The tamper would prevent flying neutrons from escaping, bouncing them instead back into the uranium. This would cause more fission, and a bigger explosion.

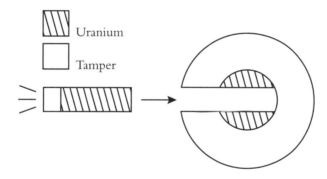

Uranium

Tamper

Major questions remained, Serber told the team. Exactly how much uranium was needed to form a critical mass? What material would perform best as a tamper? How fast would the lumps of uranium need to be brought together inside the gun? How big an explosion would this type of bomb cause? And, of course, would this design even work?

"We started working immediately," said Richard Feynman.

•  •  •

99

OUTSIDE THE WORKROOMS, Los Alamos was a disaster.

"The site itself was a mess," said Robert Serber. "It was a shambles," agreed Hans Bethe. "It was a construction site. You stumbled over kegs of nails, over posts, over ladders."

Melting snow sank into the dirt roads, turning them to sticky black mud. And while views of the surrounding mountains and deserts were spectacular, the army built high fences around the entire lab—making the scientists feel like prisoners.

"The first thing I noticed," remembered Edward Teller, "was that we were all going to be locked up together for better or for worse."

"I was shocked by the isolation," Bethe said. "Clearly we were very far from anything, very far from anybody."

Oppenheimer and his wife moved into one of the five log cabins that had originally been built for school directors, a little group of houses known as "Bathtub Row"—they had the only tubs on the Hill. Younger scientists crowded into bunk beds in an old school building while new dorms were being built. "Bob Christy and his wife had to go to the bathroom through our bedroom," recalled Feynman. "So that was very uncomfortable."

As construction continued, Oppenheimer was often seen strolling the streets of his growing town in jeans and a Western shirt, his thumbs tucked into his belt. New scientists were arriving all the time, and when the director saw someone he didn't know, he'd stride up to the newcomer.

"Welcome to Los Alamos," he'd say, smiling. "And who the devil are you?"

TO GET TO WORK, scientists struggled through the mud to the half-finished Tech Area, which housed labs and offices and was surrounded by another fence, nine feet high, with barbed wire strung along the top. Military police guarded the only gate twenty-four hours a day. To gain entrance, scientists had to show their white badges—only the scientists were issued these special photo IDs.

Oppenheimer arrived at the gate of the Tech Area each morning at 7:30, flashed his white badge, and walked to his office. This was a big change from his Berkeley days. A lover of late-night parties, he'd never scheduled classes before 11:00 a.m. But Oppenheimer knew that it wasn't just his reputation and career on the line at Los Alamos—it was the outcome of the biggest war in human history.

And in case the pressure wasn't intense enough, President Roosevelt spelled it out in a personal note. "Whatever the enemy may be planning, American science will be equal to the challenge," Roosevelt wrote to Oppenheimer. "With this thought in mind, I send this note of confidence and appreciation."

Oppenheimer thanked Roosevelt for the kind words, adding, "There will be many times in the months ahead when we shall remember them."

Then came a memo from General Leslie Groves. Given Oppenheimer's vital importance to the country, wrote Groves, "it is requested that:

(a) you refrain from flying in airplanes of any description; the time saved is not worth the risk.

(b) you refrain from driving in an automobile for any appreciable distance (above a few miles) and from being without suitable protection on any lonely road.

(c) in driving about town, a guard of some kind should be used, particularly during hours of darkness."

These were sensible precautions, but the truth is that Groves had more than safety on his mind. Many of Groves's intelligence officers still didn't trust the Los Alamos director. They believed he was secretly a Communist, and perhaps even in touch with Soviet agents. They wanted him under constant surveillance.

Army Counter-Intelligence Corps (CIC) agents hid microphones in Oppenheimer's office. They listened in on his phone calls and read his mail.

Even Oppenheimer's personal driver and bodyguard—the one Groves insisted he have—was actually an undercover agent. Oppenheimer sensed he was being watched, but he never guessed how closely.

On June 12, he traveled to Berkeley to recruit more brains for Los Alamos. CIC agents followed him every step of the way.

# LABORATORY NUMBER 2

BY EARLY 1943, the Soviet army had finally halted the massive German invasion just short of the Soviet cities of Stalingrad, Moscow, and Leningrad. "The greatest military achievement in all history," praised Douglas MacArthur, a top American general.

But the fighting raged on, with some of the biggest battles in the history of war taking place on the blood-soaked Soviet soil that spring. Joseph Stalin, the Soviet premier, called desperately for the Americans and British to launch an invasion of German-held Western Europe. This would force Hitler to fight on two fronts, taking pressure off the Soviets.

President Franklin Roosevelt and British Prime Minister Winston Churchill told Stalin it was coming. American and British troops were just beginning their attack on Germany's ally, Italy. And American forces were locked in ferocious battles with Japan all over the Pacific. A major invasion of Western Europe was still a year away.

Americans continued shipping weapons to the Soviets, but the atomic bomb remained a secret. In fact, Roosevelt and Churchill signed a special agreement, vowing to keep it that way. It was the job of Army Counter-Intelligence to guard the world's most dangerous secret—not just from the Germans, but from the Soviets as well. So CIC officers were determined to investigate any suspicious behavior.

Especially when it came from the director of Los Alamos.

ON JUNE 14, CIC agents tailed Oppenheimer onto a train heading from Berkeley to San Francisco. At the San Francisco station, they watched as Oppenheimer was greeted by a tall woman with dark hair. They recognized her as Jean Tatlock, a former girlfriend of Oppenheimer's and a member of the Communist Party.

Oppenheimer and Tatlock walked arm in arm to Tatlock's car, got in, and drove off. The agents followed the car to a Mexican restaurant in San Francisco. Oppenheimer and Tatlock went inside, had dinner and drinks, then drove to her apartment, and entered together. The agents sat in their car, watching the windows. Tatlock's lights went out at 11:30. "Oppenheimer was not observed until 8:30 a.m. next day," the agents reported, "when he and Jean Tatlock left the building together."

The agents sent their report to Lt. Colonel Boris Pash, the top army intelligence officer on the West Coast. He'd already suspected Oppenheimer of disloyalty. Now he was seriously alarmed.

Pash reported to General Groves's office in Washington, D.C., suggesting that the "subject still is or may be connected with the Communist Party." Pash believed that Oppenheimer was either handing secrets directly to the Soviets, "or he may be making that information available to his other contacts"—Jean Tatlock, for instance.

Pash strongly recommended that Oppenheimer "be removed completely from the project and dismissed from employment by the U.S. Government."

Groves refused. He had no idea what Oppenheimer and Tatlock had been up to in her apartment. He didn't want to know. He trusted Oppenheimer's loyalty. Besides, his number one worry was to build an atomic bomb before Hitler did. For this, he said, "Oppenheimer is irreplaceable."

"If anything happens to Oppenheimer," he added, "the project will be set back at least six months."

Groves's word was final. But if Army Counter-Intelligence couldn't get rid of Oppenheimer, they could certainly let him know how they felt.

"In the future, please avoid seeing your questionable friends," Colonel Kenneth Nichols told Oppenheimer. "And remember, whenever you leave Los Alamos, we will be tailing you."

This frightened Oppenheimer. He had no idea how long intelligence agents had been following him, or what they already knew about his private life. Suddenly worried about losing his position at Los Alamos, he decided to tell Colonel Pash about the time, six months earlier, that his friend Haakon Chevalier had approached him about sharing information with the Soviets. Oppenheimer repeated the brief conversation he had had with Chevalier. He assured Pash the subject had not come up again.

Oppenheimer hoped this confession would convince Pash of his loyalty. Instead, Pash was more suspicious than ever. *Had the Chevalier meeting really been that innocent*? Pash wondered. *If so, why did Oppenheimer wait so long to tell us about it*?

Pash dashed off another memo to Groves, this time accusing Oppenheimer of "playing a key part in the attempts of the Soviet Union to secure, by espionage, highly secret information which is vital to the security of the United States."

Again, Groves defended the man he'd chosen.

ARMY COUNTER-INTELLIGENCE and the FBI still believed Oppenheimer was sneaking information to the Soviets. There's no evidence that he was. Soviet memos and cables from the time show that the KGB never gave up hope of cultivating Oppenheimer—but never made any progress, either.

Meanwhile, the Soviet atomic bomb project was moving ahead. In mid 1943, the Soviet government established "Laboratory Number 2," a secret lab in the pine woods outside Moscow. The job of building the Soviet bomb was put in the hands of a forty-year-old physicist named Igor Kurchatov.

With resources short during wartime, Kurchatov and his team badly needed help from Soviet spies. Intelligence was still coming in from Klaus Fuchs in Britain, and it was good stuff. "The material as a whole," reported Kurchatov, "shows that it is technically possible to solve the entire uranium problem in a much shorter period than our scientists believed."

But what Kurchatov really needed was specific information on bomb design, and there was only one place to get it. "It is extremely important," he said, "to receive detailed technical material on this problem from America."

In Moscow, KGB officers were intensely frustrated by how little they'd uncovered about the Manhattan Project. "In the presence of this research work," Moscow cabled its spies in America, "vast both in scale and scope, being conducted right here next to you, the slow pace of agent cultivation in the USA is particularly intolerable."

What exactly were the Americans doing? The Soviets would never know—not until the KGB could get a scientist *inside* the Manhattan Project.

Then, in late 1943, the KGB got its first big break. It happened because the work at Los Alamos was proving even more difficult than Oppenheimer had expected. He needed more talent, and fast. The British government agreed to send Oppenheimer a team of top physicists.

In November Klaus Fuchs sailed for America.

A FEW WEEKS LATER, Harry Gold got a call from his KGB contact, Semyon Semyonov. Gold was needed in New York City right away.

Gold hurried to the meeting place, a dark restaurant. He saw right away that Sam was "extremely excited—more so than I had ever seen him before."

Gold asked if this had something to do with the industrial spies he'd been picking up information from over the past couple of years.

"Forget them," Semyonov said. "Forget everything you ever knew about them. You are never to see them or meet them or have anything to do with them again."

Gold was too stunned to respond.

"Something has come up," the Russian continued, "and it is so big and so tremendous that you have got to exert your complete efforts to carrying it through successfully. You have got to concentrate on it completely. Before you make a single move in connection with this, you are to think, think twice, think three times. You cannot make any mistakes."

# FERRY JOB

**FOR MONTHS AFTER THE ATTACK** on the heavy water plant at Vemork, Knut Haukelid stayed hidden in the mountains of Norway. "It was an uncommonly hard winter," he later said, "with vast amounts of snow."

German troops swarmed the area in search of the saboteurs. Haukelid and Arne Kjelstrup managed to stay a step ahead of them, but game was scarce in the barren, snowy mountains. Cold weather causes the body to burn calories quickly in an attempt to create heat. Haukelid and Kjelstrup simply couldn't find the calories.

"One day I managed to kill a squirrel with my skiing stick," remembered Haukelid. "When I ate him, he was just as miserably thin and undernourished as we were."

They starved through winter and into spring, dodging German patrols, waiting for their next job.

"When this war is over," said Kjelstrup after yet another unsatisfying meal, "I shall spend all my money on food. I shan't spend any on girls."

Haukelid licked his long-since empty spoon.

"Same here," he said.

FROM HIS OFFICE IN WASHINGTON, D.C., General Leslie Groves followed the news from Norway. "The first reports on this action were most encouraging," said Groves of the Gunnerside raid. The heavy water equipment had been destroyed, dealing a serious blow to German bomb research.

But by the summer of 1943 things had changed. Sources inside the Vemork plant—Norwegian workers who fed information to the resistance network—reported that the Germans were furiously rebuilding the equipment. In August, Vemork again began shipping heavy water to Germany, under heavy guard.

Groves was alarmed. If the Germans wanted heavy water that badly, he figured, they must be using it in their atomic bomb program. The supply must be cut off.

Just before noon on November 16, about a hundred U.S. Air Force bombers appeared two miles above the Vemork plant. Prepared for an air raid, German soldiers turned on smoke machines, which clouded the blue sky. The bombers released seven hundred bombs into the gorge on which the Vemork plant was perched.

The five-hundred-pound bombs exploded all over the gorge and the nearby town of Rjukan. One hit a bomb shelter, killing sixteen Norwegians. Several landed around Vemork, with just two hitting the heavy water plant. The high concentration room, deep in the basement of the steel and concrete structure, was unscratched.

Yet the bombing was a success, in an unexpected way. German authorities realized their precious heavy water would never be safe in Norway.

In early February 1944, more news reached London and Washington: The Germans were beginning to empty the heavy water machines. All the heavy water—far more than had ever been shipped before—was being loaded into barrels. Very soon it would be taken to Germany.

Groves demanded that those barrels be stopped before reaching German soil. British intelligence gave the job to the man in Norway with the most experience in sabotage: Knut Haukelid.

HAUKELID ENLISTED the help of another underground fighter, Rolf Sörlie. In need of much more information, the two snuck into Rjukan, the town near the Vemork plant. In the dark street, they met Kjell Nielsen, an engineer at the plant, and a man they knew could be trusted.

"Haukelid was awful to look at," Nielsen later said, "with a dense beard, and marked by the tough life in the mountains."

They hurried to Nielsen's rented room and went inside to talk. Yes, Nielsen confirmed, about forty large barrels were being filled with heavy water. In a few days, they'd be loaded onto railway cars and taken by train from the plant. At Lake Tinn, the rail cars would slide onto a ferryboat for the trip down the long, narrow waterway. Then the cars would continue by rail to the coast, where the barrels would be transferred to a ship and taken across the North Sea to Germany.

The Germans knew an attack was likely. The barrels would travel under heavy guard, and German planes would fly overhead to watch the land on either side of the tracks.

Haukelid relayed the details to British intelligence in London, saying that the job would be tricky and might result in the loss of civilian lives.

"Case considered," came the immediate reply from London. "Very urgent that heavy water be destroyed. Hope this can be done without too serious consequences. Send our best wishes for good luck in the work."

HAUKELID GAVE SÖRLIE a quick course in sabotage and explosives. In need of a third man for the job, they recruited Knut Lier-Hansen, a surveyor who lived in Rjukan. "A tough young fellow who did not know what nerves meant," was how Sörlie described Lier-Hansen. "Seldom have I seen anyone become so enthusiastic at the prospect of being involved in an action that might be dangerous."

In a series of secret meetings, each in a different location, the three men reviewed their options. One was to try another Gunnerside-style commando raid. This was unlikely to succeed, since the Germans now had extra soldiers on patrol. If Haukelid could gather a trained crew of twenty or thirty, he'd give it a try. "But the time was too short for that," he said.

Another option was to lay dynamite on the track and blow up the train somewhere along the route. But could they plant the charges without being spotted? What if the Germans sent scouts ahead of the train to inspect the rails? Would the explosion be certain to destroy the heavy water? "There were so many unknown factors that we had to give up the plan," said Haukelid.

They went over the route again—and spotted the weak link. At Lake Tinn, the train cars would be loaded onto a ferryboat. If they could sink the boat over the deepest part of the lake, the barrels of heavy water would come to rest 1,300 feet below the surface.

The Vemork engineer Kjell Nielsen got Haukelid the word. The shipment would be traveling in a few days: Sunday morning, February 20.

Haukelid dressed as a workman and walked around the docks on Lake Tinn. He found out that a boat called *Hydro* would be used Sunday morning. He bought a ticket and traveled down the lake on *Hydro*, leaning over the rail, with one eye on the minute hand of his watch.

Thirty minutes after leaving the dock, the boat was over the deepest part of the lake.

AT 1:00 A.M. ON FEBRUARY 20, Lier-Hansen parked his car under a clump of trees about a mile from the ferry dock. He cut the headlights, and he, Haukelid, and Sörlie got out and started toward the water with guns, grenades, and explosives hidden under their long coats.

"The bitterly cold night set everything creaking and crackling," recalled Haukelid. "The ice on the road snapped sharply as we went over it."

They saw the *Hydro* tied up at the dark dock. From scouting the area, they knew there were about thirty German guards at the nearby railway station. There was no one guarding the waterfront.

The men hurried along the dock and jumped onto the boat. Sounds of shouting and laughing rose from the crew's quarters below deck. "Almost the entire ship's crew was gathered together below," Haukelid said, "playing poker rather noisily."

Haukelid led the way down ladders to a hatch leading to the bilge—the ship's lowest compartment. As he opened the hatch he heard footsteps approaching. The men dove behind chairs as the Norwegian night watchman walked up. Lier-Hansen recognized the watchman and stepped out.

"You here, Knut?" asked the startled guard.

"Yes, John," said Lier-Hansen. "With some friends."

Haukelid and Sörlie stepped out from their hiding places. The guard looked them over.

"Hell, John, we're expecting a raid," Lier-Hansen improvised, hoping the guard would assume they needed to hide supplies from the Germans—and hoping he'd sympathize.

The guard pointed to the hatch leading to the bilge, and said, "No problem."

LIER-HANSEN STAYED ABOVE, chatting with the guard, while Haukelid and Sörlie climbed into the bilge.

"It was an anxious job," Haukelid remembered, "and it took time."

Through the freezing, foot-deep water sloshing around at the ship's bottom, they crawled to the front of the ferry. Blowing a hole here, they knew, would cause water to rush in. The front of the boat would sink, forcing the back to rise out of the lake. The ship's propeller would spin uselessly in the air.

Haukelid pulled the bomb out from under his long coat—nineteen pounds of plastic explosive molded into a long sausage shape. He and Sörlie taped it to the ship's metal side. Near the explosive they taped two specially adapted alarm clocks—two, just in case one malfunctioned. The clocks were connected by wire to four flashlight batteries.

Then came the dangerous part: connecting the fuse between the clocks and the explosive. Each clock had a little metal hammer that rang its alarm bell. The bells had been removed, but the hammers were still in place. When the hammer hit a metal plate on the clock, electricity would flow from the batteries through the clocks to the fuses, igniting the explosive. Each bell hammer was set just one-third of an inch above the metal plate. "There was a one-third of an inch between us and disaster," said Haukelid.

Haukelid wound the clocks. He set the alarms to ring at 10:45. He and Sörlie could hear the clocks ticking as they scurried back toward the hatch.

They passed the guard again on their way off the ship. If the man was curious about why they'd taken so long to hide supplies, he showed no sign.

"You on watch now?" Haukelid asked casually.

"Yes," said the guard, "but I go off when the train arrives."

Haukelid smiled and said, "Lucky man."

A FEW HOURS LATER, German soldiers lashed flat train cars carrying forty barrels of heavy water to the deck of the *Hydro*. The ferry pulled away from the dock at 10:15, right on time. There were fifty-three people aboard, about half of them Norwegian civilians. For the first half hour, the lake crossing was routine.

The captain was on the bridge, enjoying the cold, clear morning when he heard the explosion. He knew right away it was a bomb.

The ferry tipped forward. The flatcars rolled down the deck, snapped the ropes holding them in place, crashed into the water, and vanished. Terrified and screaming, civilians and German soldiers tumbled and leaped into the icy water, grabbing for chairs, oars, life vests.

The captain saw there was nothing he could do. "I jumped into the water and swam about fifteen feet from the ship," he later said. "By then the stern was very high and the propeller was still turning."

Just four minutes from the moment of the explosion, it was all over.

"She went down," recalled the captain, "bow first, in the deepest part of the lake."

# DIRTY WORK

**THE NEXT DAY** Knut Lier-Hansen showed up for work in Rjukan, like it was a normal Monday morning. Rolf Sörlie skied back into the mountains and disappeared. Knut Haukelid took a train to the capital city of Oslo. If anything had gone wrong with the ferry job, his mission was to try again to destroy the heavy water before it sailed for Germany.

On a busy Oslo street Haukelid stopped at a newsstand. It was front-page news in every paper: RAILWAY FERRY HYDRO SUNK

He bought a paper and read. The wrecked ferry lay 1,300 feet below the lake's surface. A rescue boat pulled twenty-seven people from the water. Twenty-six, many of them Norwegian civilians, went down with the ferry. The papers said nothing—knew nothing—about the ferry's cargo.

Haukelid slipped across the border to Sweden, beyond the reach of the German search for the ferry saboteurs. In the capital city of Stockholm, he took warm baths and put on clean clothes and ate in brightly lit restaurants. But he was in no mood for such luxuries.

"I was thoroughly tired of being there," he said, "and longed to get back to the mountains and our comrades in Norway."

Haukelid skied back across the border and rejoined the resistance. He would continue battling the German army until the end of the war.

LESLIE GROVES WAS PLEASED by the news from Norway. Pleased, not satisfied.

Yes, he'd managed to deny key material to the Germans. But the bottom line was this: He still had no idea what was going on inside German weapons labs. "We were truly in the dark then about their progress in atomic development," Groves later said.

The biggest danger, Groves figured, came from world-class German physicists. "Unless and until we had positive knowledge to the contrary," he explained, "we had to assume that the most competent German scientists and engineers were working on an atomic program with the full support of their government."

Groves talked it over with Oppenheimer and other scientists at Los Alamos, many of whom had studied and worked in Germany before the war. Groves wanted to know the names of the most brilliant German physicists—the ones most likely to succeed in giving Hitler an atomic bomb.

They all agreed on one name: Werner Heisenberg.

"The position of Heisenberg in German physics is essentially unique," Oppenheimer said. He'd be at the head of any serious German program.

The German-born physicist Hans Bethe even had an idea of what to do about it. "Kidnapping Heisenberg," said Bethe, "would greatly limit the German project."

Groves considered the idea. Kidnapping was not part of his job description, but he was ready to do whatever it took to win this race. He passed the suggestion on to a fellow general, asking the man to raise the subject with Army Chief of Staff, General George Marshall.

Marshall's reply came back: "Tell Groves to take care of his own dirty work." Groves took careful note of the wording. Marshall didn't want to know about Groves's dirty work.

But he didn't tell Groves not to get dirty.

THIS WAS A JOB for a new top-secret government agency, the Office of Strategic Services (OSS). Specifically, it was a job for Colonel Carl Eifler.

The thirty-seven-year-old Eifler already had a reputation for reckless bravery. Wounded by flying metal scraps earlier in the war, he'd pulled out his pocketknife and dug the steel from his thigh. His idea of fun was to shoot cigarettes out of his friends' mouths.

In late 1943, Eifler was working for the OSS somewhere in the jungles of southeast Asia. Fighting behind Japanese lines, he organized hit-and-run raids on enemy troops. He enjoyed the work and was disappointed to receive a mysterious order: "On or about 9 December 1943 you will proceed from Nazira [India] to Headquarters Office of Strategic Services Washington, D.C., for temporary duty." Eifler flew to Washington, wondering what he could possibly do so far from the action.

Soon after arriving, he pulled a clean uniform over his muscular 250-pound frame and drove to the OSS building. He walked in and was headed toward the director's office when he spotted a man he knew, a young lawyer who'd once dared to criticize Eifler in an official report.

Eifler lunged at the small man, seized him by his jacket, lifted him off the floor, and smacked his back into the wall. Eifler leaned in close, glaring in the man's eyes.

"Listen, you son of a bitch," he growled. "If you ever interfere in my activities again, I'll kill you."

Eifler set the lawyer down, turned, and walked to his meeting.

HE WAS GREETED by Major Robert Furman, General Groves's top intelligence officer.

"What can you tell me of my new assignment?" asked Eifler.

Without getting into specifics, Furman explained that the United States and Germany were racing to make a new kind of bomb. If the Germans won the race, they'd win the war. At this point, said Furman, the most dangerous tool the Germans had was between the ears of a physicist named Werner Heisenberg. Eifler had no idea who Heisenberg was and didn't ask.

Instead he said, "You want me to bump him off?"

"By no means," said Furman. "Our purpose is to deny the enemy his brain."

Eifler waited for more.

"Colonel Eifler," began Furman, "do you think you can kidnap this man and bring him out to us?"

"When do I start?"

"By God!" shouted Furman, banging the table, "That's the most refreshing thing I've heard in this whole damned war!"

Several days later Eifler was back at OSS headquarters, meeting this time with director General William Donovan and two of his top officers.

"Carl," said Donovan, "this new operation will not even be given a code name. It is one of the biggest items of the war to date. We cannot even tell you much about the men you will be working with."

Eifler raised no objection.

Colonel Ned Buxton asked, "Well, Eifler, have you selected a plan?"

"Yes, sir," said Eifler. "I have."

Buxton gestured for Eifler to continue.

"I will go in through Switzerland," said Eifler. He explained how he'd sneak across the border into Germany, grab Heisenberg, and drag him back to Switzerland. From there, said Eifler, "I'll take him to a certain airport where you will fly him out."

Buxton pointed out that the Swiss, who were neutral in the war, would raise a stink at having their territory used this way—well, he said, they'd just have to get over it. He agreed to send in an army plane to pick up Eifler and Heisenberg and fly them over the open Atlantic Ocean.

"Once clear of the European coast," said Buxton, "you and the scientist will be dropped to one of our submarines, which will take you aboard for return to the United States."

"If the timing of the plane and submarine are off," said Eifler, "or the submarine is being chased by German subs, or a hurricane is blowing when we get ready to ditch—what of these possibilities?"

Buxton and Donovan exchanged glances, smiling. "Eifler," said Buxton, "you're the last person in the world to be talking of risks."

Eifler conceded the point. But he did have one tactical question.

"I've kidnapped this man and smuggled him safely back to Switzerland," he said. "Now suddenly I'm surrounded by Swiss police and can't get him to the airfield. What are my orders?"

"Very simple, Colonel," said Buxton. "You are to deny Germany the use of his brain."

"The only way to do that is to kill him," said Eifler. "So I kill him, and the Swiss police arrest me—what then?"

"Then we've never heard of you."

# SECRET CITIES

**CARL EIFLER FLEW FROM WASHINGTON TO LONDON** in early 1944. From there he would make his way to Switzerland.

Oppenheimer did what he could to assist, helping the OSS find recent photographs of Heisenberg. Beyond that, the German bomb project was beyond his control. All Oppenheimer could do was build his own bomb as quickly as possible.

By 1944 the stress of the race was taking a visible toll. He was smoking more than ever, as much as four or five packs a day. Violent, purple-faced coughing fits punctured his sentences. He shed more weight from his bony frame, dropping to an almost skeletal 115 pounds.

And yet, somehow, the pressure was making him stronger. He spent long days pacing the Tech Area, popping his head into labs long enough to help solve problems, dropping into offices to join the ever-raging debates.

"It was clear to all of us," remembered Hans Bethe, "that he knew everything that was important to know about the technical problems of the laboratory, and he somehow had it well organized in his head."

When he asked scientists for updates, they'd hand him fifteen- or twenty-page technical papers, dense with formulas and calculations.

"Well," he'd say, "let's look this over and we'll talk about it."

He'd flip through the pages for five minutes—then lead a discussion on the paper's key points.

"He had a remarkable ability to absorb things so rapidly," said the physicist Lee Dubridge. "I don't think there was anything around the lab of any significance that Oppie wasn't fully familiar with."

"Each of us could walk in, sit on his desk, and tell him how we thought something could be improved," remembered Joe Hirschfelder, a chemist. "We all adored and worshipped him."

Robert Wilson expressed a theme echoed by many at Los Alamos: Oppenheimer inspired them to do things they didn't think they could. "In his presence, I became more intelligent," Wilson said, "more vocal, more intense."

"He brought out the best in all of us," agreed Hans Bethe.

Everyone worked day and night, Monday through Saturday. Oppenheimer insisted people take Sundays off to rest and recharge. Scientists fished for trout in nearby streams, or climbed mountains and discussed physics while watching the sunrise. "This is how many discoveries were made," one scientist said.

Oppenheimer unwound by jumping on his horse, Chico, and taking long rides in the hills. Armed guards rode two steps behind.

WHEN OPPENHEIMER CALLED Richard Feynman into his office, the twenty-six-year-old Feynman must have thought he was in trouble again. Several times already he'd been ordered to the office of the army censors. Censors read all incoming and outgoing mail, to ensure it contained no secret information. Feynman drove them crazy by having his family write to him in code. He enjoyed cracking the codes. Army censors did not.

Then he found a new hobby: picking locks on filing cabinets around the Tech Area and removing top-secret documents. "Whenever I wanted somebody's report and they weren't around," confessed Feynman, "I'd just go in their office, open the filing cabinet, and take it out."

When he was done, he'd hand the papers back to the scientist and say, "Thanks for your report."

"Where'd you get it?" they'd ask.

"Out of your filing cabinet."

"But I *locked* it!"

"I know you locked it. The locks are no good."

This kind of stuff infuriated Leslie Groves. "Here at great expense," he moaned to Oppenheimer, "the government has assembled the world's largest collection of crackpots."

"He caused a lot of trouble," Oppenheimer's secretary said of Feynman. "But," she added, "Oppie made allowances." Even in a city of geniuses, Feynman's brain stood out. And now Oppenheimer needed him for an urgent job.

By 1944, Los Alamos was just one small part of the Manhattan Project. The government was also building a massive factory at Oak Ridge, Tennessee—a secret city with eighty thousand workers living in trailers around the plant. It was their job to prepare the uranium for the bomb being designed at Los Alamos.

But there was a serious danger, Oppenheimer told Feynman. The army liked to keep everything secret. So the Oak Ridge workers knew very little about uranium—and almost nothing about how to handle the stuff safely. Feynman would have to go there, inspect the factory, and help them prevent a catastrophic nuclear accident.

"Now, the following people are technically able down there at Oak Ridge," said Oppenheimer, naming scientists Feynman should talk to. "I want you to make sure that these people are at the meeting, that you tell them how the thing can be made safe, so that they really understand."

"What if they're not at the meeting?" asked Feynman, feeling suddenly overwhelmed. "What am I supposed to do?"

"Then you should say, 'Los Alamos cannot accept the responsibility for the safety of the Oak Ridge plant!'"

"You mean me, little Richard, is going to go in there and say that?"

"Yes, little Richard, you go and do that."

Feynman collected top-secret reports on uranium and strapped the papers to his back, under his shirt. Then, for the first time in his life, he boarded an airplane.

"I really grew up fast!" he said.

FEYNMAN INSPECTED OAK RIDGE. Conditions were worse than Oppenheimer had feared. Feynman wrote up a report about the safety problems and how to solve them. The next day the Oak Ridge directors gathered to hear his findings, but right before the meeting an army colonel warned Feynman not to discuss any secret information about how the atomic bomb might work.

"It's impossible for them to obey a bunch of rules unless they understand how it works," objected Feynman.

The colonel repeated his order.

Feynman's mind flashed back to his talk with Oppenheimer. He took a deep breath and shouted, "Los Alamos cannot accept responsibility for the safety of the Oak Ridge plant!"

The colonel was silent for a while.

"All right, Mr. Feynman," he said finally. "Go ahead."

Feynman explained the basics: how uranium atoms split when hit with neutrons, how they give off energy, how a chain reaction could lead to an explosion. It wouldn't work with just any uranium, though. The nucleus of a uranium atom usually has a total of 238 protons and neutrons. It's called U-238. When hit with a speeding neutron, U-238 does not fission. It's useless to bomb makers. But a small percentage of uranium atoms—about 1 out of every 130—have a total of 235 protons and neutrons. This is U-235. When U-235 is hit by neutrons, it *does* split and release energy. The incredibly

123

difficult job of the Oak Ridge plant was to separate U-235 atoms from U-238 atoms, sending just the U-235 to Los Alamos.

Feynman explained how much uranium could be brought together before it became dangerous, and how to use cadmium to absorb neutrons and stop a chain reaction. "All of this was elementary stuff at Los Alamos," he recalled, "but they had never heard of any of it, so I appeared to be a tremendous genius to them."

The Oak Ridge directors agreed to redesign the factory with this new information in mind. "That was good," said Feynman. "The plant would have blown up if nobody had paid attention."

OAK RIDGE CONTINUED producing U-235, but very slowly. If everything went well, by the summer of 1945, they'd have enough fuel for just one atomic bomb.

Determined to build a bigger arsenal, Leslie Groves ordered the construction of another secret city, this one in Hanford, Washington. The Hanford plant was based on something else scientists had learned about fission. When U-238 atoms are hit with flying neutrons, they *absorb* the neutrons. That is, the neutrons stick in the nucleus of the uranium. This causes the uranium to change into an entirely new element, one that doesn't occur in nature—scientists named it plutonium. Plutonium, they discovered, will fission even faster than U-235, so it could also be used for building atomic bombs. The Hanford plant was created to produce plutonium as quickly as possible.

Between Los Alamos, Oak Ridge, Hanford, and other secret labs around the country, the Manhattan Project was employing more than 300,000 people. The government was spending hundreds of millions of dollars—yet the project was so secret, President Roosevelt chose not to tell Congress where all the money was going.

A senator from Missouri named Harry Truman began to get curious. "I had known," Truman later said, "something that was unusually important was brewing in our war plants." But what? Worried that the government was wasting taxpayer money, Truman decided to send investigators to Oak Ridge and Hanford.

Very soon after this, Truman's phone rang. It was Secretary of War Henry Stimson.

"I told him that I would come to his office at once," recalled Truman. "He said he would rather come to see me."

The seventy-seven-year-old Stimson walked into Truman's office. He lowered himself into a chair beside Truman's desk and got right to the point. Truman needed to stop asking questions about the secret war plants.

"Senator," said Stimson, "I can't tell you what it is, but it is the greatest project in the history of the world. It is most top secret. Many of the people who are actually engaged in the work have no idea what it is, and we who do would appreciate your not going into those plants."

"Well, all right then," said Truman.

"All right," agreed Stimson.

"You assure me that this is for a specific purpose."

"Not only for a specific purpose," corrected Stimson, "but a unique purpose."

"I'll take you at your word," said Truman, disappointed. "I'll order the investigations into those plants called off."

Truman couldn't help himself, though. He continued poking around for information about where all the money was going.

"Truman is a nuisance," Stimson griped. But nothing the senator did changed Stimson's position. Knowledge of the atomic bomb was available on a strictly need-to-know basis.

Harry Truman did not need to know.

# MAN WITH FOUR GLOVES

ON THE FREEZING AFTERNOON OF FEBRUARY 5, 1944, Harry Gold walked the streets of New York City's Lower East Side. He was wearing gloves and holding a second pair in his hand. This was according to Semyon Semyonov's directions—the gloves were a recognition signal for the man he was to meet. The other man, Gold was told, would be carrying a tennis ball.

A few minutes before four, Gold turned onto Henry Street. He always tried to get to a meeting spot a little early, just to have a look. He liked what he saw. The narrow street was lined with four- and five-story brick tenement buildings, many of them in the process of being torn down and replaced.

"The place had been very well chosen," said Gold. "It was beautifully deserted."

A few blocks away, Klaus Fuchs climbed the concrete stairs of a Manhattan subway station and stepped up onto the streets of the Lower East Side. He pulled out a folded map, took a quick look, and started walking.

As he turned onto Henry Street, he took a tennis ball from the pocket of his long coat. This was according to Ruth Werner's instructions—before leaving Britain, she had told him where and when to meet his American contact. She told him to carry a tennis ball and to look for a man holding an extra pair of gloves. Fuchs did not know the man's real name and was not to ask.

Sure enough, as Fuchs approached the designated spot, there was a man with four gloves, pacing the sidewalk to keep warm. The man glanced at Fuchs, and at the ball in his hand. He stepped forward.

"What is the way to Chinatown?" asked Gold.

"I think Chinatown closes at five o'clock," Fuchs responded.

With this exchange of passwords, each knew for certain he was dealing with the right man.

Gold introduced himself as "Raymond." Fuchs used his real name, since there was no secret about his identity. They shook hands, then began walking together.

"We strolled a while and talked," Gold later reported to Semyonov. "He is about five-foot-ten, thin, pale complexioned, and at first was very reserved in manner."

Gold suggested they get something to eat. Fuchs agreed.

"As I kept talking about myself," reported Gold, "he warmed up and began to show evidence of getting down to business."

Fuchs told Gold he was proud to be helping the Soviet Union. He told Gold where he was living, where the British team was working, and who was on it. He described as much as he knew about the organization of the Manhattan Project, saying he'd heard that the bomb design was happening at a secret site somewhere in New Mexico.

They made arrangements to meet again and agreed to a few basic rules. To avoid drawing attention, they would never meet in the same place twice, and "under no circumstances," said Gold, "were we to wait any longer than four or five minutes at any of the meeting places."

• • •

ABOUT A MONTH LATER, they met again on a Manhattan street corner and walked together toward the East River. Gold asked Fuchs for specifics about his work in America.

Fuchs explained that he and the British team were working out the details of how best to separate U-235 from U-238. The actual work was being done at a factory in the Southeast—the Oak Ridge plant, though Fuchs didn't know that detail yet. Fuchs described some of the complex challenges of separating uranium atoms. With his experience in chemistry, Gold was able to follow the basic science. "At the first opportunity," said Gold, "I put this material in writing, and later handed it over to John."

John was a KGB agent named Anatoly Yatzkov. Gold's long-time contact, Semyon Semyonov, had been under extremely close FBI surveillance lately, making it too risky for him to be closely involved with a source as valuable as Fuchs. Gold's new contact, Yatzkov, worked as a clerk at the Soviet consulate in New York. Soon after receiving Gold's report, Yatzkov slipped away from his desk, walked up to the KGB office on the top floor, coded the report, and sent it to Moscow.

Top officials at KGB headquarters were thrilled. *Finally*, they had a high-level physicist inside the Manhattan Project.

JUST AS HE'D BEEN IN BRITAIN, Fuchs was a bit of a loner in New York. He bought a violin and spent his evenings playing music in his apartment. On weekends, he enjoyed hiking on trails outside the city.

Each weekday he went to his office near Wall Street, where he worked with a team of British physicists. The other scientists liked Fuchs and respected his work, but didn't pay much attention to him. No one noticed him slipping notes and handwritten drafts of technical papers—documents he would have no reason to take home—into his briefcase. "I personally furnished all of the drafts," he later said, "directly to the individual known to me as Raymond."

Fuchs and Gold set a third meeting for March on Park Avenue in Manhattan. It was a chilly day, and both wore overcoats. Fuchs and Gold spotted each other and knew what to do.

"We immediately turned into one of the dark deserted side streets," Gold recalled.

Gold walked up behind Fuchs. Fuchs took an envelope from his overcoat pocket and passed it quickly to Gold, who dropped it inside his coat. They walked together to the next corner, then separated.

"The whole affair took possibly thirty seconds or one minute," Gold said. That was standard tradecraft—when documents were to be exchanged, meetings should be very short. "Approximately fifteen minutes later," said Gold, "I turned over the information to John."

Fuchs and Gold met again in late March in the Bronx. While they had dinner, Fuchs told Gold that the atomic bomb was being designed at a place called Los Alamos. At several more meetings in May and June, Fuchs delivered packages of documents with technical information on his work. Gold took the packages directly to Anatoly Yatzkov.

After one of his pick-ups from Fuchs, Gold arrived early for the hand-off to Yatzkov. "I still had about five minutes," he said. He felt the large envelope in his pocket. Inside was information about the most closely guarded secret on earth. The temptation was too great. Gold stopped on the street, in front of a drug store. He looked all around. No one was watching. He slipped the envelope from his jacket pocket, reached in, pulled out the papers, and tilted them toward the faint light coming through the store window. He began to read.

"This was in a very small but distinct writing," he said, "it was in ink, and consisted mainly of mathematical derivations."

Gold didn't understand a word of it.

129

IN LATE JULY, Gold arrived at the Bell Cinema in Brooklyn for a meeting with Fuchs. Fuchs never showed.

Their backup meeting was scheduled for a couple weeks later on the corner of Ninety-Sixth Street and Central Park West in Manhattan. Again, Gold waited. Again, no Fuchs.

"On this second occasion I became very worried," said Gold. "The area is very close to a section of New York where muggings often occur."

Yatzkov told Gold to try to find out if Fuchs was still in New York. Gold wrote Fuchs's name and address in a book and took it to the scientists' building. He was let in by a woman who was cleaning the lobby. Gold showed her the book, explaining he'd borrowed it from his friend, Klaus Fuchs, and was here to return it.

Fuchs was gone, the woman said. He'd left town suddenly and didn't say where he was going.

Gold passed the bad news to Yatzkov. KGB officials in Moscow were furious. After years of frustration they'd finally gotten a source inside the American bomb project—and now they'd lost him. "A stern warning and reprimand must be made," Moscow cabled its New York office, "for losing contact with such a source."

The Soviets never could have guessed that a second source was about to walk in the door.

# BORN REBEL

**WHEN THEODORE HALL GRADUATED** high school at the age
of thirteen, he listed his three top career options: comedian, journalist, physicist.

At just fourteen, Hall entered Queens College in New York City. Finding
the work too easy, he transferred to Harvard and loaded up on the toughest
math and physics courses available. The challenging subjects were "delightful" and "hot stuff," he told his brother. Physicist jumped to the top of his
dream job list.

Ted Hall turned eighteen in 1944. He was about six feet tall and very thin,
with wavy black hair. He was about to finish college and assumed he'd be
drafted into the army as soon as he graduated. The government had other
plans.

One afternoon, Hall was asked to report to a meeting room in the physics
lab building on campus. When he walked in he saw that the shades were
drawn, the lights dim. There was a long table in the room, but only one man

sat at the table. He introduced himself as a physics professor who now worked for the government in Washington, D.C.

"There is a project," the man told Hall. "It's doing quite important work, and they need some more hands."

Hall asked for a bit more detail. The man shook his head, saying only that the project was war-related and top secret.

After the meeting, Hall walked back to his dorm. He talked with a friend from down the hall, a fellow physics student who had also been recruited by the mysterious man from Washington. They took turns guessing what they were being asked to do and where they'd go to do it.

Hall's roommate, Saville Sax, listened to the whole conversation. Sax was a dedicated Communist, and he knew Hall had shown interest in communism as well.

"If this turns out to be a weapon that is really awful," Sax said, "what you should do about it is tell the Russians."

Hall glared at Sax. Sax said nothing more.

HALL RODE THE TRAIN to New Mexico and found his way to 109 East Palace Avenue in Santa Fe. He walked through a courtyard, knocked on a door, and entered a small office. There at a desk sat a smiling Dorothy McKibben. She made an ID badge for Hall and a quick phone call. A car came, and Hall was driven to the top of a nearby mesa and through the gates of Los Alamos.

At a brief orientation, Hall was told he'd be helping to build an atomic bomb. He was given a secret little book known as "The Los Alamos Primer," made up of copies of the lectures Robert Serber had given the year before. He got a white ID badge, giving him unrestricted access to the Tech Area.

After spending a few days studying atomic bomb physics, Hall went to work with a team led by the Italian-born physicist Bruno Rossi. The team was given a tiny amount of pure U-235, one of the first samples to arrive from the Oak Ridge plant. Rossi asked Hall to carefully place the thin uranium strip inside a specially built machine that would bombard the uranium with neu-trons. The more senior scientists watched while Hall worked the uranium into place. If he dropped the sample and contaminated it, they'd have to wait weeks for more U-235.

"It wasn't the easiest gadget to work with," Hall said later. "As I mounted the specimen, I remember my hands were shaking. I don't know whether they were shaking enough for anyone else to see."

Hall got the sample into place, and Rossi's machine bombarded it with neutrons. They figured out how many of the neutrons hit uranium atoms and caused fission. This was part of the process of determining exactly how much U-235 would be needed to make a uranium bomb.

Impressed with his youngest team member, Rossi recommended Hall for even more important work. And in the summer of 1944, Oppenheimer needed all the help he could get.

THE CRISIS BEGAN THAT SPRING, remembered the mathematician Stanislaw Ulam. Ulam was working in his office when he heard footsteps and turned toward his open door.

"I saw Robert Oppenheimer running excitedly down a corridor holding a small vial in his hand," Ulam said. "Doors opened, people were summoned, whispered conversations ensued, there was great excitement."

Ulam ran into the hall and was told that Oppenheimer was holding the first samples of plutonium to arrive at Los Alamos. It was just a few grams, but it was enough to start some important experiments.

The plan for the uranium bomb was to fire one lump of uranium at another inside a gun barrel. Oppenheimer's scientists assumed this same gun assembly method would work for plutonium. But experiments proved them wrong.

Fission occurred even faster than expected in plutonium, causing a chain reaction to begin more quickly than in uranium. So, in a gun assembly bomb, the chain reaction would start even *before* the two lumps of plutonium came completely together. Enough energy would be released to blow the plutonium apart—but only with about as much force as a normal bomb. The critical mass of plutonium would not stay together long enough to create a massive atomic explosion.

"The terrible shock, and an inescapable one, was that the gun assembly method could not be used for plutonium," John Manley remembered. "A gun just would not assemble plutonium fast enough."

What made this such a serious crisis was that Oak Ridge *might* be able to produce enough U-235 for one atomic bomb by the middle of 1945. If Oppenheimer was going to make more than one bomb—and Groves was *demanding* that he do so—the bombs would have to be made with plutonium, which was easier to produce that U-235. The bottom line: Oppenheimer now had to figure out a whole new design for an atomic bomb.

The timing only added to the pressure. Allied forces landed in France in June 1944 and began battling east across French territory toward Germany. The Allies were finally winning the war—but Hitler could still turn it around by winning the race for the atomic bomb.

"The only way we could lose the war," said physicist Philip Morrison, "was if we failed in our jobs."

STILL EIGHTEEN, Ted Hall was the youngest scientist at Los Alamos. By summer he'd learned the basics of the uranium bomb. Then Bruno Rossi put him to work experimenting with components of the new plutonium bomb.

The challenge of the top-secret work was thrilling. "Living conditions are still poor here and will remain so," Hall wrote to his family, "but I would be willing to live on whale blubber alone in an igloo at the South Pole for a crack at the same job."

Hall felt relaxed enough at Los Alamos to be himself, which meant doing things his own way. Once, late at night, a fellow physicist came into Hall's office to look for some papers. He saw a ten-foot high stack of crates in the middle of the room. On top of the leaning tower sat Hall, cross-legged, lost in thought.

"He was interested in tweaking the system," said one scientist. "He was a natural-born rebel."

On Sundays, Hall sometimes went on hikes or played a little Ping-Pong. But he spent most of his time off lying on the bed in his tiny room, listening to classical music and thinking. And not about science.

"I shared the general sympathy for our allies, the Soviet Union," Hall explained. "After they were attacked, everybody knew that they were bearing the main load in the fight against Nazi Germany."

It looked like the Germans would be defeated, but what then? Hall tried to imagine what the post-war world would be like.

"I shared a common belief that the horrors of war would bring our various leaders to their senses and usher in a period of peace and harmony," Hall said. But what if this didn't happen? What if Americans succeeded in building atomic bombs and they were the only ones to have them? Would the United States be more likely to use atomic bombs, knowing no one else could strike back? Wouldn't the world be safer if a second major power also knew how to build atomic bombs? That way, neither country would use the bomb— knowing they'd have the bomb used on them.

"It seemed to me," Hall said, "that an American monopoly was dangerous and should be prevented."

Looking back at his younger self, Hall would later call himself a "rather arrogant" teenager. That helps explain why he decided to change the course of history.

"My decision about contacting the Soviets was a gradual one," he said, "and it was entirely my own."

# TWO  INSIDE

IN MID-OCTOBER 1944, Ted Hall left Los Alamos and took the train home for two weeks of leave. He celebrated his nineteenth birthday with his parents in New York City.

The next day, October 21, Hall went to visit Saville Sax, his former college roommate. Ted found Sax at Sax's mother's small Manhattan apartment. While his mother ironed in one room, Sax led Hall to another and closed the door. In hushed voices, Hall told his friend about his decision. But, Hall wondered, how does one go about handing military secrets to the Soviet Union?

Sax had no idea. They talked over options and made a plan.

Later that day, Hall walked to the offices of a company called Amtorg, a Soviet import/export business. This was the company KGB agent Semyon Semyonov had worked for; many of the Amtorg employees doubled as Soviet spies. Hall didn't know this. It just seemed like a good place to start.

Hall entered the building and found himself in a warehouse. He saw a worker stacking boxes and approached him.

"I want to speak to someone about an important military issue," Hall said.

The worker knew the FBI kept watch on the building. He told Hall to leave immediately.

Hall persisted, asking if there was someone else he could talk to.

The man quickly gave Hall a name, Sergei Kurnakov, along with a phone number. Then he turned back to his boxes.

Hall recognized Kurnakov's name—he was a Soviet journalist based in New York. Hall had read his articles. Was he also a secret agent for the KGB? Hall didn't know, but at least it was a lead.

Hall called the number. Kurnakov invited the young man to drop by his apartment.

THE NEXT DAY Hall and Kurnakov sat in the Soviet journalist's living room. As soon as Hall began talking, Kurnakov realized his young guest had "an exceptionally keen mind."

The young man was also clearly nervous, making aimless small talk and biting his nails. Kurnakov filled two small glasses with vodka. Hall downed his drink. Kurnakov poured him another.

"T. H. is nineteen years old," Kurnakov reported to his KGB contact in New York—Kurnakov was, in fact, a spy. "Pale and slightly pimply face, carelessly dressed; you can tell his boots haven't been cleaned in a long time; his socks are bunched up around the ankles."

Beginning to relax, Hall turned the conversation to Los Alamos. He was working there, he told Kurnakov, alongside some of the world's most famous scientists. They were trying to build a secret weapon.

Kurnakov listened, asking himself: *Can this pimply kid really be a physicist? Does he really have access to top-secret information?*

Reaching for a pile of newspaper clippings, Kurnakov showed Hall an article about a new type of missile being developed by the United States. He asked if this is what Hall was working on.

137

"No," Hall said. "It's much worse than that."

Kurnakov told him to continue.

Hall said he was helping to build an atomic bomb. He was starting to explain its destructive power when Kurnakov cut him off.

"Do you understand what you are doing?" Kurnakov demanded. "What makes you think you should reveal the USA's secrets for the USSR's sake?"

"The Soviet Union is the only country that can be trusted with such a terrible thing," said Hall. "But since we can't take it away from other countries, the USSR ought to be aware of its existence and stay abreast of the progress of experiments and construction."

"Well," said Kurnakov, "how do we know that you're not just an agent of the U.S. government trying to trap me?"

"You don't."

"Why don't you just write your ideas, or whatever you want to tell us, and give it to me."

"I've already done that."

Hall pulled out a folder and handed it to Kurnakov. Inside was what Kurnakov described as a "neatly written report" outlining the basic scientific principles of the atomic bomb.

"Show this to any physicist," Hall said, pointing to the papers. "He'll understand what it's about."

Kurnakov still couldn't figure out if he was being set up by the FBI or handed the gift of a lifetime. He stepped into the next room and asked his wife to go outside and check for signs that the building was being watched. She walked around the block, seeing nothing to make her suspicious.

Kurnakov decided the potential payoff was worth the risk. He took Hall's folder, promising to check into everything and get back to Hall very soon.

Hall explained he'd be leaving in three days for Los Alamos, and, once there, would be nearly impossible to reach. Army censors read the mail and listened to the phone calls. Maybe they could use his friend Saville Sax as a courier, Hall suggested. Then he left.

Kurnakov handed Hall's folder to his wife. He put on his coat, stepped into the street, and started to walk. If American agents *were* watching the building, he figured, they'd follow him.

A few minutes later his wife walked out of the building with Hall's folder in her purse.

ON HIS LAST DAY IN NEW YORK, Hall went to lunch with his father and then on to Penn Station to catch his train. He was standing in the busy station, chatting with his dad, when he noticed someone watching him. It was Sergei Kurnakov.

He walked to Kurnakov. Their lowered voices were drowned out by surrounding conversations and the echo of footsteps on marble floors.

Hall's offer to provide information had been accepted by the KGB, Kurnakov said. Saville Sax would act as courier between Hall and the Soviets.

Hall boarded his train and headed west. His "neatly written report" headed east, to Moscow.

The KGB's chief of foreign intelligence, Pavel Fitin, said Hall's information "is of great interest to us." That was a massive understatement. Top Soviet officials like Fitin lived in terror of Joseph Stalin. Anyone who angered or disappointed the Soviet dictator could wind up in a Siberian prison camp—or with a bullet in the brain. Now, after years of agonizing frustration, Fitin could boast of having a physicist not just inside the Manhattan Project, but inside Los Alamos itself.

It was pure luck, but he'd take it.

MEANWHILE, Harry Gold and his KGB contact Anatoly Yatzkov were still looking for Klaus Fuchs.

"Our principle trouble," Gold later said, "was to decide whether Klaus, for some reason, was unable to keep the meetings if he was still in New York, or whether he had actually left New York."

From the KGB offices in Moscow, Yatzkov learned that Fuchs had a sister named Kristel Heineman living in Cambridge, Massachusetts. She was a Communist and knew her brother was in touch with the Soviets. If a Soviet agent ever needed to reach Fuchs, secret passwords had been arranged by which the agent could make himself known to Heineman.

In early November, Gold took the bus to Cambridge and found Heineman's house. He rang the front door bell. The door was opened, Gold recalled, by "an exceedingly beautiful woman."

"I bring you greetings from Max," said Gold.

"Oh," Kristel Heineman responded, "I heard Max had twins."

"Yes, seven days ago."

Now Heineman knew her visitor had come from the Soviets. She invited Gold inside and introduced him to her three young children. Gold asked if she knew where her brother was.

Yes, she said, he had been transferred somewhere in the Southwest United States. He'd be in Cambridge for a visit sometime around Christmas.

"So I can see him then," Gold reported to Yatzkov. "I was so overjoyed that I stayed for lunch."

THE MOMENT HE'D HEARD "Southwest United States," Gold figured Fuchs must be at Los Alamos. He was right.

When Oppenheimer realized he needed to design a new type of plutonium bomb, he'd called for extra help. Fuchs and the British team had moved from New York to Los Alamos in August 1944. Once there, Fuchs was unable to contact Gold, knowing the army listened to phone calls and read the mail. But he knew the Soviets. He knew they would find him.

Fuchs got to work and quickly became a valuable member of the Los Alamos team. "He worked days and nights," Hans Bethe would later say. "He contributed very greatly to the success of the Los Alamos project."

Fuchs was given a tiny Tech Area office overlooking a pond. He got there before eight every morning and stayed late into the night. At lunchtime, he stood at the pond feeding ducks, alone.

"He's all ears and no mouth," a fellow Los Alamos physicist complained. "You talk about your work to him, but you never feel he's giving you anything back."

After work, Fuchs walked back to his room in Bachelor Dormitory Number 102. The wife of an Italian physicist used to watch him march slowly past their window, his pale, owlish face turned down toward the muddy path. She named him "Poverino"—the pitiful one.

In the dorm, Fuchs's only visitor was the scientist in the adjoining room, Richard Feynman. They often sat up late together, Fuchs smoking, Feynman sipping orange juice.

"Klaus," Feynman teased, "you're missing a lot of fun in life."

In spite of Fuchs's reserve, people liked him. He seemed so gentle and generous. Women often asked him to babysit on Saturday nights, and Fuchs always agreed. He put the kids to bed, then sat and read, listening to classical music.

And Fuchs did open up a bit over time. He bought a beat-up blue Buick and gave people rides into Santa Fe. He tagged along on hikes and picnics. At one late-night party, he stunned everyone by downing a bottle of whisky and leading a conga line. Then he excused himself politely, stepped behind the bar, and passed out. Friends tucked a sheet over him and went on with the party.

"In the course of this work, I began naturally to form bonds of personal friendship," Fuchs later said. "I had to conceal from them my inner thoughts." The solution, he explained, was to establish two separate compartments in his mind. "One compartment in which I allowed myself to make friendships, to have personal relations, to help people, and to be in all personal ways the kind of man I wanted to be." This is the Fuchs people saw. They sensed there was something more, something beneath the surface. No one guessed it was Fuchs's "second compartment"—the one he used for his secret mission.

"Everyone thought of him as a quiet, industrious man who would do just about anything he could to help our project," Hans Bethe said. "If he was a spy, he played his role beautifully."

141

PAUL TIBBETS (BACK ROW, THIRD FROM LEFT) AND THE CREW OF THE ENOLA GAY

DAVID GREENGLASS U.S. Army Sergeant and spy for the Soviets

GEORGE KISTIAKOWSKY Manhattan Project chemist

HARRY TRUMAN U.S. President, 1945-1953

LONA COHEN
courier and
spy for the
Soviets

# PART 4: FINAL ASSEMBLY

MOE BERG
former ball
player; OSS
operative

TRINITY TEST
SITE

# THE PILOT

**LATE IN THE SUMMER OF 1944,** at the Alamogordo Air Force Base in New Mexico, a fighter pilot named Paul Tibbets got a strange phone call from his father in Miami.

"Are you in some kind of trouble, son?" his father asked.

Tibbets could hear the concern in his father's voice. "Not that I know of," he answered. "What makes you think so?"

"Well . . ." his father began, sounding unsure of whether or not to continue. "I hear some investigators—I think they were from the FBI—have been down here asking questions about you."

Tibbets assured his father it was just a routine check. But he knew better. This was not normal.

Twenty-nine years old, Colonel Paul Tibbets was an experienced pilot who'd flown combat missions over Europe and North Africa. Now he was

*Paul Tibbets stands in front of the* Enola Gay *on Tinian Island, August 6, 1945.*

back in the States working as a test pilot, helping engineers design the new B-29 bomber. He was one of the best flyers in the country. So he couldn't help but wonder: *What exactly have I done wrong?*

The mystery intensified a few days later when he got another call, this one from Air Force General Uzal Ent, telling him to report right away to Ent's office in Colorado Springs, Colorado.

"He told me to pack my bags," Tibbets recalled. "I would not be returning."

TIBBETS FLEW TO COLORADO AND WALKED into Ent's headquarters the next morning. He was met by Colonel John Lansdale of Army Counter-Intelligence. Lansdale led Tibbets into a small side office.

"I'd like to ask you a couple of questions before we go in to see General Ent," said Lansdale.

"Without explaining his purpose, he began talking about my personal history," remembered Tibbets. "His 'couple of questions' stretched into an interrogation from which I soon discovered that he knew more about me than I could possibly remember about myself."

"Have you ever been arrested?" Lansdale finally asked.

Tibbets's mind raced back ten years to a night on the beach in Florida. He and his girlfriend had driven to a dark spot and climbed into the backseat. A while later they were startled by the sudden glare of a policeman's flashlight. Could Lansdale really know about that? *He must*, figured Tibbets, *he knows everything else.*

Tibbets decided to tell Lansdale the story. Lansdale listened without comment.

Then he stood and said, "Now let's go see General Ent."

Tibbets followed Lansdale into Ent's office, where the general sat at his desk. There were two other men there: a naval officer and a man in a suit.

Ent introduced Tibbets to Navy Captain William Parsons and Dr. Norman Ramsey, a professor of physics.

"I'm well satisfied with Colonel Tibbets," Lansdale announced.

"That's good," said Ent. "I felt sure you would be."

Ent then told Tibbets he had been chosen for a vital mission. A top-secret mission. Everything Tibbets was about to hear, Ent cautioned, would have to be concealed, even from his wife—even from the pilots and crews who would be working under him.

Then Ent turned to Professor Ramsey, saying, "Now you take over."

Ramsey asked Tibbets: "Did you ever hear of atomic energy?"

OPPENHEIMER'S SCIENTISTS had not yet built an atomic bomb. It was far from certain they could. But U.S. military planners had to think ahead. If a bomb were built in time to affect the outcome of the war, it would need to be dropped by plane. A pilot needed to be chosen and given special training. Paul Tibbets got the job.

Tibbets learned the basics of how the atomic bomb would work and approximately how powerful the explosion might be. Using this information, it was his task to devise a strategy for flying the bomb over enemy territory, releasing it on target, and getting away before the massive blast killed everyone in the plane.

Given the freedom to pick his own training site, Tibbets selected a base in Wendover, Utah, a remote spot surrounded by salt flats. "There was no place nearby for fun-loving men with six-hour passes to get into trouble and possibly leak information," explained Tibbets.

Then Tibbets chose his flight crews, hand-picking many of the men he'd flown with earlier in the war. He wouldn't tell them what their new mission was and warned them never to ask. "We didn't want them even to speculate," said Tibbets, "or to give out a hint that our operation was different from any other."

Known as the 509th Composite Group, Tibbets's mysterious team was officially activated on December 17, 1944. "At the age of twenty-nine, I had

**147**

been entrusted with the successful delivery of the most frightful weapon ever devised," Tibbets recalled. "Although the weapon was beyond my comprehension, there was nothing about flying an airplane that I did not understand. If this bomb could be carried in an airplane, I could do the job."

# SWISS DEAL

CARL EIFLER STOOD ON THE BALCONY of the Office of Strategic Services office in the city of Algiers, Algeria. Loud honks and shouts rose from the hectic street below. OSS director General William Donovan stepped onto the balcony. He closed the door behind him.

Eifler had spent the past few months perfecting his plan to kidnap the German physicist Werner Heisenberg and putting together his team for the job. Everything was set, he told Donovan, for "my proposed entry into Country X."

"Carl, there's a change in your orders," Donovan informed Eifler. "We have broken the atom secret with our Manhattan Project. We beat the Nazis. Your mission is scrubbed."

"I see, sir," said Eifler, blinking back tears of disappointment.

Donovan assured Eifler he'd be given a new assignment, one just as dangerous, penetrating Japanese-held territory in Korea.

Eifler walked back to the room he was sharing with another OSS operative. Unable to sleep that night, he paced the room, muttering, "I can't get him out of my mind . . . I can't get him out of my mind . . ."

"Who?" asked the other man, annoyed at being kept awake.

"The last guy I bumped off," said Eifler.

"Well,"—the roommate yawned—"what can you do about it?"

"Bump off another one."

"Oh, for heaven's sake, Carl! Turn out the light and go to bed."

DONOVAN HAD not been truthful with Eifler. The Americans had not yet "broken the atomic secret" and did not know if they would "beat the Nazis" to the atomic bomb. Donovan just wanted to take Eifler off the job without hurting the man's feelings.

But the job was still on.

By December 1944, American and British forces were driving toward Germany from the west. The Soviets were coming on fast from the east. Hitler was about to be crushed—unless he could pull out an atomic bomb. So it was still necessary, reasoned Donovan, to target German physicists, especially Heisenberg.

But Donovan had changed his mind about Eifler's fitness for the mission, worried the man's loose-cannon style could draw unwanted attention to the delicate operation. He gave the job instead to a forty-one-year-old former baseball player named Moe Berg.

Berg had been a mediocre ballplayer at best, hitting .243 over fifteen big league seasons as a backup catcher. To Berg, baseball had just been a way to make a living. In the off-season he worked as a lawyer, studied languages, and traveled the world. In 1943, his playing days over, he took his talents to the OSS.

Berg was soon assigned to a secret operation, code-named Alsos. The Alsos mission's job was to follow close behind advancing Allied forces in Europe, searching for any scraps of information about the German atomic bomb program.

Berg spent some time in London studying atomic physics. In early December he was told to report to Paris. Walking the streets, he was spotted by a sportswriter he knew from his previous career. The man smiled with surprise and opened his mouth to speak.

"Don't ask me what I'm doing here," Berg warned.

Actually, he didn't know himself. He found out the next day at a meeting at the Ritz Hotel with Samuel Goudsmit, a physicist who was the scientific head of the Alsos mission. Goudsmit told Berg that based on reliable information coming out of Germany, Werner Heisenberg would be leaving the country on or about December 15, traveling to Switzerland for a scientific conference. He would be giving a lecture at Zurich University on December 18. Berg, explained Goudsmit, would be there too.

"Nothing spelled out," Berg wrote in his notes. "But Heisenberg must be rendered *hors de combat*"—French for "out of the battle."

What exactly was Berg being ordered to do? Neither he nor Goudsmit ever talked publicly about the secret mission referred to in OSS documents as the "Swiss Deal." But after the war, Berg confided in a fellow secret agent, Earl Brodie.

"He'd been drilled in physics, to listen for certain things," Brodie explained. "If anything Heisenberg said convinced Berg the Germans were close to a bomb then his job was to shoot him—right there in the auditorium. It probably would have cost Berg his life—there would have been no way to escape."

WITH HIS DARK complexion and gift for languages, Moe Berg had the ability to pass for a number of nationalities. On one earlier assignment he'd been a French merchant; on another an Arab businessman. On the afternoon of December 18, 1944, in Zurich, Switzerland, Berg was a Swiss student, curious to hear a lecture by the great German physicist Werner Heisenberg.

He found the building where Heisenberg was scheduled to talk, entered, located the correct room, and hung his hat and coat in the hall. He walked into the room holding a notebook in his hand. Tucked in one pocket was a pistol. In another was a cyanide tablet, in case he needed to kill himself before being captured.

Berg looked around the small lecture hall. There were about twenty people in the room, most of them professors or graduate students. The room was freezing, due to wartime fuel shortages. Berg sat in the second row.

Heisenberg opened by explaining the basics of a complex mathematical theory called S-matrix, quickly filling the blackboard with a jumble of symbols and formulas. Berg was instantly lost.

"Don't trouble yourself," called a professor in the front row. "We all know that."

So Heisenberg moved on to an even more advanced description of S-matrix theory. Unable to follow Heisenberg's math, Berg focused on the man.

"Thinnish," Berg wrote in his notebook, "heavy eyebrows . . . sinister eyes."

Heisenberg paced as he spoke, a piece of chalk in his right hand, his left hand buried in his jacket pocket for warmth. He noticed the man in the second row staring at him.

"H. likes my interest in his lecture," Berg jotted.

If he heard anything that led him to believe Heisenberg was close to developing an atomic bomb, Berg's orders were to take the man *hors de combat*. He was prepared to do so. But, as far as Berg could make out, Heisenberg was talking about a completely different subject.

"As I listen, I am uncertain . . . what to do?" wrote Berg. "If they knew what I'm thinking . . ."

Heisenberg ended the lecture, and the other professors and students began discussing his theories. Berg's pistol stayed in his pocket.

IT WAS STILL there a few days later when Berg showed up at a dinner party at a physics professor's house in Zurich. He spotted Heisenberg inside, surrounded by party guests.

Talk turned from science to the war, and several of the guests started grilling Heisenberg, demanding to know how he could live and work under Hitler, a monster who enslaved countries, murdered Jews.

"I'm not a Nazi," said Heisenberg defensively, "but a German."

"Now you have to admit," one guest challenged, "that the war is lost."

"Yes," Heisenberg sighed, "but it would have been so good if we had won."

Many of the guests were disgusted by this, but Berg was glad to hear it. If the Germans were about to finish an atomic bomb, would Heisenberg really believe the war was lost?

Heisenberg grabbed his coat and headed for the door. Berg followed close behind, catching up to Heisenberg outside. He introduced himself as a Swiss student, and they walked together, chatting in German.

The narrow streets were dark and quiet. There was no one around. It was the perfect moment to kill Heisenberg. But Berg had found no evidence that the man really presented a threat to the Allies.

"Oh, it's so boring here in Switzerland," Berg said, trying to draw Heisenberg into a political discussion. Berg said he'd rather be in Germany, fighting in the war.

Heisenberg disagreed, politely. He said goodnight and walked into his hotel. The next day he left for Germany.

Berg wrote up his report on the mission and sent it to the OSS. Heisenberg's belief that Germany would lose was another piece of evidence suggesting that Hitler was not about to unleash atomic bombs.

But it was not *conclusive* evidence. Heisenberg and the other German scientists were still in Germany, where fission had been discovered. They were still working—but on what?

"If only we could get hold of a German atomic physicist," said Samuel Goudsmit, "we could soon find out what the rest of them were up to."

153

# IMPLOSION

**ONE NIGHT IN LATE DECEMBER 1944,** Ted Hall sat alone in his room at Los Alamos, writing a letter. Beside him on the desk lay an open copy of Walt Whitman's famous book of poems *Leaves of Grass*. Hall carefully copied a line of poetry into his letter.

The letter was addressed to Hall's friend Saville Sax, who would take the message to Soviet agents in New York City. Back in New York, Hall and Sax had agreed to set a meeting date using what's known in tradecraft as the "book code." Each had an identical copy of *Leaves of Grass*. When Hall copied a line of poetry into his letter, Sax would find the line in his book. He'd take careful note of the line number, and then check the table of contents to see how many poems had come before this one. These details gave the date of the meeting. If the passage, for example, was from the twelfth line on the page, Sax would know to meet Hall in December, the twelfth month of the year. If the passage was from the twentieth poem in the book, the meeting would be on the twentieth day of the month. The time of day and location had been agreed upon ahead of time.

Army censors read Hall's letter and passed it on to the post office. They had no reason to suspect its true purpose.

When Sax got the letter, he went to the main branch of the New York Public Library and took out a catalogue listing courses offered at the University of New Mexico. He was thinking of studying there, he told friends, and was preparing for a visit to the campus. With this credible alibi in place, he bought a ticket for the three-day cross-country bus ride.

Sax arrived in Albuquerque and walked to the appointed meeting spot. Hall was just arriving from the opposite direction, and together they turned down a quieter street. Sax reached into his shoe and pulled out a piece of paper—a technical question from Soviet scientists. Hall handed Sax two pages of handwritten pages—everything he'd learned about the plutonium bomb so far.

Back in his hotel room, Sax copied Hall's notes onto a newspaper using milk for ink—milk makes good invisible ink because once it dries it can't be seen unless the paper is heated. He burned Hall's handwritten pages, tucked the newspaper into his travel bag, and got on a bus headed back to New York.


IN FEBRUARY 1945, American forces crossed the Rhine River and began slicing into Germany. Samuel Goudsmit and the Alsos team followed right behind. In the city of Heidelberg, Goudsmit cornered a physicist named Walther Bothe, a man he'd known before the war.

"I am glad to have someone here to talk physics with," Bothe said, smiling and shaking Goudsmit's hand. He began telling Goudsmit about some interesting research he'd been doing.

"Tell me," Goudsmit cut in. "How much did your laboratory contribute to war problems?"

Bothe's expression changed from friendly to nervous.

"We are still at war," Bothe said. "It must be clear to you that I cannot tell anything which I promised to keep secret."

"I understand your reluctance to talk," said Goudsmit. "But I should appreciate it if you will show me whatever secret papers you may have."

"I have no such papers. I have burned all secret documents. I was ordered to do so."

Goudsmit didn't buy it. "The fear of a German atom bomb development superior to ours still dominated our thinking," he said later, "and as we had obtained no real information of their uranium project in all our investigations so far, we were still mighty uneasy."

The Alsos team learned that Werner Heisenberg, and whatever work he was doing, had recently been moved to a town called Haigerloch.

Goudsmit had only one option. "We had to go farther into Germany."

At Los Alamos, Robert Oppenheimer was still losing weight. He hurried around the lab with an anxious, distracted look, sometimes not even noticing when people stopped to greet him.

His scientists were wrestling with the challenge of building a plutonium bomb. Since firing two pieces of plutonium together inside a gun was too slow, the only solution, they reluctantly decided, was to blast the pieces of plutonium together with explosives—a process known as "implosion." Basically, the idea was to take several pieces of plutonium, about the size of a grapefruit all together. Explosives would be arranged around the plutonium, like a very thick skin around a fruit. The explosives would blast the plutonium together at tremendous speed, creating a critical mass and setting off a chain reaction—and an atomic explosion.

It was a nice theory—but scientists doubted it would actually work. For an implosion bomb to succeed, the inward blast had to be perfectly symmetrical. That is, the force driving the pieces of plutonium together had to be exactly the same from every angle. One scientist suggested a comparison: Imagine surrounding an unopened beer can with explosives and trying to blow the can in on itself without spilling a drop of liquid. That was the challenge of implosion. If the shock waves moving in on the plutonium were not perfectly even, some plutonium would squirt out, instead of being driven in. A critical mass would not be achieved, and the bomb would fizzle.

Oppenheimer reorganized the entire lab, assigning everyone available to various aspects of the implosion puzzle. He gave the hardest job, that of figuring out how to create a perfectly symmetrical explosion, to a chemistry professor named George Kistiakowsky—Kisty for short.

Kisty's first reaction: "Dr. Oppenheimer is mad to think this thing will make a bomb."

Then he got to work.

KISTY QUICKLY REALIZED that he would need to mold his own plastic explosives. His design called for "a hundred or so pieces," he explained, "which had to fit together to within a precision of a few thousandths of an inch." Each piece would have to explode at the exact same time, within one millionth of a second, or the bomb would fizzle.

Getting implosion right required a lot of trial and error. That put Ted Hall at the center of the action.

Hall's new job was to help figure out what happened to a ball of metal when it was surrounded by explosives and blown inward. Working in a small wooden cabin, he assembled test bomb cores that were about the size of a basketball. He hung each heavy core from the ceiling, made a series of measurements, then took the core down.

"Twice I dropped the damn object on my toe," Hall recalled. "I did it once and everyone was very sympathetic, and then I did it again."

Hall and a team of scientists took the core to a canyon a couple of miles from the lab. They ringed it with explosives, ducked behind a shelter, and set off the bombs.

Hall then took the bomb core back to his cabin, hung it up again, and performed more tests. The results helped convince Oppenheimer that a plutonium implosion bomb might work. There were hundreds of details to hammer out, but the basic design was set.

"Now we have our bomb," Oppenheimer told Leslie Groves in late February.

Very few people knew more about it than Ted Hall.

IN NEW YORK CITY, Saville Sax delivered Hall's report to his KGB contact, Anatoly Yatzkov. The information was cabled to headquarters in Moscow, which reported that the technical details were of "great interest."

But Hall's report also caused concern—Soviet spies worried they were being given disinformation. Was Hall really an American double-agent, feeding false data to the Soviets in order to make them waste their time and resources on bomb designs that wouldn't work? This is what Stalin's dreaded head of secret police, Lavrenti Beria, suspected.

"If this is disinformation," Beria warned KGB chiefs, "I'll put you in the cellar."

To save their jobs, and probably their lives, Soviet spies needed a second source to corroborate Hall's report. They needed Klaus Fuchs.

On a snowy February morning, Harry Gold was at home in Philadelphia, getting ready for work, when he got a phone call from "John"—the name by which he knew Anatoly Yatzkov. Yatzkov was at a nearby gas station and needed to see Gold right away.

Gold bundled up, left the house, and found Yatzkov at the station, wet and freezing. They hopped on a streetcar and talked just loud enough to hear each other over the car's clanking wheels. Yatzkov's message was short and to the point: Fuchs was in Cambridge. Gold was to go see him right away.

Gold jumped off the streetcar. He traveled to Massachusetts on February 21 and found Fuchs at his sister's home.

"K. welcomed me most warmly," Gold later reported.

Fuchs led Gold to an upstairs bedroom. He explained that he'd been unable to get away at Christmas as planned; things were just too busy at Los Alamos. Then he gave Gold a packet of papers, "a report," Fuchs later said, "summarizing the whole problem of making an atomic bomb." The papers, he said, "included a statement on the special difficulties that would have to be overcome in making a plutonium bomb."

Fuchs explained that he wouldn't be able to get another leave from Los Alamos—everyone was needed for the final push to finish the bomb. Future meetings would have to be in Santa Fe. He unfolded a street map of the city and showed Gold the Castillo Street Bridge. They would meet there, said Fuchs, on the first Sunday in June, at exactly 4:00 p.m.

On directions from Yatzkov, Gold tried to hand Fuchs an envelope with $1,500 in tens and twenties. Fuchs brushed the money aside.

"It was quite obvious that by even mentioning this, I had offended the man," Gold reported. "He flatly refused to accept it."

Gold apologized, picked up the money and papers, and left.

WHEN FUCHS'S REPORT reached Laboratory Number 2 near Moscow, it was read eagerly by Igor Kurchatov, lead physicist of Stalin's atomic bomb program. Through Hall and Fuchs, Kurchatov learned that a gun assembly bomb with plutonium would not work. This saved the Soviets from going down the same dead end as Oppenheimer's team. Kurchatov also learned that it might be possible to build bombs using the principle of implosion. "Very valuable," Kurchatov said of the material provided by the KGB. "Exceptional importance."

"There is no doubt," he added, "that the implosion method is of great interest."

# FALLING STARS

ON THE AFTERNOON OF APRIL 12, 1945, Vice President Harry Truman strode through the Capitol Building in Washington, D.C., dressed in his usual gray suit and bow tie.

Until about a year before, Truman had been a senator from Missouri. Then President Roosevelt surprised the nation by picking Truman to be his running mate in the 1944 election. They won easily. But Truman soon realized that FDR had wanted him to help win votes in the Midwest—not to help run the country. By April 1945, Truman had been vice president for three months. Roosevelt had invited him to a total of two private talks.

At about five that afternoon, Truman stepped into the office of the Speaker of the House for a scheduled meeting. The secretary looked up from her desk.

"Steve Early wants you to call him right away," she said.

Truman picked up the phone and dialed the number for Roosevelt's press secretary.

"This is the V.P.," Truman told Early.

"Please come right over."

Something in the tone of Early's voice caused the blood to drain from Truman's face. "Jesus Christ and General Jackson," he said as he hung up.

Truman jumped in a car and told the driver to take him to the White House. "I thought I was going down there to meet the president," he later said. "I didn't allow myself to think anything else." But he suspected the worst. Roosevelt had not been looking well. "His eyes were sunken," Truman remembered. "His magnificent smile was missing from his careworn face. He seemed a spent man."

Truman hurried into the White House and was taken up to the second floor, to an office used by Eleanor Roosevelt, the president's wife.

Eleanor stepped forward and put her arm around Truman's shoulder.

"Harry," she said, "the president is dead."

Truman stood silent for a long moment. He finally managed to ask, "Is there anything I can do for you?"

Eleanor smiled sadly at Truman. "Is there anything *we* can do for *you*? For you are the one in trouble now."

TRUMAN CALLED the members of Roosevelt's cabinet, told them the news, and asked them to come right to the White House. Then he called Harlan Fiske Stone, Chief Justice of the Supreme Court. He asked Stone to come swear him in as president.

After taking the oath of office, Truman met with the cabinet members. He assured them he would continue Roosevelt's policies. "I made it clear, however, that I would be president in my own right," he said later, "and that I would assume full responsibilities for such decisions as had to be made."

The meeting lasted just a few minutes. Truman watched everyone get up and silently file out—everyone except Secretary of War Henry Stimson, who walked around the long table and up to the president.

"Stimson told me that he wanted me to know about an immense project

161

that was underway—a project looking to the development of a new explosive of almost unbelievable power," recalled Truman. "It was the first bit of information that had come to me about the atomic bomb."

Just two years before, Stimson had decided Truman wasn't important enough to know about the Manhattan Project. Now, if an atomic bomb could be built, it would be Truman's job to decide how to use it.

"If you ever pray, pray for me now," Truman told reporters when they surrounded him the following day. "I don't know whether you fellows ever had a load of hay fall on you, but when they told me yesterday what had happened, I felt like the moon, the stars, and all the planets had fallen on me."

BY APRIL, HITLER'S ARMIES were in complete collapse. Allied forces were pouring into Germany from east and west. But the question remained: How close was Hitler to getting an atomic bomb?

On April 23, a squad of Alsos mission soldiers led by Lt. Colonel Boris Pash—the same man who had grilled Oppenheimer about his loyalty to America—raced ahead of advancing armies into the town of Haigerloch.

"As we approached," reported Pash, "pillowcases, sheets, towels and other white articles attached to flagpoles, broomsticks and window shutters flew the message of surrender."

But Pash wasn't there to take the town—he was there to find Heisenberg's secret lab. The search led to an eighty-foot cliff, where Pash found a doorway carved into the rock. The steel door was padlocked.

Pash's soldiers asked around, found the lab manager, and dragged him to the door. Pash told the man to unlock the lab. The man hesitated.

"Shoot the lock off," Pash ordered his soldiers. Gesturing to the manager he added, "If he gets in the way, shoot him."

The manager unlocked the door.

The doorway opened on a dark cave. In the floor, dug into the rock, was a hole about ten feet across, covered by a heavy metal shield. Pash had picked up enough physics to know he was looking at the heart of Germany's atomic research.

"A German prisoner," reported Pash, "confirmed the fact that we had captured the Nazi uranium 'machine' as the Germans called it—actually an atomic pile."

In this cave, Heisenberg had been trying to build an atomic pile, similar to the one made by Enrico Fermi on the squash court in Chicago. He'd been trying to create a chain reaction in uranium—the first step on the road to an atomic bomb. But where Fermi had succeeded, Heisenberg had failed.

The Germans were more than two years behind.

German physicist Kurt Diebner, a leader of Hitler's bomb project, later explained why: "It was the elimination of German heavy-water production in Norway that was the main factor in our failure to achieve a self-sustaining atomic reactor before the war ended."

"THE PIECES of the puzzle were beginning to fall into place at last," said a relieved Leslie Groves. American soldiers found Germany's entire supply of uranium at a nearby farm, freshly plowed under the soil. It was packed into fruit barrels and shipped to the United States.

"The capture of this material," Groves reported, "would seem to remove definitely any possibility of the Germans making any use of an atomic bomb in this war."

That race was over—but another was just beginning.

Germany did not have the atomic bomb. Now Groves was determined to keep the Soviet Union from getting it. "Our principle concern," he explained, "was to keep information and atomic scientists from falling into the hands of the Russians."

Alsos teams rounded up the top German scientists. Otto Hahn, the man who had discovered fission, was found sitting at a desk in his office, a packed suitcase beside him.

"I have been expecting you," he said in English.

A few days later, Boris Pash tracked down Werner Heisenberg in a mountainside cabin. When the Americans arrived, Heisenberg was sitting on the porch, waiting. He sighed and stood, feeling, he later said, "like an utterly exhausted swimmer setting foot on firm land."

"He was worth more to us than ten divisions of Germans," said Groves. "Had he fallen into Russian hands, he would have proven invaluable to them."

OVER THE FOLLOWING FEW WEEKS, teams of Soviet soldiers sped through Germany on an Alsos-style mission of their own. They were under orders to grab important papers from German labs and capture top German physicists. The Soviets wanted to know how far the German bomb project had gotten, and they wanted German scientists—willing or not—to help them with their own bomb.

As Soviet soldiers ransacked German labs, they realized two things. One, the Germans had not come close to building an atomic bomb.

Two, all the scientists were gone.

# LAND OF ENCHANTMENT

**HARRY GOLD AND ANATOLY YATZKOV** sat at a small table in the back of Volk's Bar in Manhattan, talking over Gold's upcoming trip to New Mexico to meet with Klaus Fuchs.

"We discussed last-minute arrangements for the transfer of information once I got back from Santa Fe," Gold said.

In case anything went wrong and either of them was unable to meet, Yatzkov set up an emergency system. If Gold got two tickets to a sporting event in the mail, with nothing else in the envelope, he was to take note of the date on the tickets. Three days after the event, he was to go to a certain bar in Queens between eight and nine at night. He was to show up a little early, check for signs of surveillance, then take a seat. A Soviet agent would join him at the table.

This was all routine to Gold by now. But then Yatzkov hit him with an additional detail.

"He wanted me to take a little side trip," Gold remembered. "He said there was a man in Albuquerque who also worked at Los Alamos and who was ready to furnish me with information."

Gold didn't like it. "I complained that it was jeopardizing the whole matter of the information I was getting from Fuchs," he said. "It represented an additional delay, an additional period or interval in which something could happen, and I just for once got up on my hind legs and almost flatly refused to go to New Mexico."

He was right to protest. "A basic rule was being broken," KGB agent Alexander Feklisov later lamented. "Namely, that two secret networks must remain compartmentalized, without communicating between one another. The person having access to both networks becomes a weak link. If that person should stumble, both parts will fall together."

Yatzkov knew the rules of tradecraft, but his neck was on the line. He could not risk sending disinformation to Moscow—he wanted this second source as a backup to Fuchs's material.

"I have been guiding you idiots every step," he snapped at Gold. "You don't realize how important this mission to Albuquerque is."

Yatzkov then gave Gold the name and address of the second source, $500 for the man, a password, and the torn half of a Jell-O box.

ADOLF HITLER COMMITTED suicide on April 30. Days later Germany surrendered. The war in Europe was over.

Scientists at Los Alamos celebrated—and for a happy moment thought their job was done. Their work had been driven by the absolute necessity of winning the bomb race with Germany. "For me, Hitler was the personification of evil, and the primary justification for the atomic bomb work," remembered the physicist Emilio Segrè. "Now that the bomb could not be used against the Nazis, doubts arose. Those doubts, even if they do not appear in official reports, were discussed in many private discussions."

The discussions were cut short by a memo from Secretary of War Stimson, which Oppenheimer distributed in early May. "The work you are doing is of tremendous importance and must go forward with all possible speed," Stimson urged. "We still have the war against Japan to win."

Only weeks before, the U.S. Marines had captured the Japanese island of Iwo Jima in some of the bloodiest fighting in the history of the American military. And the war would only get more ferocious as the Allies battled closer to the Japanese mainland.

Pushing any doubts out of his mind, Oppenheimer worked his scientists harder than ever. The design for the uranium bomb was complete, and the plutonium bomb was nearly done. The next big question: Was it necessary to test the atomic bomb to make sure it actually worked?

The uranium bomb couldn't be tested. By July 1945, Los Alamos would have just enough U-235 for one bomb, and it couldn't be wasted on a test. But plutonium was a little easier to make, and the plutonium bomb design was far more complicated. Oppenheimer was convinced a test was essential. Leslie Groves disagreed.

"To test or not to test the plutonium bomb was a very hot issue," George Kistiakowsky remembered. "Oppenheimer and I were pleading with General Groves that there *had* to be a test because the whole scheme was so uncertain. But General Groves said he couldn't afford to lose all that plutonium."

Oppenheimer won the argument by insisting that without a test, "the use of the gadget over enemy territory will have to be done substantially blindly." He selected a section of flat New Mexico desert near the Alamogordo Air Force Base. He named the site Trinity. The test was set for mid-July.

As temperatures soared over 100 degrees, scientists and soldiers moved into tents at the test site. Each morning they shook tarantulas and scorpions from their boots and tied handkerchiefs over their mouths in a hopeless effort to keep out the flying sand. They worked twenty-hour days, setting up instruments to measure the blast, and building a 100-foot steel tower to hold the bomb.

Robert Oppenheimer's younger brother, Frank, also a physicist, helped prepare for the test at Trinity. "People were feverishly setting up wires all over the desert," he said, "building the tower, building little huts in which to put cameras and house people at the time of the explosion."

No one told Dorothy McKibben what was going on, but she was able to figure it out. More trucks than ever were rumbling past her Santa Fe office, more scientists were checking in. And she kept getting calls from top government and military officials in Washington asking about hotel rooms in the area.

"The voices on the telephone showed strain and tautness," she said. "I sensed we were about to reach some sort of climax."

HARRY GOLD GOT to Santa Fe a little after noon on June 2. With a few hours to kill before his meeting with Fuchs, he strolled through a local history museum. While there he picked up a street map entitled "New Mexico: Land of Enchantment." He checked the map for the spot he was to meet Fuchs and marked it with a pen. He was glad not to have to ask for directions, making it that much less likely anyone would remember he was ever in town.

Later that afternoon he walked to the Castillo Street Bridge, a gray arch over the narrow trickle called the Santa Fe River. "Hardly more than a creek," Gold said to himself as he waited in the bright sun.

He checked the watch on his sweaty wrist. It was 4:05 p.m. Fuchs should have been there five minutes ago. He looked around, feeling conspicuous on the empty bridge. It was, he said, "no place for a stranger to be standing around doing nothing."

Standard Soviet tradecraft was to wait no more than five minutes at a public meeting spot—any longer could attract attention. But Gold had had to plead with his boss to get time off. He didn't know when he'd be able to make it back to New Mexico. He decided to wait a little longer.

Finally, at 4:20, Fuchs's blue car pulled up. Gold ducked into the passenger seat and Fuchs drove off.

Fuchs apologized, saying he'd gotten a flat tire. Gold glanced over at the physicist. He was looking healthier. His usually pale skin had some color, and he'd put on a little weight.

Fuchs stopped the car at a deserted spot. He gave Gold a quick update on the progress at Los Alamos and the upcoming test. They set their next meeting for September, the soonest Gold thought he could get away from work again. Then Fuchs handed over what Gold described as "a considerable packet of information."

"I did what I consider to be the worst I have done," Fuchs would say several years later. "Namely, to give information about the principle of the design of the plutonium bomb."

GOLD CLIMBED ONTO A BUS with the plans for an atomic bomb in his travel bag. His head was pounding, and he wasn't sure if it was from stress or the altitude—Santa Fe is over 7,000 feet above sea level.

When he got to Albuquerque, Gold was told every hotel room in town was booked. He wandered for hours. Near midnight, in desperate need of rest, he asked a passing policeman where he could spend the night. The cop directed him to a rooming house, where he was given a cot in the hall. He couldn't sleep. Every police siren, every drunken hoot—every sound that night triggered the same thought: "They might be coming for me."

The next morning Gold walked to the address given to him by Anatoly Yatzkov, entered the building, walked up to the second floor apartment, and knocked. The door was opened by a young man wearing army pants and a pajama shirt. He had curly black hair and a goofy grin.

"Mr. Greenglass?" Gold asked.

"Yes."

"I come from Julius."

Hearing this phrase, Greenglass turned back into the tiny apartment. He picked up his wife's purse and took out the torn half of a Jell-O box. Gold took out his half of the Jell-O box and handed it to Greenglass. Greenglass held the torn pieces together. They fit perfectly—clearly two halves of the same box.

Gold stepped into the apartment and introduced himself to Greenglass and his wife as "Dave from Pittsburgh." He asked for the package.

Greenglass said it wasn't ready—he needed a few hours to write up his report. Gold sighed angrily.

"You know," Greenglass said, still smiling, "there are several men at Los

169

Alamos who might also be willing to furnish information. If you want me to, I can go right ahead and talk to them."

"The devil you can!" Gold hissed, infuriated by this source's lack of trade-craft training. "You don't approach people like that and say, 'Say, can you get me information on the atom bomb?'"

Greenglass apologized, said he was just trying to help.

Gold said he'd be back in a few hours. Exhausted and annoyed, he walked down the stairs muttering to himself, "Who in the world ever got this guy into this business? Does this poor baby know what the heck he is fooling with?"

THOUGH GOLD DIDN'T KNOW THE DETAILS, David Greenglass was an army sergeant assigned to Los Alamos. He worked in a machine shop on the Hill, helping to build the super-precise explosive molds needed for the implosion bomb. Greenglass wasn't a scientist and didn't know nearly as much about the bomb as Klaus Fuchs or Ted Hall. Still, his knowledge was useful—and the Soviets wanted every scrap of information they could get.

Gold returned to Greenglass's apartment later that afternoon. Greenglass gave him an envelope containing about ten pages of notes and rough sketches, and Gold handed the soldier $500 in cash.

Gold traveled by train to Chicago, caught a plane to Washington, D.C., and jumped on a train up to New York City. From there, he took the subway to Queens and found his way to a deserted area near a cemetery. Anatoly Yatzkov was there.

"We met for a matter of seconds," Gold recalled. "I turned over the information."

# TRINITY

THE SUN BAKED LOS ALAMOS THAT JUNE, and no rain fell. The grass turned brown. The wells dried up. "We brushed our teeth with Coca-Cola," an army nurse remembered.

Oppenheimer's teams were working through the night, grabbing a few hours of sleep in their Tech Area offices. A new crisis erupted nearly every day with at least one of the bomb's five-hundred-plus components.

On July 2, George Kistiakowsky x-rayed his custom-made plastic explosives, just to make sure they were perfect. When he held the films up to the light, the shapes were dotted with tiny dark spots. Air holes.

Oppenheimer got on the phone to Washington. Between coughing fits, he pleaded with Leslie Groves to authorize a delay of the test. Groves refused. President Truman was leaving in a few days for Potsdam, Germany, where he was going to meet with Joseph Stalin to begin talking about post-war plans. It was becoming clear that when the war ended the United States and the Soviet Union would be the only world powers left standing—and that they'd be rivals. Potsdam would be Truman's first meeting with the famously intimidating Soviet leader. Truman wanted to *know* that the United States had a working atomic bomb. He wanted to stun Stalin with the news.

Oppenheimer begged for just a few more days. The chances of a successful test before July 20, he said, were fifty-fifty at best. Groves demanded the test go ahead on July 16.

"Time and time again we had in the technical work almost paralyzing crises," Oppenheimer later said. "Time and again the laboratory drew itself together and faced the new problems and got on with the work."

This time the solution came from a steady-nerved George Kistiakowsky. "I got hold of a dental drill," he said. Kisty knew the explosives were extremely unstable—any sudden jolt could set them off. "Not wishing to ask others to do an untried job, I spent most of one night, a week before the Trinity test, drilling holes in some faulty casings so as to reach the air cavities."

He mixed a batch of liquid explosives and, drop by drop, gently filled the holes.

"You don't worry about it," he said. "I mean, if fifty pounds of explosives goes in your lap, you won't know it."


ON JULY 3, several cars drove up to a brick mansion surrounded by gardens, meadows, and woods. The car doors opened and out stepped a few British soldiers, followed by ten of Germany's best scientists. Otto Hahn was there. So was Werner Heisenberg.

The Germans asked the British where exactly they were, and why they'd been brought there. They got no answers.

Instead, they were taken inside and each given a pretty, private room. They were told they could walk in the garden, play volleyball on the lawn, listen to the radio, eat and drink as much as they wanted. They could do anything at all—except leave.

What the Germans learned only later was that they were at an estate called Farm Hall, in the countryside of southeast England. They'd been taken there to keep them out of the hands of the Soviets, but there was more to it. The goal was to isolate the Germans, to keep them from even mentioning the words *atomic bomb* in public. If the Allies were going to use the bomb against Japan, they wanted it to have maximum shock value—they wanted it to come out of nowhere.

The Americans and British were also eager to learn exactly how much these German scientists had figured out about building atomic bombs. Before the Germans arrived, British intelligence officers set up hidden microphones all over Farm Hall. The first conversation the mics picked up was an exchange between Heisenberg and the physicist Kurt Diebner.

"I wonder whether there are microphones installed here?" Diebner asked.

"Microphones installed?" Heisenberg said, laughing. "Oh, no, they're not as cute as all that."

ON JULY 5, Oppenheimer sent a telegram to top Manhattan Project physicists in Berkeley and Chicago: "Any time after the fifteenth would be a good time for our fishing trip."

This was their prearranged code—the test was on, and anyone who wanted to see it had better get out to New Mexico right away. On July 11 Oppenheimer kissed his wife goodbye and drove out to the desert.

The next day Philip Morrison, one of Oppenheimer's former students, removed the plutonium bomb core from a vault in the Los Alamos Tech Area. He carefully set the pieces into two padded suitcases equipped with thermometers. If a chain reaction began, the rising temperature would be the first clue.

Morrison carried the suitcases outside to a waiting army car. He set them on the back seat and sat down beside them. A driver started the engine and drove through the gates. "I was just thinking about what an extraordinary

173

thing it was to be driving along there in just an ordinary car," remembered Morrison, "and yet we were carrying the core of the first atomic bomb."

Five hours later the car arrived at the Trinity site and stopped in front of an abandoned adobe ranch house. Morrison carried the cases past armed guards and into the building. The inside of the house was spotless. The window frames were covered with black tape to keep out flying dust.

Morrison set the plutonium down next to a table by the wall. Then he tried to get some sleep. Final assembly of the bomb would be done in the morning.

AT ABOUT NOON THE NEXT DAY, an army truck bumped and bounced very slowly down the dirt road leading to the Trinity site. In the back of the truck were George Kistiakowsky's molded explosives.

The truck backed up to the steel tower that was built to hold the bomb. Kisty jumped down. Using a large crane, soldiers eased the five-foot-wide ball of explosives out of the truck bed and set it down on the sand. Then they began putting up a white tent around the bomb.

At the same time, at the ranch house, the physicist Robert Bacher supervised the assembly of the bomb's plutonium core. Eight scientists dressed in white surgical coats stood around a table putting the pieces together. Outside the door sat four army jeeps, engines running, in case a quick getaway became necessary.

Several times Oppenheimer stuck his head into the room to check on the progress, like an anxious husband whose wife was in labor. Bacher finally asked him to stay away—he was making everyone even more nervous.

The phone in the ranch house rang at about three o'clock. It was Kistiakowsky calling from the tower to say the explosives were ready. Bacher drove the plutonium to the tower.

In the tent by the tower, Philip Morrison used a long pair of pincers to steady the plutonium core as it was lowered on a wire into a metal tamper inside the huge ball of explosives.

It didn't fit.

Several men cursed. Oppenheimer leaned forward and peered into the bomb. "We halted our efforts in order not to damage the pieces," remembered one of the physicists. "Could we have made a mistake?"

No problem, Bacher assured everyone. The plutonium had expanded in the heat of the ranch house. If they left it out for a few minutes it would cool off and contract again.

They waited several minutes in silence. They tried again. The plutonium slid right in.

EARLY THE NEXT MORNING, at Los Alamos, Major Robert Furman and Captain James Nolan loaded a three-hundred-pound lead bucket into the back of an army truck. Furman signed a receipt and got into one of the seven cars surrounding the truck.

Inside the bucket was uranium 235. It was on its way to the American air base on the Pacific island of Tinian. The pilot Paul Tibbets and his crew were already there. Whether the plutonium bomb worked or not, the plan was to have one uranium bomb assembled and ready for use by early August.

The convoy drove to Kirtland Air Force Base in Albuquerque and from there flew to Hunter's Point Naval Shipyard, near San Francisco, where the cruiser USS *Indianapolis* was docked, ready to take sail west.

THAT MORNING, at the tower at Trinity, Oppenheimer watched as scientists and army engineers worked together to attach a steel cable to the test bomb. When everything was set, a motor-powered crane lifted the five-ton round metal bomb off the ground. Soldiers ran under the bomb and tossed down a thick pile of cotton mattresses—low-tech protection in case of a potentially disastrous fall.

The bomb swayed and turned in the breeze as it was lifted, just a foot a minute, toward the top of the tower. At the top, two engineers helped ease it down onto a wooden platform and secured it in place. A team of scientists climbed the tower and began attaching wires and detonators all over the bomb's surface.

JULY 15 was a day for final checks. At about four that afternoon, after weeks of blue skies, dark clouds rolled over the desert. Lighting flashed above the distant mountains.

Early in the evening, Oppenheimer climbed the steel tower alone. On the top of the wooden platform was a metal shack with three walls, open on the fourth side. Inside the shack was the fully assembled bomb, a huge gray globe held together by bolts, with wires snaking in and out all over its surface. Oppenheimer looked over his work. The test was set for four the next morning. There was nothing more he could do—nothing but imagine last-second problems.

"Oppenheimer was really terribly worried," remembered the chemist Donald Hornig. "He thought someone had better babysit it right up until the moment it was fired."

The twenty-five-year-old Hornig got the job. He grabbed a book and climbed the tower. On the platform beside the bomb was a folding chair. A single 60-watt bulb hung from the roof of the open metal shack. There was a telephone, in case of trouble.

"By then there was a violent thunder and lightning storm," said Hornig. "The possibility of lightning striking the tower was very much on my mind."

He calmed himself with the knowledge that if lighting struck, the tower's steel frame would most likely conduct the electricity harmlessly into the ground. Or, perhaps, the electrical burst would set off the bomb.

176

"And in that case, I'd never know about it," he said. "So I read my book."

GENERAL GROVES ARRIVED at the Trinity site later that night, got out of his car, and looked angrily at the sky. Rain was falling, wind whipping, lightning flashing.

He found Oppenheimer, and they discussed the weather. It was a serious problem. They needed clear skies to get a good look at the explosion, but far more worrisome was the danger of spreading radioactive fallout. When the uranium atoms in the bomb split, some would break down into other radioactive elements—atoms that would continue shooting out particles. If the wind blew this deadly fallout into rain clouds, it could literally rain down on nearby towns. Without a break in the wind and rain, the test could not go forward.

Groves and Oppenheimer agreed to meet again at one in the morning to assess the situation.

"Get some sleep," said Groves. Then he found a cot and shut his eyes.

Oppenheimer walked to the mess tent. He sat on a bench, drinking coffee and smoking, reading poetry and listening to rain pound the canvas roof.

# TEST SHOT

THAT NIGHT, AT LOS ALAMOS, Klaus Fuchs splashed down a muddy path to the road where three busses were waiting. He climbed onto one and found a seat in the back. Richard Feynman walked back and sat next to Fuchs. All three buses drove down the hill and through the dark, starless night.

"There were about ninety of us in that strange caravan, traveling silently in the utmost secrecy," said William Laurence, a *New York Times* reporter, and the only non-scientist in the group. He'd been invited by Groves to witness the Trinity test, though he was under strict orders to keep everything he saw secret, until told otherwise.

The buses reached Trinity early on the morning of July 16. They stopped at their assigned spot, Compaña Hill, a rise in the desert twenty miles from the blast tower. The bus doors opened and Laurence and the other men stepped out onto the sand.

"The night was still pitch black, save for an occasional flash of lightning in the eastern sky," Laurence recalled.

Military police came forward to check IDs. The scientists shivered in the rain. "With the darkness and the waiting in the chill of the desert, the tension became almost unendurable," said Laurence.

A searchlight swept quickly across the bottoms of the thick clouds. Laurence looked toward the source of the light, twenty miles to the southeast. The bomb was there, he knew, sitting atop a steel tower. He wondered aloud how he was supposed to report on a story from twenty miles away.

"Don't worry," a scientist said, patting Laurence on the back. "You'll see all you need to."

TED HALL SAT with a group of soldiers in the back of an army truck on the edge of the Trinity test site.

Hall wasn't important enough to get an invitation to see the test up close. Instead, he was assigned to an army rescue crew. If radioactive fallout started spreading through the sky, it would be Hall's job to help evacuate people from local farms and villages.

Hall spent the early morning hours listening to nervous soldiers trying to distract themselves. "The guys discussed all sorts of things," he remembered, "like marriage, divorce, the high divorce rate among Hollywood stars."

The cold, rainy night passed slowly.

AT ONE IN THE MORNING, Groves rolled out of his cot, pulled on a shirt, and walked through rain and wind to the mess hall. Oppenheimer was still there.

Together they walked through puddles toward a concrete bomb shelter. They studied the sky, searching for pinpricks of starlight through the drifting clouds.

"If we postpone," Oppenheimer said, "I'll never get my people up to pitch again." It would be extremely difficult to get everyone—not to mention the bomb itself—to this point of readiness again.

"Naturally he was nervous," Groves recalled, "although his mind was working at its usual extraordinary efficiency."

179

At two-thirty, the head meteorologist, Jack Hubbard, came to the bomb shelter for a quick conference.

"What the hell's wrong with the weather?" demanded Groves.

Hubbard began to explain that a tropical air mass was moving in from—

Groves cut Hubbard off. He didn't want the science. He wanted to know if the rain would stop by 4:00 a.m.

No, said Hubbard, but there would probably be a window of clear skies from about 5:00 to 6:00 a.m.

"You'd better be right on this," said Groves, "or I will hang you."

Groves made Hubbard sign his forecast. Then he and Oppenheimer set the test for five-thirty.

A FEW MINUTES AFTER FIVE, George Kistiakowsky stood below the steel blast tower, a flashlight in his hand. The rain had slowed to a thin mist. The wind was dying down.

Kisty pointed a beam of light at a metal box beneath the tower. Kenneth Bainbridge crouched down and unlocked it. Inside was a switch. Bainbridge threw the switch, shut the box, and replaced the padlock. The bomb was armed—and set to explode in twenty minutes.

Kisty, Bainbridge, and the last few scientists at the tower jumped into jeeps and sped away. From that point on, everything would be run from the control room in Oppenheimer's bomb shelter, six miles from the blast site.

"The scene inside the shelter was dramatic beyond words," recalled General Thomas Farrell, who was there with Oppenheimer. Scientists sat on the edge of stools in front of tables loaded with electronic panels, dials, switches, and blinking lights. At the first sign of trouble, they could shut the bomb down.

A physicist named Sam Allison sat in the corner of the bunker, a telephone in his hand. He lifted the receiver and spoke into the mouthpiece: "It is now zero minus twenty minutes."

The countdown was broadcast to bomb shelters all over Trinity.

"We were told to lie down on the sand, turn our faces away from the blast, and bury our heads in our arms," remembered Edward Teller, who was on Compaña Hill. "No one complied. We were determined to look the beast in the eye."

"Zero minus fifteen minutes," announced Allison.

Teller warned the others on the hill to be careful of sunburn. He took out a tube of suntan lotion, squeezed a bit onto his hand, and passed the tube on.

The reporter William Laurence looked on in shock. "It was an eerie sight," he said, "to see a number of our highest-ranking scientists seriously rubbing sunburn lotion on their faces and hands in the pitch-blackness of the night, twenty miles away from the expected flash."

Allison's voice came over the radio: "Zero minus ten minutes."

Then scientists passed around thick pieces of dark glass, the kind used in welder's masks. The plan was to watch the blast through the glass. Klaus Fuchs took a piece of glass and held it up to his eyes.

Feynman refused the glass, instead climbing into the cab of a truck. The windshield, he figured, would protect his eyes by filtering out the blast's harmful ultraviolet light—and would give him a better view than the welder's glass.

A green flare shot into the sky and arced over the desert—the five-minute signal.

Ted Hall saw the flying green flame from his spot in the truck. He and the others turned their back to the blast site. They covered their faces with their arms.

IN HIS BUNKER, Oppenheimer leaned against a wooden beam, glancing back and forth from the sky to the scientists at the control panels.

"Zero minus two minutes."

"Lord," Oppenheimer said to no one in particular, "these affairs are hard on the heart."

181

Groves lay on the ground in a separate bunker, his eyes facing away from the blast site. "As we approached the final minute, the quiet grew more intense," he remembered. "I thought only of what I would do if, when the countdown got to zero, nothing happened."

"Zero minus one minute."

"As the time interval grew smaller and changed from minutes to seconds, the tension increased by leaps and bounds," recalled General Farrell.

Unable to stay still a moment longer, George Kistiakowsky jumped up and ran to the top of the bomb shelter. "I put on dark glasses and turned away from the tower," he said. "I didn't think anything would happen to me."

"Zero minus ten seconds, nine, eight, seven . . ."

Oppenheimer lay on the ground in the bunker. His brother Frank lay on one side of him, General Farrell on the other.

"We were lying there, very tense, in the early dawn," said Isidor Rabi. "You could see your neighbor very dimly. Those ten seconds were the longest ten seconds that I ever experienced."

"Four, three, two . . ."

"Oppenheimer, on whom had rested a very heavy burden, grew tenser as the last seconds ticked off," remembered Farrell. "He scarcely breathed. He held on to a post to steady himself. For the last few seconds he stared directly ahead."

Allison shouted, "Zero!"

"AND THEN, without a sound, the sun was shining. Or so it looked."

That's how the physicist Otto Frisch described the first instant of the explosion. Isidor Rabi's account was similar: "There was an enormous flash of light, the brightest I have ever seen or that I think anyone has ever seen."

"The whole country was lighted by a searing light with the intensity many times that of the midday sun," recalled General Farrell. "It lighted every peak, crevasse, and ridge of the nearby mountain range with a clarity and beauty that cannot be described."

"I was looking directly at it, with no eye protection of any kind," said Robert Serber, who watched from Compaña Hill. "I saw first a yellow glow, which grew almost instantly to an overwhelming white flash, so intense that I was completely blinded." It was thirty seconds before he could see again.

"The thing that got me was not the flash but the blinding heat of a bright day on your face in the cold desert morning," remembered Philip Morrison. "It was like opening a hot oven."

Richard Feynman had known the flash was coming, and that he was safe behind the truck windshield—but it was so sudden and so bright, he instinctively ducked behind the dashboard.

"I look back up," described Feynman, "and I see this white light changing into yellow and then into orange. A big ball of orange . . . a ball of orange that starts to rise and billow a little bit and get a little black around the edges."

"An enormous ball of fire," said Rabi, "which grew and grew and it rolled as it grew."

"Up it went," reported William Laurence, "a great ball of fire about a mile in diameter, changing colors as it kept shooting upward, from deep purple to orange, expanding, growing bigger, rising as it expanded."

The fireball continued rolling and rising, twisting itself into an enormous mushroom shape, glowing dark purple thousands of feet above the desert. In the bomb's eerie light, General Farrell watched Oppenheimer's reaction. "His face," said Ferrell, "relaxed into an expression of tremendous relief."

Frank Oppenheimer thought he heard his brother whisper, "It worked."

183

THEN, ABOUT THIRTY SECONDS after the blast, came the sound. Since light travels much faster than sound, the sight of the blast reached observers almost instantly, while the sound rumbled toward them at about five seconds per mile. The bomb's thunderclap bounced off the mountains and echoed back and forth across the desert.

The blast knocked George Kistiakowsky into a muddy puddle. He got up in time to see scientists scrambling out of the bunker. "Oppenheimer and the others rushed to join me," Kisty remembered. "I slapped Oppenheimer on the back."

"A loud cry filled the air," wrote William Laurence of the scene on Compaña Hill. "The little groups that hitherto had stood rooted to the earth like desert plants broke into dance."

In the back of an army truck, Ted Hall sat among shocked soldiers, watching the shimmering mushroom cloud rise and begin to fade. "I had rather expected that it would work," Hall said.

Oppenheimer and Farrell jumped in a jeep, drove to Groves's bunker, and leaped out.

"I'll never forget the way he stepped out of the car," Isidor Rabi said of Oppenheimer. "I'll never forget his walk . . . this kind of strut. He had *done* it."

People were pouring whisky into paper cups, passing them around. Groves rushed up to Oppenheimer.

"I am proud of you," said Groves as they shook hands.

"Thank you," said Oppenheimer.

"The war is over," Farrell said.

"Yes," Groves agreed, "as soon as we drop one or two on Japan."


"NATURALLY, we were very jubilant over the outcome of the experiment," Rabi later said of the mood among scientists that morning. "We turned to one another and offered congratulations—for the first few minutes. Then, there was a chill, which was not the morning cold."

It was the chill of knowing they had used something they loved—the study of physics—to build the deadliest weapon in human history. Oppenheimer was feeling the chill too.

"It was extremely solemn," he recalled. "We knew the world would not be the same. A few people laughed, a few people cried. Most people were silent."

Oppenheimer thought of a line from the ancient Hindu scripture, the *Bhagavad-Gita*, a dramatic moment in which the god Vishnu declares: "Now I am become death, the destroyer of worlds."

# LITTLE BOY

**THE TRINITY BLAST WAS HEARD IN EL PASO**, Texas, 150 miles from the explosion. The shock wave rattled windows in Silver City, New Mexico, 200 miles from Trinity. People in Amarillo, Texas, 450 miles away, saw the flash.

Newspapers and radio stations all over the region were flooded with calls demanding information. The reporters, of course, had no idea what had happened. But that morning they received a statement from the army—one General Groves had prepared weeks before.

The news went out: "The explosives dump at the Alamogordo Air Base has blown up. No lives are lost. The explosion is what caused the tremendous sound and the light in the sky. I repeat for the benefit of the many phone calls coming in: the explosive dump at the Alamogordo Air Base has blown up."

THAT MORNING at Hunter's Point Naval Shipyard on San Francisco Bay, sailors on the USS *Indianapolis* watched a crane lower a fifteen-foot wooden crate to the ship's deck. On the side of the crate was stenciled: "Secret—U.S. Government." Inside was the gun assembly for the uranium bomb.

At the same time, Major Robert Furman and Captain James Nolan carried the uranium onto the ship in their three-hundred-pound lead bucket. They took it to their cabin and locked the door. Then they bolted the bucket to the floor.

Shortly before noon the *Indianapolis* steamed under the Golden Gate Bridge and headed out to sea. The trip to Tinian would take ten days. Furman and Nolan were under strict orders to stay with the U-235 at all times, trading four-hour shifts in the cabin. They flipped a coin to see who got the first shift.

IT WAS EARLY EVENING IN POTSDAM, Germany, when news of the Trinity test reached President Truman.

"Operated on this morning," read the coded telegram. "Diagnosis not yet complete but results seem satisfactory and already exceed expectations. . . . Dr. Groves pleased."

The meaning was clear: The test had been a success.

"We have discovered the most terrible bomb in the history of the world," Truman wrote in his diary.

A few days later, Groves sent a more complete report to Potsdam. Truman sat in stunned silence as Harry Stimson read aloud. The bomb had exploded with the almost unbelievable force of eighteen thousand tons of TNT, an explosive used in regular bombs. The heat of the blast completely vaporized the steel tower holding the bomb. For hundreds of feet in all directions, sand was melted into a greenish glass. Instruments a mile from the blast measured temperatures of 750 degrees Fahrenheit. Not a plant or animal in this radius was left alive.

As Stimson read, he could see that Truman was "tremendously pepped up" by the report. "It gave him an entirely new feeling of confidence."

It was time to shock Joseph Stalin.

After a long day of meetings, Truman stopped the Soviet premiere as he was leaving the conference room. "I casually mentioned to Stalin that we had a new weapon of unusual destructive force," Truman recalled.

Truman was hoping to see fear on Stalin's face. But the man just nodded politely—his expression never changed.

"Glad to hear it," Stalin said through an interpreter. "I hope you'll make good use of it against the Japanese." Then he left the room.

Winston Churchill, equally eager to intimidate Stalin, stepped quickly to Truman.

"How did it go?" he whispered.

Truman shrugged. "He never asked a question."

Truman assumed Stalin hadn't understood. He never guessed that Stalin already knew all about the American bomb project.

Back in his private room, Stalin told his foreign secretary, "We'll have to have a talk with Kurchatov today about speeding up our work."

THE BOMB WORKED—NOW Truman had to decide what to do with it.

It all came down to the progress of the war with Japan. In late June, American forces had finally taken the island of Okinawa, 340 miles from the Japanese mainland. More than 12,000 Americans were killed in the 82-day fight, as 100,000 Japanese soldiers defended every inch of the island to the death. Meanwhile, American bombers were pounding Japan night after night, flattening and burning entire cities. One single bombing raid over Japan's capital of Tokyo set off a firestorm that killed 100,000 people. Japan's military had taken such a beating by this point, the country was nearly defenseless against American air raids. And yet Japan refused to surrender.

As a next step, American troops were preparing for an all-out invasion of Japan. The Japanese had an estimated 2.5 million troops ready to defend the islands. Truman asked General George Marshall how many Americans were likely to be killed or wounded. "It was his opinion," recalled Truman, "that such an invasion would cost at a minimum a quarter of a million American casualties."

For Truman, that settled it. If the atomic bomb could shock Japan into giving up, it had to be used. "It was a question of saving hundreds of thousands of American lives," he later explained. "I couldn't worry about what history would say about my personal morality. I made the only decision I ever knew how to make. I did what I thought was right."

ON JULY 26, the *Indianapolis* arrived at Tinian with the uranium bomb's gun assembly and U-235. That same day Truman and Churchill issued the Potsdam Declaration—a final demand that Japan end the fighting. There was no mention of the atomic bomb, but the document closed with a harsh warning: "We call upon the government of Japan to proclaim now the unconditional surrender of all Japanese armed forces. . . . The alternative for Japan is prompt and utter destruction."

When the message reached Tokyo the next morning, Japanese leaders debated options. Policy decisions were not usually made by Japan's emperor, Hirohito. Instead, a group known as the Big Six—the country's three top political and three top military leaders—met to argue and hammer out decisions. When it came time to consider surrender, the Big Six were split. Political leaders were open to the idea of accepting the Potsdam demand. Military leaders urged immediate rejection. They especially feared unconditional surrender, which would allow foreign soldiers to take over their country with no conditions. This, they felt, was too disgraceful to even consider.

Prime Minister Baron Suzuki called reporters together. "As for the government, it does not find any important value in it," Suzuki said of the Potsdam Declaration. "There is no other recourse but to ignore it entirely and resolutely fight for the successful conclusion of the war."

"In the face of this rejection," Stimson later said, "we could only proceed to demonstrate that the ultimatum had meant exactly what it said."

The order went out to Colonel Tibbets on Tinian: "The 509 Composite Group, 20th Air Force, will deliver its first special bomb as soon as weather will permit visual bombing after about 3 August 1945."

ROBERT SERBER AND A TEAM of physicists flew from Los Alamos to Tinian. On August 1, in an air-conditioned hut, they assembled the uranium bomb. Ten feet long and painted dark gray, it looked like a small submarine. They nicknamed it Little Boy.

The bomb was ready on August 2. Tibbets was just waiting on the weather.

"The word came Sunday morning, August 5," he remembered. "After three days of uncertainty, the clouds that hung over the Japanese islands for the past week were beginning to break up. Conditions were 'go' and tomorrow was the day."

That afternoon, Little Boy was loaded into Tibbets's plane, which he had named *Enola Gay*, for his mother.

At midnight, Tibbets gathered his crew for a final briefing on the mission. "The usual jesting that takes place before a briefing was missing," reported William Laurence, who'd come to Tinian to witness the event.

"Tonight is the night we have all been waiting for," Tibbets began. "We are going on a mission to drop a bomb different from any you have ever seen or heard about. This bomb contains a destructive force equivalent to twenty thousand tons of TNT."

"He paused, expecting questions," Laurence reported. "But there was silence in the room, a look of amazement and incredulity on every face."

AT 1:37 A.M., three B-29s rumbled down the runway on Tinian, took off, and headed for Japan. Each would check the weather over a specific Japanese city—potential targets approved by President Truman. The planes would radio the reports to Tibbets, who, based on weather conditions and visibility, would choose from the list of targets.

"Our orders were for a visual bombing run," Tibbets explained. He was not permitted to use radar. If he couldn't see the target, he was not to release his irreplaceable bomb.

Beside the runway, Tibbets walked around the *Enola Gay*, making the final preflight checks. Then he and his eleven hand-picked crew members climbed into the plane. "First we checked all the instruments and radio equipment," recalled Tibbets. "Now it was time to fire the engines."

Tibbets taxied the plane to the end of the runway. "More than a mile and a half of chipped coral runway stretched out before me in the darkness," he said. Just the night before, four B-29s had crashed attempting to take off. Tibbets could see the planes' black, twisted skeletons still lying beside the runway. It was never easy to get these massive machines safely off the ground. And the *Enola Gay* was loaded with extra fuel and the bomb—fifteen thousand pounds more cargo than the B-29 was designed to carry. Tibbets knew he'd need every inch of the runway to build up enough speed to get his heavy plane into the air.

"I like to think that my reputation for keeping cool in moments such as this was deserved," Tibbets said. "But now I found myself gripping the controls with a nervous tension I hadn't experienced since that first combat mission."

*This is the moment*, he told himself. *This is the reason they chose me.*

"Gradually we picked up speed—75, 100, 125 miles an hour," he said. "The end of the runway was approaching fast and the lights on both sides of the paved surface were running out."

In the nearby control tower, William Laurence and a very tense General Thomas Farrell watched Tibbets's plane bouncing along the runway. With less than 100 feet left, they saw the plane ease off the ground and begin to climb.

Farrell exhaled. "I never saw a plane use that much runway," he said. "I thought Tibbets was never going to pull it off."

"IT WAS A PLEASANT TROPICAL NIGHT," Tibbets remembered. "Around us were cream-puff clouds, their edges outlined by the faint glow of a crescent moon."

The flight over the Pacific was easy and uneventful. Tibbets and the crew watched the sun rise as they passed over Iwo Jima. "And now we were winging toward Japan," he said, "surrounded by scattered clouds that were edged with reddish gold from the slanting light of the newly risen sun."

At 8:30 a.m., reports started coming in from the weather planes. The radio operator wrote down the coded messages and handed them to Tibbets. The copilot took control of the plane while Tibbets decoded and read the notes.

Then he lifted the intercom and announced to the crew: "It's Hiroshima."

# HIROSHIMA

"IT WAS A CLEAR but sultry morning," remembered Yohko Kuwabara, who was a thirteen-year-old girl on the morning of August 6, 1945. "The midsummer sun was so bright it almost hurt my eyes."

She had just finished breakfast at her family's home in Hiroshima when she noticed the time. "It was already past seven. 'I'll be late for school!' I started getting ready for school in a hurry."

Yohko raced down the street to the streetcar stop near her home. A streetcar soon came, and she climbed onto the crowded car. "I pushed my way through until I was standing behind the driver," she said. "Through the windshield I looked at the pedestrians hurrying on their way."

"WE WERE EIGHT MINUTES away from the scheduled time of the bomb release when the city came into view," recalled Paul Tibbets. "The early morning sunlight glistened off the white buildings in the distance."

Through 31,000 feet of clear sky, Hiroshima looked just like the pictures

Tibbets had studied. Located on the southeastern coast of Japan, the city stood on six long, flat islands. Between the islands ran branches of the Ota River as it fanned out into a delta near the sea. This was Japan's eighth largest city, and the location of an important army base. On August 6, there were about 280,000 civilians living in Hiroshima, and 43,000 soldiers.

Tibbets's bombardier, Thomas Ferebee, pressed his left eye against his bombsight, giving him a magnified view of the city below. It was his job to aim the bomb at the T-shaped Aioi Bridge—a centrally located feature that could be identified from high in the air.

"Okay, I've got the bridge," announced Ferebee.

Ferebee pointed toward the target. Theodore Van Kirk, the navigator, looked down, comparing the view from the nose of the plane with the photo of Aioi Bridge in his hand.

"No question about it," Van Kirk agreed.

Tibbets guided the plane toward the bridge.

"We're on target," said Ferebee.

Tibbets picked up the intercom and said: "Put on your goggles. Place them up on your forehead. When the countdown starts, pull the goggles over your eyes and leave them there until after the flash."

At 8:15 the bomb bay doors opened. The bomb dropped out and fell toward the city.

"With the release of the bomb, the plane was instantly nine thousand pounds lighter," Tibbets said. "As a result, its nose leaped up sharply and I had to quickly execute the most important task of the flight: to put as much distance as possible between our plane and the point at which the bomb would explode."

FORTY-THREE SECONDS after dropping from the plane, at an altitude of 1,900 feet above Hiroshima, the bomb's two pieces of uranium slammed together, setting off an explosive chain reaction. The blinding flash and raging fireball looked just like the ones at Trinity—only this time, there was a city underneath.

The blast heated the ground beneath the explosion to over 5,000 degrees. Nearly every person within 1,000 yards in all directions was instantly killed. Many were vaporized.

A ten-year-old boy named Shintaro Fukuhara was standing outside his school with his younger brother at the moment of the explosion. "I saw a red dragonfly winging along and finally alighting on the wall right in front of me," he remembered. "Just as my brother reached out to catch the dragonfly, there was a flash. I felt I'd suddenly been blown into a furnace. . . . When I opened my eyes after being flung eight yards, it was still dark as if I were facing a wall painted black."

Yohko Kuwabara was still on the crowded streetcar, headed for school. "I was blinded for a moment by a piercing flash of bright light," she later said, "and the air filled with yellow smoke like poison gas. Momentarily, it got so dark I couldn't see anything. There was a loud, dull, thunderous noise. The inside of my mouth was gritty, as if there were sand in it, and my throat hurt."

Described by survivors all over the city, the sudden darkness was caused by the enormous amount of dust and debris thrown into the air by the force of the blast.

"The view, where a moment before all had been so bright and sunny, was now dark and hazy," said a doctor named Michihiko Hachiya. Pushing and wriggling out from under fallen pieces of his home, Hachiya stood. He was bleeding badly, his skin pieced with splinters and broken glass. Like people all over Hiroshima, he assumed a large, but ordinary bomb had fallen right near him.

"Yaeko-san!" he called to his wife. "Where are you?"

She rose from the rubble, bleeding, her clothes torn.

"We'll be all right," he told her. "Only let's get out of here as fast as we can."

Together they ran to the street. Hachiya tripped over something, looked down, and saw it was the body of a soldier, crushed under a fallen gate. Then he looked out at the neighborhood—and knew this had been no ordinary bomb. Everywhere houses were swaying and falling, flames rising from the ruins.

YOHKO KUWABARA TUMBLED out of the streetcar. Buildings all around her were on fire. "I picked my way through the rubble and made it out to the main street," she said. "I stood there dumbfounded. . . . I heard children crying, buildings collapsing, men and women screaming. I saw the bright red of blood and people with dazed expressions on their faces trying to get away. Where should I go?"

The ten-year-old boy, Shintaro Fukuhara, also felt the need to move, to get away. "I had unconsciously taken my brother's hand and started running," he said. "I just ran home as fast as I could."

He passed people with horrible burns, their faces swollen, their blackened skin hanging in strips. Bodies on the ground, and bodies floating in the river. "I cannot describe the countless tragic things I saw," he said.

An image that haunted many in Hiroshima was the horrific parade of victims on the streets. "They stagger exactly like sleepwalkers," said one survivor; "like walking ghosts" said another.

"They held their arms out in front of their chest like kangaroos," said a high school girl, "with only their hands pointed downward."

Dr. Hachiya saw this as he was wobbling toward the hospital where he worked. "They moved as though in pain, like scarecrows, their arms held out from their bodies with forearms and hands dangling," he said. "These people puzzled me until I suddenly realized that they had been burned and were holding their arms out to prevent the painful friction of raw surfaces rubbing together. . . . One thing was common to everyone I saw—complete silence."

"IF I LIVE A HUNDRED YEARS, I'll never quite get these few minutes out of my mind," said Robert Lewis, copilot of the *Enola Gay*.

The plane was nine miles from the explosion when the bomb's shock wave hit.

"The plane bounced," Theodore Van Kirk remembered, "it jumped and there was a noise like a piece of sheet metal snapping."

Tibbets held tight to the controls. The plane was undamaged.

"Now that I knew we were safe from the effects of the blast, I began circling so that we could view the results," said Tibbets. "We were not prepared for the awesome sight that met our eyes."

The men saw a purple-gray mushroom cloud rising above Hiroshima, its top reaching three miles above their plane. The cloud boiled and writhed, they said, like a living thing.

"Even more fearsome was the sight on the ground below," said Tibbets. "At the base of the cloud, fires were springing up everywhere amid a turbulent mass of smoke that had the appearance of bubbling hot tar. . . . The city we had seen so clearly in the sunlight a few minutes before was now an ugly smudge."

The entire city, said Van Kirk, looked like "a pot of boiling black oil."

"A feeling of shock and horror swept over all of us," said Tibbets.

Robert Lewis picked up his pencil and made a note in his logbook: "My God, what have we done?"

After turning back toward Tinian, Tibbets wrote out a coded report and handed it to the radio operator. "Clear-cut successful in all respects. Visual effects greater than Trinity. . . . Proceeding to regular base."

As the plane headed home, the crew felt a mix of emotions, including relief that the job was done and hope that the war would now end. But something else entered the mix, a thought Paul Tibbets would never forget.

"We were sobered by the knowledge that the world would never be the same," he said. "War, the scourge of the human race since time began, now held terrors beyond belief."

# REACTION BEGINS

PAUL TIBBETS'S REPORT was relayed from Tinian to Leslie Groves's office in Washington, D.C. Groves picked up his phone and called Los Alamos. Robert Oppenheimer lifted the receiver to his ear.

"I'm proud of you and all of your people," Groves said.

"It went all right?" asked Oppenheimer.

"Apparently it went with a tremendous bang."

"I extend my heartiest congratulations," Oppenheimer said. "It's been a long road."

"Yes, it has been a long road, and I think one of the wisest things I ever did was when I selected the director of Los Alamos."

"Well, I have my doubts, General Groves."

"Well, you know I've never concurred with those doubts at any time."

PRESIDENT TRUMAN WAS ON A SHIP back to the United States, eating lunch with the crew. An officer walked in and handed him a message that had just come in from Secretary of War Stimson, along with a map of Japan. On the map, circled in red, was the city of Hiroshima.

Truman read the note. He jumped up, grabbed a fork from beside his plate, and began banging it against the side of his water glass. Everyone in the mess hall turned to the president.

"Keep your seats, gentlemen," Truman said, an excited smile on his face as he waved the note in his hand. "I have an announcement to make. We have just dropped a new bomb on Japan which has more power than twenty thousand tons of TNT. It has been an overwhelming success!"

The room erupted in cheers.

In Washington, the White House released a statement that Truman had prepared ahead of time. "An American airplane dropped one bomb on Hiroshima," Truman announced to the world. "We are now prepared to obliterate more rapidly and completely every productive enterprise the Japanese have above ground in any city. . . . Let there be no mistake; we shall completely destroy Japan's power to make war. . . . If they do not now accept our terms they may expect a rain of ruin from the air, the like of which has never been seen on this earth."

AT LOS ALAMOS, most scientists first heard the news over the public address system.

"Attention please, attention please," announced a voice over the Tech Area intercom. "One of our units has just been successfully dropped on Japan."

Richard Feynman described his first reaction as "very considerable elation and excitement."

"There was a sudden noise in the laboratory, of running footsteps and yelling voices," remembered Otto Frisch. Scientists ran from door to door shouting, "Hiroshima has been destroyed!"

Frank Oppenheimer, who was standing outside his brother's office, remembered thinking, "Thank God it wasn't a dud." But a second thought followed quickly. "Before the whole sentence of the broadcast was finished, one suddenly got this horror of all the people who had been killed."

Frisch saw fellow scientists rushing to the phone to make reservations at Santa Fe restaurants to celebrate. "Of course they were exalted by the success of their work, but it seemed rather ghoulish," he later said. "I still remember the feeling of unease, indeed nausea."

As the news spread, children of scientists grabbed pots and pans and ran outside banging them together and shouting. Parties started all over the mesa.

Feynman sat on the hood of a jeep, playing bongos as people danced in the dirt streets. "I was involved in this happy thing," he remembered, "with the excitement running over Los Alamos—at the same time as the people were dying and struggling in Hiroshima."

Almost everyone was feeling that same strange mix of pride and horror. That night Oppenheimer went to a party in one of the men's dorms, carrying in his hand a message from Washington with more details on the destruction in Hiroshima. As he showed the note around, the mood in the room darkened. The party broke up early. As Oppenheimer walked home, he saw one of his scientists bent over a bush, vomiting.

He thought to himself, "The reaction has begun."

JUST BEFORE DINNER time at Farm Hall, the English mansion at which Germany's top scientists were being held, a British officer named T. H. Rittner asked to speak to Otto Hahn in private.

Hahn had discovered fission less than seven years before. Now Rittner told him the news: The Americans had just dropped an atomic bomb on Hiroshima.

200

"Hahn was completely shattered by the news, and said he felt personally responsible," Rittner reported. "He told me that he had originally contemplated suicide when he realized the terrible potentialities of his discovery and he felt that now these had been realized and he was to blame."

Rittner forced Hahn to gulp down a glass of whisky. Slightly calmer, Hahn walked to the dining room, where the other German scientists were gathered for dinner. He announced the news.

"The guests were completely staggered," recalled Rittner. "At first they refused to believe it."

Rittner excused himself and shut the door. With no idea they were being recorded, the Germans talked freely.

"Did they use the word *uranium* in connection with this atomic bomb?" Heisenberg asked.

Hahn said he wasn't sure.

"Then it's got nothing to do with atoms," insisted Heisenberg. The Allies may have used a very powerful bomb, he said, but not a *real* atomic bomb, not a bomb based on the fission of uranium atoms.

"If they have really got it," said Hahn, "they have been very clever in keeping it secret."

"I still don't believe a word about the bomb," said Heisenberg, "but I might be wrong."

A little later that night they turned on a radio and heard Truman's official announcement. Forced to concede that an atomic bomb had destroyed Hiroshima, the German scientists began trying to figure how the bomb had been made. They discussed the technical challenges and lack of key materials that had slowed their own bomb-making efforts.

Then they began trying to convince themselves they could have built the bomb—if they had really wanted to.

"If we had all wanted Germany to win the war, we would have succeeded," claimed Carl von Weizsacker.

"I don't believe that," said Hahn, "but I am thankful we didn't succeed."

"The Americans could do it better than we could, that's clear," added Horst Korsching.

Weizsacker wasn't convinced. "If they were able to complete it in the summer of 1945," he said, "we might have had the luck to complete it in the winter of 1944–1945."

"The result would have been that we would have obliterated London but still would not have conquered the world," said Karl Wirtz. "And then they would have dropped them on us."

"I thank God on my bended knees that we did not make the uranium bomb," said Hahn.

Heisenberg said, "I would like to know what Stalin is thinking this evening."

THE SOVIET DICTATOR WAS FURIOUS.

"Stalin had a tremendous blow up," recalled one top official, "losing his temper, banging his fists on the table and stamping his feet." He had known the American bomb was coming, of course. But reports of its devastating power shocked him.

"Hiroshima has shaken the whole world!" he shouted to his advisors. "The balance has been destroyed." Stalin wanted his own atomic bomb—and he wanted it quickly. "Provide us with atomic weapons in the shortest possible time. It will remove a great danger from us."

Stalin called Igor Kurchatov to his office and chewed him out for not *demanding* the resources he needed to move more swiftly.

"So much is destroyed, so many people perished," said Kurchatov. "The country is on starvation rations and everything is in shortage."

Yes, Stalin admitted, thousands of Soviet towns and factories lay in ruins. More than twenty million people had been killed in the war with Germany. But that wouldn't stop the Soviet Union from building an atomic bomb.

"If the baby doesn't cry, the mother doesn't know what he needs," Stalin lectured Kurchatov. "Ask for anything you need. There will be no refusals!"

And just to make sure Kurchatov and his team understood what was at stake, Stalin placed his head of secret police, Lavrenti Beria, in charge of the bomb project. Beria was to be Stalin's Leslie Groves—but with additional powers.

"One gesture of Beria," said a Soviet scientist, "was sufficient to make any of us disappear."

THE FIRST REPORTS to reach the Japanese capital of Tokyo were panicked and sketchy. Some kind of catastrophe had occurred at Hiroshima, but no one knew the details. Government officials tried to contact the army command center in Hiroshima. There was no response.

Then came Truman's announcement that the Americans had dropped an atomic bomb. And the next morning a telegram from southern Japan reached Tokyo: "The whole city of Hiroshima was destroyed instantly by a single bomb."

General Torashiro Kawabe immediately sent an officer to the lab of Yoshio Nishina, Japan's top atomic physicist. When the war began, the government had put Nishina in charge of fission bomb research in Japan. But the country never made building the bomb a high priority.

Now, the moment Nishina walked into Kawabe's office, the general demanded, "Could you build an atom bomb in six months? In favorable circumstances we might be able to hold out that long."

Nishina shook his head. "Under present conditions six years would not be long enough. In any case we have no uranium."

Kawabe then asked if there was any defense against the bomb.

"Shoot down every hostile aircraft that appears over Japan," said Nishina.

Both knew that was impossible.

Government and military leaders gathered to discuss the next question: Was it time to accept the Potsdam Declaration—and unconditional surrender?

Yes, urged foreign minister Shigenori Togo, because America's atomic bomb "drastically alters the whole military situation."

"Such a move is uncalled for," countered Korechika Anami, the war minister. "Furthermore, we do not yet know if the bomb was atomic."

General Seizo Arisue, the army's chief of intelligence, was sent to investigate. As Arisue's plane circled above what appeared to be a smoking, ash-gray desert, the pilot pointed down.

"Sir," he said, "this is supposed to be Hiroshima. What should we do?"

"Land," Arisue said.

The moment he stepped out of the plane, Arisue was hit by the horrible stench of burning flesh. It would take time to compile official statistics, but he could see that the city was gone. Of the 76,000 buildings that had stood two days before, 70,000 were completely destroyed. About 70,000 people were dead already. Over 100,000 more would die of wounds, burns, and radiation poisoning.

Yoshio Nishina toured Hiroshima on August 8. "I decided at a glance," he later said, "that nothing but an atomic bomb could have created such devastation."

That same day, the Soviet Union declared war on Japan, eager to grab a piece of the dying empire. And still, the debate continued in Tokyo. Political leaders urged surrender. Military leaders refused.

IN TRUMAN'S OFFICE in the White House, Secretary of War Stimson handed the president photographs of the ruins of Hiroshima, taken by American planes. Truman studied the pictures. "He mentioned the terrible responsibility that such destruction placed upon us," Stimson remembered.

"We ought to proceed with Japan in a way which will produce as quickly as possible her surrender," Stimson told the president.

Truman agreed—but aside from dropping another bomb, what options were there?

Reword the Postdam Declaration, Stimson suggested. Tell Japanese leaders they could keep their emperor—as long as it would get them to surrender.

Not possible, Truman insisted. Ever since Japan had attacked Pearl Harbor, the United States had been demanding *unconditional* surrender. Now, after the enormous sacrifices American fighters had made, Truman felt he could not back down from that demand. Political worries played a role too. If Truman began negotiating with Japan now, it could be seen as a sign of weakness. Political opponents would attack him for flinching under pressure.

Truman decided he'd wait to hear from Japan. Until then, the atomic bombs would continue to fall.

Another day passed with no word from Tokyo.

"BACK ON TINIAN, the second atomic bomb was being assembled even as the world was learning about the first," remembered Paul Tibbets. Known as Fat Man, this was a large, round plutonium implosion bomb similar to the one tested at Trinity.

Unless Tibbets heard otherwise, his orders were to drop the bomb as soon as weather conditions permitted. "The use of a second bomb the same week," he said, "was calculated to indicate that we had an endless supply of this super weapon for use against one Japanese city after another."

Tibbets assigned the mission of dropping the second bomb to a pilot named Charles Sweeney. Fat Man was loaded into a B-29, and Sweeney and his crew took off and flew toward Japan early on the morning of August 9.

Sweeney reached his target, the city of Kokura, at about ten-thirty. The city was covered with clouds, invisible from the sky. Sweeney circled the plane, looking for an opening.

"Two additional runs were made, hoping that the target might be picked up after closer observation," weaponeer Frederick Ashworth wrote in his flight log. "However, at no time was the aiming point seen."

Japanese anti-aircraft guns opened fire on the B-29. "We had some flack bursts," said Jacob Beser, the radar operator. "Things were getting a little hairy."

"We'll go on to secondary target, if you agree," announced Sweeney. Ashworth nodded.

"Proceeding to Nagasaki."

Fat Man exploded over the city of Nagasaki with the force of 22,000 tons of TNT. At least 40,000 people were instantly killed, and tens of thousands more fatally wounded or poisoned with radiation.

"People were saying that Tokyo would be next," remembered a Tokyo resident named Yukio Mishima. As he walked the streets of Japan's capital, Mishima could feel the agonizing suspense in the air; he could see it in passing faces. "It was just as though one was continuing to blow up an already bulging toy balloon, wondering, 'Will it burst now? Will it burst now?'"

"If it had gone on any longer," he said, "there would have been nothing to do but go mad."

In Washington, Leslie Groves told Truman a third atomic bomb "should be ready for delivery on the first suitable weather after 17 or 18 August."

Truman was hoping not to use it. "It is not to be released on Japan without express authority from the president," George Marshall ordered Groves.

Japan's Big Six leaders gathered in Tokyo for an emergency meeting. Once again, the top generals resisted surrender. The desperate debate lasted late into the night before Emperor Hirohito stepped in. The emperor did not normally make policy decisions, but in times of crisis his word was final.

"I cannot endure the thought of letting my people suffer any longer," he said. "The time has come when we must bear the unbearable."

That ended the argument. Japan surrendered on August 15. World War II was over.

# END GAME

**WHILE AMERICANS CELEBRATED VICTORY,** a woman in her early thirties, with short, dark hair stepped off a train in the tiny town of Las Vegas, New Mexico. She walked to a boarding house and asked for a room, explaining to the clerk that she suffered from tuberculosis and that her doctor had told her to spend some time breathing dry desert air.

Actually, Lona Cohen was perfectly healthy. She was an experienced spy and courier for KGB agents in New York, and she was in New Mexico to meet Ted Hall.

Stalin was screaming for the bomb, and Soviet scientists still needed more information from Los Alamos—they needed final reports on how the atomic bombs had been made. A meeting had already been arranged with Hall, but Anatoly Yatzkov decided not to use Hall's friend Saville Sax as a courier. This mission was too important to trust to an amateur.

On the first Sunday after arriving in New Mexico, Lona Cohen took a three-hour bus ride to Albuquerque and walked across the University of

New Mexico campus to the spot where she was to meet Hall. She'd seen a photo of him, so she knew what to look for. He wasn't there.

Trained not to wait more than five minutes, she walked back to the bus stop and returned to Las Vegas. Both Cohen and Hall had been told that if either missed the first meeting, they should try again the next Sunday, at the same time and place.

Cohen returned the following Sunday. No Hall. She came back the week after. He didn't show.

AT LOS ALAMOS, the British team of scientists began packing up to head home. Before leaving, they scheduled one last party in honor of their American hosts. Someone needed to drive to Santa Fe to pick up the liquor. Klaus Fuchs volunteered.

He drove his dented Buick through the gates and down the hill. "I stopped somewhere on the way in the desert," he remembered, and "drove off the highway to a solitary place."

Fuchs took out a pen and a half-written report. Sitting in his car, he quickly finished the paper, which included vital details on plutonium bomb design, as well as a technical description of the uranium bomb used at Hiroshima. He shoved the papers into an envelope and drove to the liquor store.

At about six that evening, Harry Gold was standing on the side of a small road on the outskirts of Santa Fe. When Fuchs drove up, Gold hopped into the passenger seat.

"We drove out into the mountains beyond Santa Fe," Gold reported. He could hear the clinking of glass bottles on the backseat.

Fuchs pulled over. "He was very nervous," Gold remembered, "and I was inwardly not too calm myself."

"Well," Fuchs began, his face twisted into an uneasy smile, "were you impressed?"

"More than impressed," said Gold. "Horrified."

Fuchs understood. The bombs had been even more devastating than he had expected. For the first time in their many meetings, Fuchs talked non-stop. He talked about the shocking site at Trinity, the chilling reports from Hiroshima and Nagasaki. He just had to talk.

"He himself was rather awestricken by what had occurred," remembered Gold, "greatly concerned by the terrible destruction which the weapon had wrought."

They watched the sky darken, the lights come on in town. Fuchs suggested that someday, maybe, they would meet again. "Meet openly as friends," he said, "and speak of music, and other matters, but not speak of war."

Gold said he hoped this would happen.

Finally, Fuchs handed Gold the papers he had prepared, then Fuchs drove Gold to the bus station. They shook hands, and Gold got out. "After a period of anxious waiting," he said, "about an hour and a half, I finally obtained a bus going back to Albuquerque."

TED HALL WAS AWARE he'd missed meetings with the Soviet courier assigned to pick up his final report. He'd been unable to get away from his work at Los Alamos.

Finally, a month after Lona Cohen arrived in New Mexico, Hall spent a quiet Sunday morning in his office, preparing the promised papers. Knowing his lab partner, Philip Koontz, was going on a picnic that day, Hall expected to be alone. He spread top-secret bomb plans on his desk so he could refer to them as he wrote up his report.

The door swung open.

Panicking, Hall clumsily swept the papers into his desk drawer as Koontz stepped in. If the man had come over to see what Hall was doing, there would have been no possible explanation.

Hall got lucky—Koontz felt guilty that he was taking time off while his partner was spending Sunday in the office. He said a quick goodbye and ducked out.

Later that day Hall took a bus to the University of New Mexico campus. He'd been told to look for a woman with a magazine poking out of her purse. She would answer to the name "Helen."

The woman with the magazine was there. When she spotted Hall, she walked up and introduced herself. They strolled together for a few minutes, like old friends.

Cohen quietly cautioned Hall that he was taking a huge risk in helping the Soviets. "Things might turn out pretty hot," she said.

Hall assured Cohen he knew of the danger.

If American agents were ever on Hall's trail, Cohen said, the KGB had told her to help arrange his transport to the Soviet Union, where he'd be given a new life.

Hall said he very much hoped that would not be necessary. Then he handed his papers to Cohen and they parted.

COHEN TOOK THE BUS back to her boarding house. She pulled the tissues out of a nearly full tissue box, crammed Hall's secret papers into the bottom of the box, replaced the tissues, grabbed her already-packed suitcase, and left.

Minutes later she stepped into the train station. The place was crawling with soldiers and FBI agents. They were searching all passengers coming in and going out.

Since the war ended, newspapers had been free to tell the public that the atomic bomb had been built by scientists at Los Alamos, led by Robert Oppenheimer. The government was determined to protect Oppenheimer and his staff—and their bomb-making secrets.

Cohen's tissue box held Hall's handwritten report, with detailed plans and sketches of an atomic bomb. It was more than enough evidence to get her *and* Hall executed for spying.

She was too well trained to panic. Rushing out of the station would be the surest way to draw attention. Instead, she set down her bag, and, glancing around casually, took a few minutes to focus her mind on the character she'd invented: a friendly, absent-minded tuberculosis patient on her way home from the desert.

When her train was nearly done boarding, Cohen stepped up to the track with her suitcase in one hand, her purse over her shoulder, the box of tissues in her other hand. An FBI agent asked to see her ticket and look in her bags. Another began asking questions about her business in New Mexico.

While answering, Cohen opened her purse and fumbled through the contents. No ticket. She laughed aloud at herself for misplacing it. She kneeled down to open her suitcase, but couldn't work the zipper with the box of tissues in her hand. The train whistle blew. Over the loudspeaker came the "all aboard" announcement—her train was about to leave.

Smiling, she passed the tissues to the government agent.

Her hands free, she opened the suitcase, rummaged, and found the ticket. The agents had a look at the contents of her bag. They nodded and gestured for her to get going.

She zipped up the bag, lifted her purse, and stepped up onto the train—without the tissues. "I felt in my bones that the gentleman himself must remind me about this box," she later said.

As the train began rolling, Cohen heard the FBI agent call to her. She turned around. He handed her the box of tissues through the open door. It was the one thing he hadn't searched.

HARRY GOLD RETURNED SAFELY to New York City with the report from Klaus Fuchs. Lona Cohen came back with the report from Ted Hall. In separate meetings, both delivered their papers to their Soviet contact, Anatoly Yatzkov.

Leonid Kvasnikov, who ran the KGB office in New York City, compared the documents from Fuchs and Hall. Both contained thorough reports on atomic bomb design. "I made a conclusion," he said, "that I myself, although I was not a very good craftsman, I could have built a bomb with this data—if I had certain materials, of course."

The best thing about the reports, Kvasnikov knew, was that the bomb plans from both Hall and Fuchs were nearly identical. That convinced the Soviets the information was correct, allowing them to move ahead quickly with bomb building. No need for the kind of costly trial and error that had taken place at Los Alamos.

By October, KGB officers in Moscow were able to produce a complete report on plutonium bomb design, containing detailed descriptions of each component of the weapon and specific materials needed. Using this, Soviet scientists immediately began building their first atomic weapon.

It was an exact copy of the American bomb.

# FATHER OF THE BOMB

**SOON AFTER JAPAN'S SURRENDER,** Robert Oppenheimer got on a train and headed east. He was "a nervous wreck," a fellow passenger observed. "Oppenheimer kept looking under the table and all around."

Everyone knew Oppenheimer now. His name was spread across newspaper headlines, his bony face and intense eyes started out from magazine covers. The press was calling him the "Father of the Atomic Bomb"—a new kind of superhero. Superman relied on his enormous physical strength; Oppenheimer could let loose the energy locked inside atoms.

Oppenheimer was torn by the attention. He relished the fame, but was terrified by the thought of what he had helped create—a world with atomic weapons.

"If you ask, 'Can we make them more terrible?' the answer is yes," Oppenheimer told a reporter. "If you ask, 'Can we make a lot of them?' the answer is yes."

This is what he was hoping to prevent. Oppenheimer got off the train in

Washington, D.C., carrying a report with his recommendations for the future. Physicists could certainly design more powerful atomic bombs, he argued. But would that necessarily make the country safer? No, because other countries could also build bombs—and there would be no way to ensure that those bombs weren't used on Americans.

"The safety of this nation," he insisted, "cannot lie wholly or even primarily in its scientific or technical prowess. It can be based only on making future wars impossible."

The only hope, he believed, was for the United States to stop building bombs and to somehow convince the Soviet Union not to start.

Truman's secretary of state, James Byrnes, replied that neither goal was realistic. Byrnes returned Oppenheimer's report, with a message for its author, "Tell Dr. Oppenheimer for the time being his proposal about an international agreement is not practical, and that he and the rest of the gang should pursue their work full force."

In other words, he wanted Oppenheimer to get back to the lab and build more bombs. That's what Leslie Groves expected, too—if things moved according to schedule, he reported, the U.S. Army would have twenty plutonium bombs by the end of 1945.

OPPENHEIMER RETURNED TO LOS ALAMOS, feeling what he described to a friend as "a profound grief, and a profound perplexity about the course we should be following."

At the lab Edward Teller showed him a design for a far more powerful atomic weapon. He wanted Oppenheimer to help get government support for the new bomb.

"I neither can nor will do so," Oppenheimer told Teller.

"It was obvious," Teller said later, "that Oppenheimer did not want to support further weapons work in any way."

That was a common feeling among the bomb makers. "We all felt that, like the soldiers, we had done our duty," said Hans Bethe, "and that we deserved to return to the type of work that we had chosen as our life's career, the pursuit of pure science and teaching."

On October 16, 1945, Oppenheimer officially resigned as director of Los Alamos. A ceremony was planned, and Dorothy McKibben drove from her office in Santa Fe up to the Hill to attend. It was a sunny fall day. McKibben saw thousands gathering in front of an outdoor stage. Beside the stage she saw Oppenheimer, pacing.

"Hello," she said.

He walked right by her.

"His eyes were glazed over," she remembered, "the way they were when he was in deep thought."

On stage a few minutes later, Leslie Groves handed Oppenheimer a scroll—a certificate of thanks from the government to Oppenheimer and the Los Alamos staff.

"It is our hope that in years to come we may look at this scroll, and all that it signifies, with pride," Oppenheimer told the crowd. "Today that pride must be tempered with a profound concern," he continued. "If atomic bombs are to be added as new weapons to the arsenals of a warring world, or to the arsenals of nations preparing for war, then the time will come when mankind will curse the names of Los Alamos and Hiroshima.

"The peoples of this world must unite or they will perish."


A WEEK LATER, Oppenheimer was back in Washington to continue his talks with top officials. Early on the morning of October 24, he walked the streets of the capital with Henry Wallace, the secretary of commerce.

"I never saw a man in such an extremely nervous state as Oppenheimer," Wallace wrote in his diary that night. "He seemed to feel that the destruction of the entire human race was imminent."

Oppenheimer complained that Secretary of State Byrnes didn't seem to understand the implications of the bomb. Byrnes seemed to think it could be used like a pistol, to scare the Soviets into behaving a certain way. "Oppenheimer believes that this method will not work," wrote Wallace. "He says the Russians are a proud people and have good physicists and abundant resources. They may have to lower their standard of living to do it but they will put everything they have got into getting plenty of atomic bombs as soon as possible."

At that point, the United States and Soviet Union would be in an arms race—each trying to produce weapons fast enough to stay ahead. Oppenheimer believed this race could still be prevented.

"Do you think it would do any good to see the president?" Oppenheimer asked.

"Yes," said Wallace.

THE NEXT MORNING, at ten-thirty, Oppenheimer walked into the Oval Office. President Truman was at his desk. He stood and shook Oppenheimer's hand. This was their first meeting.

They sat and began to talk. The conversation started awkwardly. Truman wanted to discuss how scientists and the military could continue working together to make more atomic bombs, while Oppenheimer tried to steer the conversation to the topic of international cooperation, and the goal of stopping the arms race before it could begin.

Truman brushed this worry aside, asking: "When will the Russians be able to build the bomb?"

"I don't know," Oppenheimer answered.

"I know."

"When?"

"Never."

Oppenheimer was stunned by Truman's confidence—unjustified confidence, Oppenheimer believed. He had planned to lay out his step-by-step strategy for preventing an arms race, backing each step with clearly reasoned arguments. But at this critical moment, he was too emotional to command his powers of persuasion.

He lifted his trembling hands in front of Truman. "Mr. President," he said, "I feel I have blood on my hands."

Truman's eyes flashed disgust. "Never mind," he mumbled, "it'll all come out in the wash." If Truman had any misgivings about using the atomic bomb, he kept them well buried.

A long silence followed.

Then the president stood. The meeting was over.

"Don't worry," Truman told Oppenheimer as they shook hands. "We're going to work something out, and you're going to help us."

Oppenheimer left the room.

"Blood on his hands, dammit," Truman grumbled as the door shut. "He hasn't half as much blood on his hands as I have. You just don't go around bellyaching about it." When aides came in to discuss other business, Truman snapped, "I don't want to see that son-of-a-bitch in this office ever again!"

Outside the Oval Office, Oppenheimer put on his hat and coat. He walked through the halls and out of the White House and toward the street. He was the father of the atomic bomb. But at that moment he knew his creation was completely—and forever—beyond his control.

# FALLOUT

ONE SUMMER DAY, three years after the end of World War II, Harry Gold fell in love. "It really happened so—just like that," he said. "Here was the girl I had been searching for all my life."

The woman was Mary Lanning, a fellow chemist. She and Gold began dating, and Gold became more and more convinced that this was his shot at happiness. Why not grab it? The war was long since over. Klaus Fuchs was back in Britain. Gold was working in a hospital lab in Philadelphia, with no access to valuable secrets and no interest in spying ever again. Why not just live a normal life?

It was wishful thinking, and Gold knew it.

Mary had no idea what was wrong, but she sensed a disturbing coolness in her boyfriend. Here was a man who was kind and generous. He said he loved her. And yet he always seemed distracted. When Gold asked Lanning to marry him, she hesitated. If he really loved her, she wondered, why the lack of passion?

It wasn't lack of passion she was sensing. It was fear. "Fear of exposure," Gold later admitted. "And fear not for myself, but a horror at the thought that the disastrous revelation might come after we had been married for three or four years, with children at home of our own."

Gold could confess, tell her everything. She might stick by him. But the basic problem remained. For most of his adult life, Harry Gold had been a spy for the Soviet Union. Was it really possible to get away with something like that?

"Who knew better than I on what a precarious, tottering house of cards my whole life rested?"

On a wet and gray morning on the plains of Kazakhstan, 2,000 miles east of Moscow, Igor Kurchatov paced back and forth in a small concrete bunker.

"Well, well . . ." muttered the head of the Soviet bomb project. "Well, well . . ."

It was a few minutes before 6:00 a.m. on August 29, 1949. Outside Kurchatov's bunker, the tall grass bent in the wind. Six miles away a steel tower rose 100 feet above the flat land. On a platform at the top of the tower sat the Soviet Union's first atomic bomb.

"Zero minus ten minutes."

The countdown echoed off the bunker's concrete walls. Kurchatov continued walking and muttering. Crowded into the bunker were other top Soviet physicists, along with the head of Stalin's secret police, Lavrenti Beria. Beria watched Kurchatov's nervous pacing. He decided to crank up the pressure.

"Nothing will come of it, Igor," Beria jabbed.

Kurchatov shook his head. "We'll certainly get it," he insisted.

For weeks the Soviet scientists had been privately discussing what would happen if this bomb test failed. Many expected to be shot.

The countdown hit ten seconds, then five, four, three, two, one . . .

And then: "On top of the tower an unbearably bright light blazed up," one of the Soviet physicists recalled. "The white fireball engulfed the tower, and expanding rapidly, changing color, it rushed upwards."

The bomb was an exact copy of the American implosion bomb tested at Trinity, and the rising, twisting, pulsing ball of fire looked just the same. The steel tower was vaporized. Tanks placed around the tower to test the bomb's strength were tossed into the air.

As he watched the bomb's glow brighten low hills in the distance, Kurchatov was hit by the same emotion that had swept over Oppenheimer at Trinity: pure relief. And his first words were identical. "It worked."

A much more excited Lavrenti Beria hugged and kissed Kurchatov, then ran to the phone and shouted for an immediate connection to Stalin's home. Stalin's secretary picked up in Moscow, where it was two hours earlier. He explained to Beria that the Soviet leader was still asleep.

Beria said, "Wake him up."

THE SOVIET UNION'S FIRST ATOMIC bomb exploded with the force of twenty thousand tons of TNT. It was too big to hide.

Just a few days later, a U.S. Air Force weather plane flying over the western Pacific detected high levels of radiation in the air. Air samples were collected and sent to labs for study. In Washington, D.C., a panel of scientists—including Robert Oppenheimer—analyzed the results. They were quickly convinced that an atomic bomb had exploded somewhere in the Soviet Union, probably on the morning of August 29.

Oppenheimer was not surprised. Just a few months before, he'd told a reporter, "Our atomic monopoly is like a cake of ice melting in the sun."

But President Harry Truman was stunned. His intelligence experts had just told him the Soviets wouldn't have the bomb until the middle of 1953. How had they built an atomic bomb so quickly?

An FBI counter-intelligence agent named Robert Lamphere asked himself the same question. "Had the Russian scientists actually been several years ahead of our estimates of their progress?" Lamphere wondered. "Or had they been aided in their effort to build it by information stolen from the United States?"

The answer lay in a stack of coded telegrams sent from America by Soviet agents during World War II. While in the United States, Soviet spies had to use an American telegraph company to send information quickly to Moscow. The KGB probably knew that the telegraph company was making copies of every telegram and handing them over to the U.S. Army. This didn't particularly worry the Soviets—the messages were always written in an extremely complex code.

In 1949, after years of failure, American code breakers cracked the code. Intelligence agents began decoding all the messages sent to the Soviet Union during the war. That's when they came across a shocking note sent from New York City to KGB headquarters in 1944.

"In this cable were data and theories that seemed to have come directly from inside the Manhattan Project," Lamphere explained. "When I read the KGB message, it became immediately obvious to me that the Russians had indeed stolen crucial research from us, and had undoubtedly used it to build their bomb."

The 1944 telegram summarized a top-secret scientific paper. The paper had been written by one of the British scientists working with Oppenheimer. A few phone calls later, Lamphere had the name of the paper's author: Klaus Fuchs.

Lamphere notified agents of MI-5, Britain's military intelligence agency.

221

AFTER THE WAR, Fuchs had returned to Britain and continued working for the government. By 1949, he'd risen to the head of the theoretical physics division at Harwell, Britain's main atomic research center.

One morning shortly after the Soviet bomb test, a tall, thin man stepped into Fuchs's office. He identified himself as William Skardon, an investigator with MI-5, and said he was just doing a routine check. Puffing on a pipe, Skardon asked Fuchs a long series of questions about the scientist's background and family.

After seventy-five minutes of friendly chatter, Skardon suddenly said, "Were you not in touch with a Soviet official or a Soviet representative while you were in New York? And did you not pass on information to that person about your work?"

There was a long silence. Fuchs sat perfectly still. Even his face remained frozen.

Finally he said, "I don't think so."

At that moment Skardon knew the man was guilty.

But he had no evidence. The coded Soviet telegrams couldn't be used in a public court, because the Americans didn't want the Soviets to know they had broken their code. Sure, Fuchs had been a Communist back in his college days, but that was hardly proof he was a Soviet spy.

Skardon repeated the charge anyway, just to get a reaction.

"I don't understand," Fuchs said. "Perhaps you will tell me what the evidence is."

Skardon declined, moved on to other subjects, and said a polite good-bye.

He questioned Fuchs several more times over the next few weeks. Fuchs continued to deny everything, though the pressure was getting to him. At home, alone at night, he considered suicide.

On January 22, 1950, Fuchs called Skardon. He said he wanted to talk. Skardon came to Fuchs's house.

"You asked to see me, and here I am," the investigator said.

"Yes," said Fuchs. "It's rather up to me now."

"When did it start?" asked Skardon.

"I started in 1942."

"Tell me, just to give me a better picture, what was the most important information you passed over?"

"Perhaps the most important thing was the full design of the atom bomb."

HARRY GOLD'S FEAR of exposure had ruined his relationship with Mary Lanning. Alone again, he tried to focus on his job—always wondering when his house of cards would come crashing down.

When he read newspaper accounts of the arrest of Klaus Fuchs in Britain, he knew it would be soon.

On Monday, May 15, 1950, FBI agents Scott Miller and Richard Brennan came to the Philadelphia hospital lab where Gold worked. "Even before they showed me their identification, I knew who they were," Gold recalled.

The agents asked Gold to come down to the Bureau offices to answer a few questions. They were curious about men Gold had worked with during the war, "and," they added, "some other matters." Gold was questioned for five hours that night, but the questions were general—there was no accusation of spying.

On Tuesday, he noticed two men in suits following him. On Wednesday, while he was at work, an agent poked his head into the lab.

"I thought I'd stop in and see what your place was like," the man said with a smile.

Gold showed the agent around. They chatted politely, but the mood was tense. Both were pretending this was just a friendly visit. But knew it wasn't. *I'm under surveillance,* Gold kept thinking. *Why? What do they know?*

Agents Miller and Brennan brought Gold to FBI offices for questioning again on Thursday. But they didn't accuse him of anything—not yet. Then, after a nine-hour session on Friday night, Brennan handed Gold a photograph.

"Do you know who he is?"

Gold looked at the photo. It was the pale, sad, owl-like face of Klaus Fuchs.

"I do not know him," Gold said, desperately trying to sound calm. "I recognize the picture as that of Dr. Fuchs, the Briton who got in trouble over there, but I don't know him. I've never been in England."

"Oh yes, you know him. You met him in Cambridge, Massachusetts."

"Never been there in my life."

As with Fuchs, the agents had no proof that Gold was a spy. Fuchs had described Gold's appearance but didn't know Gold's real name. Fuchs had also told investigators that his American contact seemed to know a lot about chemistry, but that was hardly evidence. The FBI needed to force Gold to confess, or they had no case.

That was why they were keeping him under constant surveillance, and conducting late-night interrogations. The agents were hoping to wear Gold down, to confuse him, to make him lose hope. It was working. After two more long interviews on Saturday and Sunday, the agents mentioned they could settle the matter once and for all by taking a quick look in Gold's house. Gold had the legal right to refuse, but decided there was no point.

"What would happen, would happen, and that was all," he later said of his thinking at this critical moment. "Possibly it was the sheer and utter exhaustion of that past week which had produced this reaction in me."

The next morning, May 22, Gold ate breakfast at home with his brother and father. When they put on their coats to leave for work, Gold was still in his pajamas.

"I have to work home today," he told them. He said goodbye, and they left.

Gold looked at the clock. The FBI would be there any moment. Shaking off his fatigue, Gold decided to make use of what little time remained. He started quickly up the stairs to his bedroom.

He had a few more minutes to destroy seventeen years of evidence.

# EPILOGUE: SCORPIONS IN A BOTTLE

KLAUS FUCHS MADE A COMPLETE CONFESSION and was taken to a prison in London to await trial. When friends came to visit, Fuchs tried to explain how he had divided his brain into two compartments: one for his commitment to Communism, and one for his personal life. His main regret, he said, was that his secret mission had caused him to lie to his friends.

"You don't know what I had done to my own mind," Fuchs said.

On the morning before his trail, Fuchs met with his lawyer in a prison cell beneath the courthouse.

The lawyer, Derek Curtis-Bennett, warned Fuchs to brace himself—he was likely to be given the maximum penalty allowed by law.

"You know what that is?" Curtis-Bennett asked.

"Yes," said Fuchs. "It's death."

*Harry Gold is escorted by federal marshalls after a meeting with a federal judge, May 31, 1959.*

"No, you bloody fool, it's fourteen years."

Fuchs was confused.

"You didn't give secrets to an enemy," the lawyer said. "You gave them to an ally." During World War II, Britain and the Soviet Union had been fighting on the same side. In the eyes of British law, Curtis-Bennett explained, that made all the difference. If Fuchs had committed treason to help an enemy, he'd face the death penalty. But the maximum sentence for passing secrets to an ally was fourteen years in prison.

After a trial lasting just two hours, Fuchs was given fourteen years. He was released from prison in 1959, thanks to a reduction in sentence for good behavior. He moved to Communist East Germany, where he got married, and continued atomic research. Fuchs died in 1988, at the age of 76.

As SOON AS the FBI found incriminating papers in his bedroom, Harry Gold cracked wide open. Seventeen years of secrets came pouring out. "Every time you squeeze him, there is some juice left," said one of the interrogating agents.

Here's where the huge mistake made five years before by the KGB came back to bite them. When Gold went to New Mexico in June 1945, he had orders from his KGB handler, Anatoly Yatzkov, to pick up information from both Klaus Fuchs *and* a second source, David Greenglass. By doing this, Gold cross-contaminated two separate spy rings. He learned about, and was therefore capable of exposing, two different operations.

That's exactly what happened. Gold told the FBI about Greenglass, who was arrested and questioned. Greenglass identified the people who had recruited him to spy for the Soviets, Julius and Ethel Rosenberg. In the most famous espionage trial of the century, the Rosenbergs were found guilty of helping to pass vital national secrets to the Soviets. They were sentenced to death—under American law, the fact that the Soviets were not enemies at the time the information was exchanged did not save them. The trial exposed the names of Soviet agents, and many had to flee the country. The KGB continued to spy on America, of course, but they were never again as effective as they had been during World War II.

Gold's confession and the Rosenberg trial also helped ignite the Red Scare of the 1950s—an obsessive hunt for Communists everywhere in American society. Gold watched it all from his jail cell. By cooperating with authorities he avoided the electric chair, getting a thirty-year sentence instead.

"I am calm," he said during his prison term, "and my mind is at peace for the first time in more than a decade and a half."

Gold was paroled from prison in 1965. He returned home to Philadelphia, where he died in 1972, at the age of 61.

Ted Hall was the one who got away.

After the war, Hall decided to return to school and began working toward his PhD in physics at the University of Chicago. There he met and fell in love with a student named Joan. Hall's approach was different from Gold's. Rather than live with secrets, he took Joan to her bedroom and shut the door. He looked around the small room, nervously.

"You don't have any microphones in here, do you?" he asked.

She assured him she didn't.

They sat on the bed. Ted told her everything. They were married soon after.

Three years later, the army code breakers who had exposed Klaus Fuchs found another curious telegram sent to KGB headquarters during World War II. It had been sent from New York City to Moscow in late 1944. The message described Ted Hall's meeting with the Soviet journalist and agent Sergei Kurnakov at Kurnakov's New York apartment—the meeting at which the nineteen-year-old Hall had first offered himself as a spy.

The information was passed on to the FBI's Chicago office. On March 16, 1951, agent Robert McQueen dropped by Hall's lab at the university. He said he needed Hall's help "with a matter pertaining to the security of the United States." Hall agreed to come to McQueen's office to answer a few questions.

The moment he began questioning Hall, McQueen knew he'd met his match. "I think he was very bright," McQueen recalled. "Very, very bright."

Expecting this day to come, Hall had long ago prepared his story. When McQueen pulled out a photo of Sergei Kurnakov, Hall calmly said he knew of Kurnakov's articles but had never met the man.

Hour after hour the questions grew more intense. McQueen finally came out and accused Hall of spying. Hall seemed confused by the charge, but not greatly upset.

"Quite calm for his age," McQueen noted. Too calm, the agent thought. "An innocent man usually says, 'Why are you asking me these questions?'"

Hall never protested. He answered the questions, then got up to leave. McQueen asked if he'd be willing to come back for another interview.

No, said Hall. He had nothing more to say.

The FBI *knew* Hall was guilty. And Hall knew they knew. But all the government had on Hall was the decoded KGB cable, and they didn't want to use that in court. Hall guessed this was the case. He simply refused to talk with the FBI—and they had no legal way to force him.

That didn't stop FBI agents from opening Hall's mail and tapping his home phone and following him everywhere.

"We knew that there was a definite chance that the world was going to collapse around us," Joan Hall remembered. She and Ted lived in fear for a couple of years—but slowly, over time, the FBI gave up.

In 1962 the Halls, with their three young children, moved to Britain, where Hall went to work in a lab at Cambridge University. It was not until 1995, when the KGB's decoded messages were finally made public, that Hall was exposed. When reporters came to his house to question him, he admitted contact with Soviet agents but declined to discuss details.

"If confronted with the same problem today," Hall acknowledged, "I would respond quite differently."

Ted Hall lived another four years, dying at the age of 74.

• • •

AFTER LEAVING LOS ALAMOS, Robert Oppenheimer moved east, taking over as director of the Institute for Advanced Study in Princeton, New Jersey. He also continued working in Washington, D.C., where he served as a scientific advisor to the government on atomic energy policy.

That's where he got in trouble.

The Soviet bomb test in 1949 seriously intensified the Cold War—the growing global rivalry between the United States and the Soviet Union that followed World War II. The United States faced a major decision: Now that the Soviets had the atomic bomb, should the Americans try to build an even more devastating weapon?

While working at Los Alamos, Oppenheimer and other top scientists had discussed the possibility of building what they called the "Super." This would be a new kind of bomb, not based on splitting atoms. The Super would get its energy from fusion, or the *joining* of atoms. At the extreme temperatures and pressures inside the sun and other stars, hydrogen atoms are fused together. This fusion process creates helium atoms—and releases vast amounts of energy. It is fusion that powers the stars.

In theory, scientists realized, it would be possible to re-create this process inside a bomb. Hydrogen could be put inside a fission bomb, like the ones used in Japan. When the fission bomb exploded, the heat and pressure should be great enough to cause the fusion of the hydrogen atoms. The power of such a bomb would have almost no limit. The more hydrogen you add, the bigger the blast.

In October 1949, Oppenheimer and other scientific advisors sat down to discuss the hydrogen bomb. Would the bomb really work? Probably, the scientists agreed. Would building it make Americans safer? No, they argued. The United States already had bombs powerful enough to wipe out Soviet cities. Building even bigger bombs would only heat up the arms race with the Soviets. The Soviets would respond by building bigger bombs themselves, putting Americans in greater danger. Oppenheimer argued that now was the time to step back from the arms race, not to accelerate it.

"We believe a super bomb should never be produced," Oppenheimer wrote on behalf of the scientists.

Another Los Alamos leader, Hans Bethe, added his own argument. "I believe the most important question is the moral one," he said. "Can we, who have always insisted on morality and human decency between nations as well as inside our own country, introduce this weapon of total annihilation into the world?"

President Truman saw it differently. The Soviet dictator Joseph Stalin was proving to be ruthless and untrustworthy. It would be dangerous—even irresponsible, Truman figured—to let the Soviets become more powerful than the United States. And, as always, there was a political angle. If the Soviets got the hydrogen bomb first, American voters might blame the president who'd let it happen.

When it came time to make the decision, Truman had one question about the hydrogen bomb: "Can the Russians do it?"

Yes, said his advisors.

"In that case, we have no choice. We'll go ahead."

On January 31, 1950, Truman announced that the country was moving forward with work on the hydrogen bomb.

"We keep saying, 'We have no other course,'" lamented Truman's advisor David Lilienthal. "What we should be saying is, 'We are not bright enough to see any other course.'"

Albert Einstein, who had first alerted President Roosevelt to the possibility of building atomic bombs, was deeply disturbed. "If successful," he said, "radioactive poisoning of the atmosphere and hence annihilation of any life on earth has been brought within the range of technical possibilities."

232    ON NOVEMBER 1, 1952, on a tiny island in the South Pacific, the United States tested the world's first hydrogen bomb. It exploded with the incredible force of 10 megatons of TNT. That's 10 *million* tons of TNT—more than 500 times more powerful than the bomb that flattened Hiroshima.

Less than a year later, in Kazakhstan, the Soviets successfully tested their first hydrogen bomb.

From this point on, there could be no such thing as winning a nuclear war. "We may be likened to two scorpions in a bottle," Oppenheimer wrote in a 1953 article, "each capable of killing the other, but only at the risk of his own life."

Quotes like this got Oppenheimer into trouble. They particularly annoyed Lewis Strauss, chairman of the Atomic Energy Commission (AEC), the government agency in charge of the country's atomic energy policy. Strauss argued that Oppenheimer's opposition to the H-bomb was an act of disloyalty to America. He suggested that maybe Oppenheimer had *always* been disloyal. As evidence, he dug up those flimsy charges the army and FBI had investigated ten years before: that Oppenheimer was secretly a Communist and maybe even a Soviet spy.

Strauss devised a plan for taking Oppenheimer down. He'd have the AEC strip Oppenheimer of his security clearance. Without this clearance, Oppenheimer would no longer be allowed to see secret information on the latest atomic weapons research. He couldn't advise the government, because he wouldn't know what was going on.

Oppenheimer had two options: demand a hearing, or simply walk away. He knew by now that nothing he did or said could stop the arms race. But there was a principle involved—he couldn't let the charges against him go unchallenged. "This course of action," he told Strauss, "would mean that I accept and concur in the view that I am not fit to serve this government that I have now served for some twelve years. This I cannot do."

Oppenheimer got his hearing, but it was bogus from the start. Strauss personally picked the panel of judges. The FBI tapped Oppenheimer's phones and listened in on conversations between him and his attorney. This illegally gathered information was used against Oppenheimer in court.

Strauss and his lead lawyer, Roger Robb, came up with two main lines of attack. First, they argued that Oppenheimer objected to the hydrogen bomb, and therefore was helping to weaken America. Second, that Oppenheimer had never come clean about the so-called Chevalier incident. This was the time in late 1942 when Oppenheimer's friend, Haakon Chevalier, had come to his house and mentioned that a Soviet agent he knew would be interested in any scientific information Oppenheimer might like to share.

Oppenheimer had hashed it all out with army security officers back in 1943. But now Robb suggested that Oppenheimer had never told the *whole* truth about the Chevalier incident. If the incident had really been so innocent, Robb asked, why hadn't Oppenheimer reported it to Leslie Groves right away?

Robb was clearly implying that Oppenheimer had closer contact with the Soviets than he was admitting. The judges were swayed—they voted to revoke Oppenheimer's security clearance. "Dr. Oppenheimer is not entitled to the continued confidence of the government," declared the AEC.

OPPENHEIMER WAS ONLY FIFTY YEARS OLD, but friends said he suddenly looked older.

"I think it broke his spirit, really," Robert Serber said of the ruling.

"I think to a certain extent it actually almost killed him, spiritually," agreed Isidor Rabi. "It achieved what his opponents wanted to achieve; it destroyed him."

During the hearing a friend mentioned that Oppenheimer, with his scientific reputation, would be welcome at any top university in Europe—why not go?

Tears glazed Oppenheimer's eyes as he said, "Damn it, I happen to love this country."

Even after the hearing, the FBI continued listening in on Oppenheimer's phone calls. When he and his family flew to the Caribbean island of St. John for a vacation, agents kept watch. "According to the plan," declared one FBI report, "Oppenheimer will first travel to England, from England he will travel to France, and while in France he will vanish into Soviet hands."

Actually, Oppenheimer sat on the beach for a few weeks. Then he went home to New Jersey.

He continued working in Princeton until his retirement in 1966. That same year he was diagnosed with cancer of the throat. He died in 1967, at the age of 62.

ALL THE WHILE the arms race expanded.

In 1954, the United States tested a massive 15-megaton hydrogen bomb on the tiny Pacific island of Bikini Atoll. A cloud of radioactive dust spread over 7,000 square miles of ocean. To this day, the radioactive soil of Bikini Atoll makes the island uninhabitable.

Soviet bomb makers responded with the biggest atomic explosion in history—an incredible 50-megaton monster. The test knocked down brick buildings 25 miles from the blast. The shock wave cracked windows 500 miles away.

Other countries decided they needed the bomb as well. Great Britain tested its first atomic bomb in 1952. France followed with its first bomb test in 1960. Then came China in 1964, and India in 1974.

The United States and Soviet Union continued racing. The race was no longer to build bigger bombs—the bombs were already too big for any possible target. The race was to build more bombs, and faster and more accurate ways to deliver them by airplane, submarine, and missile. By the mid-1980s the two sides had a total of 65,000 nuclear bombs. Each side could now destroy the other's cities within minutes of the start of war. The rivals had enough bombs to destroy all human life—many times over.

The world has since stepped back a bit from this cliff.

In the late 1980s, the United States and U.S.S.R. began negotiating treaties to reduce the number of atomic weapons. The reductions have continued since the end of the Cold War. Together, the United States and Russia now have about 22,000 atomic weapons.

But other countries have joined the nuclear club. Pakistan tested a uranium fission bomb in 1998. North Korea has had the bomb since 2006. Israel may have about eighty atomic bombs, though it will not officially confirm or deny its bomb program. In 2011, United Nations inspectors announced that they had found evidence that Iran was very likely working, in secret, to build its own atomic arsenal.

The big question is: Will any of these bombs ever be used?

Most of the world's atomic bombs are still in the hands of the United States and Russia. And while our two countries are not exactly friendly, tensions are far lower than they were during the Cold War. For now, at least, it's hard to imagine a realistic series of events that could lead to a massive exchange of atomic bombs.

But other dangers exist. One is the nightmare scenario of a terrorist group getting hold of an atomic weapon. Another is that an actual government—like the secretive rulers of North Korea—might just be crazy enough to lash out with atomic bombs. Or long-time enemies India and Pakistan could go to war, as they have several times, and this time the shooting could escalate into a nuclear battle.

And if you think atomic explosions in Asia wouldn't affect Americans, consider this. A study published in *Scientific American* in 2010 looked at the probable impact of a "small" nuclear war, one in which India and Pakistan each dropped fifty atomic bombs. The scientists concluded that the explosions would ignite massive firestorms, sending enormous amounts of dust and smoke into the atmosphere. This would block some of the sun's light from reaching the earth, making the planet colder and darker—for about ten years. Farming would collapse, and people all over the globe would starve to death. And that's if only half of one percent of all the atomic bombs on earth were used.

236

In the end, this is a difficult story to sum up. The making of the atomic bomb is one of history's most amazing examples of teamwork and genius and poise under pressure. But it's also the story of how humans created a weapon capable of wiping our species off the planet. It's a story with no end in sight.

And, like it or not, you're in it.

RACE TO TRINITY

Albert Einstein
Old Grove Rd.
Nassau Point
Peconic, Long Island

August 2nd, 1939

F.D. Roosevelt,
President of the United States,
White House
Washington, D.C.

Sir:

Some recent work by E.Fermi and L. Szilard, which has been com-
municated to me in manuscript, leads me to expect that the element uranium may be turned into a new and important source of energy in the immediate future. Certain aspects of the situation which has arisen seem
to call for watchfulness and, if necessary, quick action on the part
of the Administration. I believe therefore that it is my duty to bring
to your attention the following facts and recommendations:

In the course of the last four months it has been made probable -
through the work of Joliot in France as well as Fermi and Szilard in
America - that it may become possible to set up a nuclear chain reaction
in a large mass of uranium,by which vast amounts of power and large quantities of new radium-like elements would be generated. Now it appears
almost certain that this could be achieved in the immediate future.

This new phenomenon would also lead to the construction of bombs,
and it is conceivable - though much less certain - that extremely powerful bombs of a new type may thus be constructed. A single bomb of this
type, carried by boat and exploded in a port, might very well destroy
the whole port together with some of the surrounding territory. However,
such bombs might very well prove to be too heavy for transportation by
air.

The United States has only very poor ores of uranium in moderate quantities. There is some good ore in Canada and the former Czechoslovakia, while the most important source of uranium is Belgian Congo.

In view of this situation you may think it desirable to have some permanent contact maintained between the Administration and the group of physicists working on chain reactions in America. One possible way of achieving this might be for you to entrust with this task a person who has your confidence and who could perhaps serve in an inofficial capacity. His task might comprise the following:

a) to approach Government Departments, keep them informed of the further development, and put forward recommendations for Government action, giving particular attention to the problem of securing a supply of uranium ore for the United States;

b) to speed up the experimental work,which is at present being carried on within the limits of the budgets of University laboratories, by providing funds, if such funds be required, through his contacts with private persons who are willing to make contributions for this cause, and perhaps also by obtaining the co-operation of industrial laboratories which have the necessary equipment.

I understand that Germany has actually stopped the sale of uranium from the Czechoslovakian mines which she has taken over. That she should have taken such early action might perhaps be understood on the ground that the son of the German Under-Secretary of State, von Weizsäcker, is attached to the Kaiser-Wilhelm-Institut in Berlin where some of the American work on uranium is now being repeated.

Yours very truly,

*A. Einstein*

(Albert Einstein)

*Previous page: Albert Einstein's letter to President Franklin Delano Roosevelt, warning of the possibility that Germany might be developing an atomic weapon. This Page: Top left: Fermi's atomic pile under construction, November 1942. Uranium was loaded into the holes in the graphite blocks. Top right: The bomb core is carried to a waiting vehicle on its way to the tower at Trinity, July 1945. Bottom right: The 100-foot tower that will house the gadget. Bottom left: The core (right) is ready for insertion into the gadget (left). Facing Page: Top left: The fully assembled gadget is raised on a pulley. Top right: The gadget*

*awaits the test at the top of the tower. Bottom left: The Trinity explosion .006 seconds after detonation. Bottom right: The explosion .127 seconds after detonation. Following Page: Top: A mushroom cloud roils over Trinity 12 seconds after detonation. Bottom left: Aerial view of the crater created by the Trinity test. Bottom right: Robert Oppenheimer and Leslie Groves survey the remains of the test tower on a visit to the site, September 9, 1945.*

# SOURCE NOTES

**AS I SAID IN THE BEGINNING,** this is a big story, and I had a lot to learn before I could pull it all together. Here's the list of books and other sources I used. If you'd like to find out more about any particular aspect of the bomb race, these sources might help.

### Bomb Race Sources

My book weaves together three basic story lines: the Americans try to build a bomb, the Soviets try to steal it, and the Allies try to sabotage the German bomb project. Each of the sources below focuses on some part of one or more of these stories. The bible on this whole subject, by the way, is Rhodes's *The Making of the Atomic Bomb*.

Conant, Jennet. *109 East Palace: Robert Oppenheimer and the Secret City of Los Alamos.* New York: Simon & Schuster, 2005.

Gallagher, Thomas. *Assault in Norway: Sabotaging the Nazi Nuclear Program.* Guilford, CT: The Lyons Press, 1975.

Haynes, John Earl, Harvey Klehr, and Alexander Vassiliev. *Spies: The Rise and Fall of the KGB in America.* New Haven: Yale University Press, 2009.

Holoway, David. *Stalin and the Bomb: the Soviet Union and Atomic Energy, 1939–1956*. New Haven: Yale University Press, 1994.

Jungk, Robert. *Brighter Than a Thousand Suns*: *A Personal History of the Atomic Scientists*. New York: Harcourt, Brace and Company, 1956.

Lamont, Lansing. *Day of Trinity*. New York: Atheneum, 1965.

Laurence, William. *Dawn Over Zero: The Story of the Atomic Bomb*. New York: Alfred A. Knopf, 1947.

Los Alamos National Laboratory Public Affairs Office. *Los Alamos 1943–1945: The Beginning of an Era*. Los Alamos, NM, 1986.

Mears, Ray. *The Real Heroes of Telemark*. London: Hodder & Stoughton, 2003.

Persico, Joseph E. *Roosevelt's Secret War: FDR and World War II Espionage*. New York: Random House, 2001.

Powers, Thomas. *Heisenberg's War: The Secret History of the German Bomb*. Cambridge, MA: Da Capo Press, 1993.

Rhodes, Richard. *Dark Sun: The Making of the Hydrogen Bomb*. New York: Simon & Schuster, 1995.

Rhodes, Richard. *The Making of the Atomic Bomb*. New York: Simon & Schuster, 1986.

Serber, Robert. *The Los Alamos Primer: The First Lectures on How to Build an Atomic Bomb*. Berkeley, CA: University of California Press, 1992.

Shirer, William, L. *The Rise and Fall of the Third Reich*. New York: Simon and Schuster, 1960.

Toland, John. *The Rising Sun: The Decline and Fall of the Japanese Empire, 1936–1945*. New York: The Modern Library, 2003.

Zoellner, Tom. *Uranium: War, Energy, and the Rock that Shaped the World*. New York: Viking, 2009.

## Character Sources

Here's a list of sources dealing with one or more of this book's important characters. I'd say *American Prometheus* is the single best Oppenheimer book, but there are a lot to choose from. Two other favorites were Moss's *Klaus Fuchs* and Hornblum's *The Invisible Harry Gold*. Albright and Kunstel's *Bombshell* is a priceless source because the authors actually met with Ted Hall before he died.

Albright, Joseph, and Marcia Kunstel. *Bombshell: The Secret Story of America's Unknown Atomic Spy Conspiracy*. New York: Times Book, 1997.

Bird, Kai and Martin Sherwin. *American Prometheus: The Triumph and Tragedy of J. Robert Oppenheimer.* New York: Vantage Books, 2005.

Cook, Haruko Taya and Theodore F. Cook. *Japan at War: An Oral History.* New York: The New Press, 1992.

Cole, K.C. *Something Incredibly Wonderful Happens: Frank Oppenheimer and the World He Made Up.* Boston: Houghton Mifflin, 2009.

Davis, Nuel Pharr. *Lawrence and Oppenheimer.* New York: Simon & Schuster, 1968.

Dawidoff, Nicholas. *The Catcher Was a Spy: The Mysterious Life of Moe Berg.* New York: Pantheon Books, 1994.

Goodchild, Peter, *J. Robert Oppenheimer: Shatterer of Worlds.* New York: Fromm International Pub. Corp., 1985.

Hall, Joan. Interview on PBS program "Secrets, Lies, and Atomic Spies." Broadcast Feb. 5, 2002.

Herken, Gregg. *Brotherhood of the Bomb: The Tangled Lives and Loyalties of Robert Oppenheimer, Ernest Lawrence, and Edward Teller.* New York: Henry Holt and Company, 2002.

Hornblum, Allen M. *The Invisible Harry Gold: The Man Who Gave the Soviets the Atom Bomb.* New Haven: Yale University Press, 2010.

Larsen, Rebecca. *Oppenheimer and the Atomic Bomb.* New York: Franklin Watts, 1998.

McCullough, David. *Truman.* New York: Simon & Schuster, 1992.

Moon, Thomas and Carl F. Eifler. *The Deadliest Colonel.* New York: Vantage Press, 1975.

Moss, Norman. *Klaus Fuchs: The Man Who Stole the Atom Bomb.* London: Grafton Books, 1987.

Norris, Robert S. *Racing for the Bomb.* South Royalton, VT: Steerforth Press, 2002.

Pais, Abraham. *J. Robert Oppenheimer: A Life.* New York: Oxford University Press, 2006.

Roberts, Sam. *The Brother: The Untold Story of Atomic Spy David Greenglass and How He Sent His Sister, Ethel Rosenberg, to the Electric Chair.* New York: Random House, 2001.

Royal, Denise. *The Story of J. Robert Oppenheimer.* New York: St. Martin's Press, 1969.

Steeper, Nancy Cook. *Gatekeeper to Los Alamos: Dorothy Scarritt McKibben.* Los Alamos, NM: Los Alamos Historical Society, 2003.

Sykes, Christopher. *No Ordinary Genius: The Illustrated Richard Feynman.* New York: W.W. Norton & Company, 1994.

Williams, Robert Chadwell. *Klaus Fuchs: Atom Spy.* Cambridge, MA: Harvard University Press, 1987.

## Primary Sources

Here's the heart of the book—firsthand accounts by participants in the bomb race, found in a huge variety of memoirs, interviews, articles, letters, speeches, hearings, secret recordings, and a few primary source collections. Leslie Groves, Richard Feynman, Knut Haukelid, Paul Tibbets, and others take you *inside* the bomb race, while Harry Gold gives his version of history in his testimony in *Scope of Soviet Activity in the United States*, a series of congressional hearings held in 1956. Oppenheimer never wrote an autobiography, but he tells his story though letters, interviews, and testimony in *In the Matter of J. Robert Oppenheimer*, the 1954 hearing that brought him down.

Alvarez, Luis. Interview conducted by Charles Weiner and Barry Richman, February 15, 1967. Recording housed at Niels Bohr Library and Archives, College Park, MD.

Anderson, Herbert L. "Fermi, Szilard, and Trinity." *Bulletin of the Atomic Scientists*, Oct. 1974, pgs. 40–47.

Badash, Lawrence, Joseph Hirschfelder, Herbert Broida, editors. *Reminiscences of Los Alamos, 1943–1945*. Dordrecht, Holland: D. Reidel Publishing Company, 1980.

Bernstein, Jeremy. *Hitler's Uranium Club: The Secret Recordings at Farm Hall*. New York: Copernicus Books, 2001.

Blum, John Morton, editor. *The Price of Vision: The Diary of Henry A. Wallace*. Boston: Houghton Mifflin Company, 1973.

Churchill, Winston. *The Hinge of Fate*. Boston: Houghton Mifflin, 1950.

Feklisov, Alexander, and Sergei Kostin. *The Man Behind the Rosenbergs: Memoirs of the KGB Spymaster*. New York: Enigma Books, 2004.

Fermi, Laura. *Atoms in the Family*. Chicago: University of Chicago Press, 1961.

Ferrell, Robert H., editor. *Harry S. Truman and the Bomb: A Documentary History*. Worland, WY: High Plains, 1996.

Feynman, Richard P. *Surely You're Joking, Mr. Feynman! Adventures of a Curious Character*. New York: Bantam Books, 1986.

Feynman, Richard P. *What Do You Care What Other People Think? Further Adventures of a Curious Character*. New York: Bantam Books, 1989.

Frisch: *What Little I Remember*. New York: Cambridge University Press, 1979.

Fuchs, Klaus. Statement made at British War Office, January 27, 1950. Available online at www.mi5.gov.uk.

Goudsmit, Samuel Abraham. *Alsos*. New York: Henry Schuman, Inc., 1947.

Groves, Leslie. *Now It Can Be Told: The Story of the Manhattan Project*. New York: Harper & Brothers, 1962.

Hachiya, Michihiko, MD. *Hiroshima Diary: The Journal of a Japanese Physician, August 6–September 30, 1945*. Chapel Hill: University of North Carolina Press, 1955.

Haukelid, Knut. *Skis Against the Atom*. Minot, ND: North American Heritage Press, 1989 (Originally published by William Kimber, 1954).

*In the Matter of J. Robert Oppenheimer: Transcript of Hearing before Personal Security Board and Texts of Principal Documents and Letters*. Cambridge, MA: MIT Press, 1954.

Kelly, Cynthia C., editor. *The Manhattan Project: The Birth of the Atomic Bomb in the Words of Its Creators, Eyewitnesses, and Historians*. New York: Black Dog & Levanthal Publishers, 2007.

Lamphere, Robert, and Tom Shachtman. *The FBI-KGB War: A Special Agent's Story*. New York: Random House, 1986.

Libby, Leona Marshall. *The Uranium People*. New York: Crane, Russak & Company, 1979.

Oppenheimer, Robert. "Oppenheimer Replies." *Bulletin of the Atomic Scientists*, May 1954, pgs. 177–191.

Osada, Arata, editor. *Children of Hiroshima*. Tokyo: Publishing Committee for Children of Hiroshima, 1980.

Pash, Boris. *The Alsos Mission*. New York: Award House, 1969.

*Pearl Harbor Remembered: Survivors Remembrances*, oral history collected by Pearl Harbor Survivors Association, Upland, CA.

Roosevelt, Franklin, D. "Day of Infamy" Speech, December 8, 1941. Original at National Archives, Washington, D.C., and viewable online at www.archives.gov.

*Scope of Soviet Activity in the United States: Hearings to Investigate the Administration of the Internal Security Act and Other Internal Security Laws*. Washington, D.C.: U.S. Government Printing Office, 1956–57.

Serber, Robert. *Peace and War: Reminiscences of a Life on the Frontiers of Science*. New York: Columbia University Press, 1998.

Smith, Alice Kimball and Charles Weiner, editors. *Robert Oppenheimer: Letters and Recollections*. Stanford: Stanford University Press, 1980.

Stimson, Henry. "Memorandum of Conference with the President" August 8, 1945, 10: 45 AM. From the Henry Lewis Stimson Diaries, reel 9, Manuscripts and Archives, Yale University Library, New Haven, CT.

Szilard, Leo. *His Version of the Facts: Selected Recollections and Correspondence*. Cambridge: MIT Press, 1978.

Teller, Edward. *Memoirs: A Twentieth-Century Journey in Science and Politics*. Cambridge, MA: Perseus Publishing, 2001.

Tibbets, Paul W., with Clair Stebbings and Harry Franken. *The Tibbets Story*. New York: Stein and Day, 1978.

Truman, Harry. "Statement by the President of the United States." Aug. 6, 1945. At Harry S. Truman Library and Museum, Independence, MO. Available online at www.trumanlibrary.org.

Truman, Harry S. *Memoirs by Harry S. Truman: Volume 1: Year of Decisions*. Garden City, NY: 1955.

Truman, Margaret, editor. *Where the Buck Stops: The Personal and Private Writings of Harry S. Truman*. New York: Warner Books, 1989.

Ulam, Stanislaw. *Adventures of a Mathematician*. Berkeley, CA: University of California Press, 1991.

Wattenburg, Albert. "December 2, 1942: The Event and the People." *Bulletin of the Atomic Scientists*, Dec. 1982, pgs. 22–32.

Werner, Ruth. *Sonya's Report*. London: Chatto & Windus, 1991.

Wigner, Eugene. *The Recollections of Eugene P. Wigner as Told to Andrew Szanton*. New York and London: Plenum Press, 1992.

Wilson, Jane. "All in Our Time: Reminiscences of Nuclear Pioneers." *Bulletin of the Atomic Scientists*, April 1974, pgs. 10–18.

# QUOTATION NOTES

**Prologue: May 22, 1950**

All quotes from Gold's testimony in *Scope of Soviet Activity*.

**Skinny Superhero**

"Are you comfortable": Kelly, *Manhattan Project*.

"My escort went for a walk": Bird, *American Prometheus*.

"Forgetful Prof Parks Girl": S.F. *Chronicle*, Feb. 14, 1934.

"very frail, very pink-cheeked": Rhodes, *Atomic Bomb*.

"A repulsively good little boy": Bird, *American Prometheus*.

"He generally would answer": Kelly, *Manhattan Project*.

"Oh, come now": Bird, *American Prometheus*.

"He spoke quite rapidly": Kelly, *Manhattan Project*.

"Not that one": Bird, *American Prometheus*.

"The trouble is": Goodchild, *J. Robert Oppenheimer*.

"Beginning in late 1936": *In the Matter of J. Robert Oppenheimer*.

**The U Business**

"Perhaps you can suggest": Rhodes, *Atom Bomb*.

"I don't believe it": Kelly, *Manhattan Project*.

"We walked up and down": Libby, *Uranium People*.

"Yes, that is what I mean": Rhodes, *Atom Bomb*.

"I feel as if I had caught": Jungk. *A Thousand Suns*.

"Oh, what idiots": Libby, *Uranium People*.

"Bohr has just come in": Rhodes, *Atom Bomb*.

"In the second section": Weiner, *Alvarez Interview*.

"That's impossible": Rhodes, *Atom Bomb*.

"The U business": Smith, *Letters and Recollections*.

"Within perhaps a week": Rhodes, *Atom Bomb*.

"I'll cook them": Shirer, *Rise and Fall*.

## Finding Einstein

"the cottage of Dr. Moore": Szilard, *His Version*.

"Perhaps I misunderstood": Jungk. *A Thousand Suns*.

"Say, do you by any chance": Szilard, *His Version*.

"I hadn't thought of that": Kelly, *Manhattan Project*.

"And Einstein was just": Wigner, *Recollections*.

"Alex, what are you up to": Rhodes, *Atomic Bomb*.

"The element uranium": Kelly, *Manhattan Project*.

"Alex, what you are after": Rhodes, *Atomic Bomb*.

## Tradecraft

"Since the outbreak": Powers, *Heisenberg's War*.

"You'd never in a million": Hornblum, *Harry Gold*.

"Black was waiting": Rhodes, *Dark Sun*.

"I am a Communist": *Scope of Soviet Activity*.

"an almost puppy-like": Hornblum, *Harry Gold*.

"And that, is how I began": *Scope of Soviet Activity*.

"I'm giving you orders": Hornblum, *Harry Gold*.

"What the hell": *Scope of Soviet Activity*.

"They had decided to drop": Rhodes, *Dark Sun*.

## Rapid Rupture

"We often tailed": Feklisov, *Man Behind*.

"Many of the men": *In the Matter of J. Robert Oppenheimer*.

"After breakfast": Oral History: *Pearl Harbor Remembered*

"You gave the right": Shirer, *Rise and Fall*.

"They caught our ships": Persico, *Secret War*.

"No matter how long": National Archives.

"Just a few weeks": Serber, *Peace and War*.

"We were aware": Oppenheimer, *Bulletin of Atomic Scientists*

## Norway Connection

All quotes from: Haukalid, *Skis Against the Atom*.

## Enormoz

"I hoped to look through": Holoway, *Stalin and the Bomb*.

"Germany and the USA": Haynes, *Spies*.

"It was difficult because": Feklisov, *Man Behind*.

"Of the leads we have": Haynes, *Spies*.

## On the Cliff

"He took me to the majestic bluffs": Churchill, *Hinge of Fate*.

"He invited me to feel": Churchill, *Hinge of Fate*.

"I was, like every other": Groves, *Now It Can Be Told*.

"He had no hesitation": Norris, *Racing for the Bomb*.

"Groves is the biggest": Kelly, *Manhattan Project*.

"I was not happy": Groves, *Now It Can Be Told*.

"We don't know": Goodchild, *J. Robert Oppenheimer*.

"A major change": *In the Matter of J. Robert Oppenheimer*.

"He's a genius": Bird, *American Prometheus*.

"No one with whom": Groves, *Now It Can Be Told*.

"He had, after all": Bird, *American Prometheus*.

"It is desired that clearance": Groves, *Now It Can Be Told*.

"permanently incapacitated": Bird, *American Prometheus*.

## International Gangster School

"Ruined houses": Haukalid, *Skis Against*.

"It was not at all like": Gallagher, *Assault*.

"During a field exercise": Haukelid, *Skis Against*.

"Interesting": Gallagher, *Assault*.

## Gliders Down

All quotes from Gallagher, *Assault in Norway*.

## Quiet Fellow

"It was pleasant": Werner, *Sonya's Report*.

"The spelling": Frisch, *What I Remember*.

"I accepted": Fuchs's *Statement*.

"A very nice": Moss, *Klaus Fuchs*.

"When I learned about": Fuchs's *Statement*.

"Once Klaus gave me": Werner, *Sonya's Report*.

"Important, very valuable": Rhodes, *Dark Sun*.

"The organizational pace": Haynes, *Spies*.

"One evening in New York": Rhodes, *Dark Sun*.

"I, personally know very little": Bird, *American Prometheus*.

"Do you know any": Herken, *Brotherhood*.

"On thinking the matter": Bird, *American Prometheus*.

"I saw George Eltenton": Rhodes, *Dark Sun.*

"That would be a frightful": Jungk, *A Thousand Suns.*

"That was the end": Rhodes, *Dark Sun.*

"no chance whatsoever": Herken, *Brotherhood.*

**Disappearing Scientists**

"This will never do": Smith, *Letters and Recollections.*

"If you go on up": Bird, *American Prometheus.*

"We didn't want to": Jungk, *A Thousand Suns.*

"This is the place": Conant, *109 East Palace.*

"a policy of absolutely": Smith, *Letters and Recollections.*

"How would you like": Lamont, *Day of Trinity.*

"People I knew well": Ulam, *Adventures.*

"What's it all about": Kelly, *Manhattan Project.*

"I traveled all over": *In the Matter of J. Robert Oppenheimer.*

"Almost everyone knew": Kelly, *Manhattan Project.*

"He wasn't supposed": Feynman, *Surely You're Joking.*

"This would be a very": Sykes, *No Ordinary Genius.*

**Chicago Pile**

"It was terribly cold": Libby, *Uranium People.*

"The scene of this test": Kelly, *Manhattan Project.*

"The balcony was": Libby, *Uranium People.*

"If the pile should": Groves, *Now It Can Be Told.*

"Go ahead, George": Fermi, *Atoms in the Family.*

"You could hear": Rhodes, *Atom Bomb.*

"This will do it": Fermi, *Atoms in the Family.*

"Then the clicks": Anderson, *Bulletin of Atomic Scientists.*

"The pile has gone critical": Rhodes, *Atom Bomb.*

"Everyone began": Anderson, *Bulletin of Atomic Scientists.*

"The controlled release": Libby, *Uranium People.*

"For some time": Libby, *Uranium People.*

**Operation Gunnerside**

"You must reckon": Mears, *Real Heroes.*

"You have a fifty-fifty": Gallagher, *Assault.*

"It was a tight fit": Haukelid, *Skis Against.*

"We were all issued": Mears, *Real Heroes.*

"No doubt the hearts": Haukelid, *Skis Against.*

"Do you know where": Gallagher, *Assault.*

"There was back-slapping": Haukelid, *Skis Against.*

"As you all know": Gallagher, *Assault.*

**High Concentration**

"The weather was": Laurence, *Dawn Over Zero.*

"The great seven-story": Haukelid, *Skis Against.*

"All right, men": Gallagher, *Assault.*

"The time seemed long": Haukelid, *Skis Against.*

"What could be holding": Gallagher, *Assault.*

"Shall I fire": Haukelid, *Skis Against.*

"The Germans still don't" Gallagher, *Assault.*

"High concentration installation": Haukelid, *Skis Against.*

## The Gatekeeper

"How would you like a job": Conant, *109 East Palace.*

"Go to 109 East Palace": Jungk, *A Thousand Suns.*

"They arrived, breathless": Conant, *109 East Palace.*

"Some amazing rumors": Groves, *Now It Can Be Told.*

"for Santa Fe purposes": Kelly, *Manhattan Project.*

"The FBI and Army": Serber, *Peace and War.*

"I can't understand": Conant, *109 East Palace.*

## The Gadget

"Buildings were still": Kelly, *Manhattan Project.*

"The object of the project": Bird, *American Prometheus.*

"He wasn't much": Conant, *109 East Palace.*

"Around Los Alamos": Serber, *Los Alamos Primer.*

"We started working": Sykes, *No Ordinary Genius.*

"The site itself": Serber, *Peace and War.*

"It was a shambles": *109 East Palace.*

"The first thing I noticed": Teller, *Memoirs.*

"I was shocked": Bird, *American Prometheus.*

"Bob Christy": Feynman, *Surely You're Joking.*

"Welcome to Los Alamos": Conant, *109 East Palace.*

"Whatever the enemy": Smith, *Letters and Recollections.*

"it is requested": *Los Alamos: 1943–1945.*

## Laboratory Number 2

"The greatest military": Goodchild, *J. Robert Oppenheimer.*

"Oppenheimer was not observed": Bird, *American Prometheus.*

"subject still is or may be": Goodchild, *J. Robert Oppenheimer.*

"Oppenheimer is irreplaceable": Herken, *Brotherhood.*

"In the future": Bird, *American Prometheus.*

"This is a pleasure": this and other quotes from Pash-Oppenheimer interview are from *In the Matter of J. Robert Oppenheimer.*

"playing a key part": Conant, *109 East Palace.*

"The material as a whole": Rhodes, *Dark Sun.*

"In the presence of this": Haynes, *Spies.*

253

"extremely excited": Hornblum, *Harry Gold*.

"Forget them": *Scope of Soviet Activity*.

### Ferry Job

All quotes from: Haukelid, *Skis Against the Atom*.

### Dirty Work

"Railway Ferry Hydro Sunk": Haukelid, *Skis Against*.

"We were truly": Groves, *Now It Can Be Told*.

"The position of Heisenberg": Powers, *Heisenberg's War*.

"On or about 9 December": Moon, *The Deadliest Colonel*.

"Our purpose is to deny": Powers, *Heisenberg's War*.

"this new operation": this and all remaining quotes in chapter from Moon, *The Deadliest Colonel*.

### Secret Cities

"It was clear to all": Smith, *Letters and Recollections*.

"Well, let's look this over": Bird, *American Prometheus*.

"Each of us could walk": Conant, *109 East Palace*.

"In his presence": Bird, *American Prometheus*.

"This is how many": Rhodes, *Atomic Bomb*.

"Whenever I wanted": Feynman, *Surely You're Joking*.

"Here at great expense": Conant, *109 East Palace*.

"Now, the following people": Feynman, *Surely You're Joking*.

"I had known": Truman, *Memoirs*.

"Truman is a nuisance": McCullough, *Truman*.

### Man with Four Gloves

"The place had been": *Scope of Soviet Activity*.

"What is the way": Hornblum, *Harry Gold*.

"We strolled a while": Haynes, *Spies*.

"We immediately turned into": Rhodes, *Dark Sun*.

"A stern warning": Haynes, *Spies*.

### Born Rebel

"delightful": Albright, *Bombshell*.

"I saw Robert": Ulam, *Adventures*.

"The terrible shock": Conant, *109 East Palace*.

"The only way": Bird, *American Prometheus*.

"Living conditions are still": Albright, *Bombshell*.

### Two Inside

"I want to speak to someone": Haynes, *Spies*.

"an exceptionally keen": Albright, *Bombshell*.

"T.H. is 19 years old:" Haynes, *Spies*.

"Well, how do we know": Hall, *Nova Interview*.

"Show this to any physicist": Haynes, *Spies.*

"Our principle trouble": Rhodes, *Dark Sun.*

"an exceedingly beautiful": Hornblum, *Harry Gold.*

"I bring you greetings": Haynes, *Spies.*

"He worked days": Bird, *American Prometheus.*

"He's all ears": Lamont, *Day of Trinity.*

"In the course of this work": Fuchs, *Statement.*

"Everyone thought of him": Moss, *Klaus Fuchs.*

## The Pilot

All quotes from: Tibbets, *The Tibbets Story.*

## Swiss Deal

"my proposed entry": Powers, *Heisenberg's War.*

"Carl, there's a change": Moon, *Deadliest Colonel.*

"Don't ask me": Dawidoff, *The Catcher.*

"He'd been drilled": Powers, *Heisenberg's War.*

"H likes my interest": Dawidoff, *The Catcher.*

"I'm not a Nazi": Powers, *Heisenberg's War.*

"If only we could get": Goudsmit, *Alsos.*

## Implosion

"I am glad to have": Goudsmit, *Alsos.*

"Dr. Oppenheimer is mad": Davis, *Lawrence.*

"a hundred or so pieces": Rhodes, *Atomic Bomb.*

"Twice I dropped": Albright, *Bombshell.*

"Now we have our bomb": Rhodes, *Dark Sun.*

"If this is disinformation": Holoway, *Stalin and the Bomb.*

"K. welcomed me": Haynes, *Spies.*

"a huge bundle": *Scope of Soviet Activity.*

"It was quite obvious": Rhodes, *Dark Sun.*

## Falling Stars

"Steve Early wants you": McCullough, *Truman.*

"This is the V.P.": Truman, *Memoirs.*

"I thought I was going": McCullough, *Truman.*

"the president is dead": Truman, *Memoirs.*

"As we approached": Kelly, *Manhattan Project.*

"A German prisoner": Rhodes, *Atomic Bomb.*

"The pieces of": Groves, *Now It Can Be Told.*

"like an utterly exhausted": Powers, *Heisenberg's War.*

"He was worth more": Groves. *Now It Can Be Told.*

## Land of Enchantment

"We discussed last-minute": *Scope of Soviet Activity.*

255

"He wanted me to take": Hornblum, *Harry Gold*.

"I complained": Hornblum, *Harry Gold*.

"A basic rule": Feklisov, *Man Behind*.

"I have been guiding": Albright, *Bombshell*.

"For me, Hitler was": Conant, *109 East Palace*.

"To test or not to test": Badash, *Reminiscences*.

"the use of the gadget": Bird, *American Prometheus*.

"People were feverishly": Rhodes, *Atomic Bomb*.

"The voices on the telephone": Royal, *Story of Oppenheimer*.

"Hardly more than a creek": Hornblum, *Invisible Harry*.

"a considerable packet": Albright, *Bombshell*.

"I did what I consider": Fuchs, *Statement*.

"They might be coming": Rhodes, *Dark Sun*.

"Mr. Greenglass": Lamont, *Day of Trinity*.

"there are several men": *Scope of Soviet Activity*.

## Trinity

"We brushed our teeth" Jungk, *A Thousand Suns*.

"Time and time": *In the Matter of J. Robert Oppenheimer*.

"I got hold": Rhodes, *Atomic Bomb*.

"I wonder whether": Bernstein, *Uranium Club*.

"Any time after": Goldchild, *J. Robert Oppenheimer*.

"We halted our efforts": Rhodes, *Atomic Bomb*.

"Oppenheimer was really": Kelly, *Manhattan Project*.

"Get some sleep": Groves. *Now It Can Be Told*.

## Test Shot

"There were about ninety": Laurence, *Dawn Over Zero*.

"Don't worry": Lamont, *Day of Trinity*.

"The guys discussed": Albright, *Bombshell*.

"Naturally he was nervous": Groves. *Now It Can Be Told*.

"What the hell's wrong": Rhodes, *Atomic Bomb*.

"The scene inside": Kelly, *Manhattan Project*.

"It is now zero": Bird, *American Prometheus*.

"We were told to lie": Rhodes, *Atomic Bomb*.

"Zero minus fifteen": Bird, *American Prometheus*.

"It was an eerie sight": Laurence, *Dawn of Zero*.

"Lord, these affairs": Lamont, *Day of Trinity*.

"As we approached": Groves. *Now It Can Be Told*.

"As the time interval": Kelly, *Manhattan Project*.

"I put on dark glasses": Badash, *Reminiscences*.

"We were lying there": Rhodes, *Atomic Bomb*.

"Oppenheimer, on whom": Kelly, *Manhattan Project*.

"And then, without a sound": Goodchild, *J. Robert Oppenheimer*.

"There was an enormous": Rhodes, *Dark Sun*.

"The whole country was lighted": Groves, *Now It Can Be Told*.

"I was looking directly": Rhodes, *Atomic Bomb*.

"I look back up": Feynman, *Surely You're Joking*.

"An enormous ball of fire": Rhodes, *Dark Sun*.

"Up it went": Laurence, *Dawn of Zero*.

"His face relaxed": Kelly, *Manhattan Project*.

"It worked": Cole, *Something Wonderful*.

"Oppenheimer and the others": Badash, *Reminiscences*.

"A loud cry": Laurence, *Dawn of Zero*.

"I had rather expected": Albright, *Bombshell*.

"I'll never forget the way": Bird, *American Prometheus*.

"I am proud of you": Groves. *Now It Can Be Told*.

"The war is over": Laurence, *Dawn of Zero*.

"Naturally, we were very": Rhodes, *Atomic Bomb*.

"It was extremely solemn": Bird, *American Prometheus*.

**Little Boy**

"The explosives dump": Conant, *109 East Palace*.

"Operated on this morning": Rhodes, *Atomic Bomb*.

"tremendously pepped up": Holoway, *Stalin*.

"I casually mentioned": Truman, *Memoirs*.

"How did it go": Toland, *Rising Sun*.

"We'll have to have": Holoway, *Stalin*.

"It was his opinion": McCullough, *Truman*.

"It was a question of saving": Truman, *Buck Stops*.

"We call upon": Rhodes, *Atomic Bomb*.

"The 509 Composite Group": Toland, *Rising Sun*.

"The word came Sunday": Tibbets, *Tibbets Story*.

"The usual jesting": Laurence, *Dawn Over Zero*.

"Tonight is the night": Tibbets, *Tibbets Story*.

"He paused": Laurence, *Dawn Over Zero*.

"Our orders were": Tibbets, *Tibbets Story*.

"I never saw a plane": Toland, *Rising Sun*.

"It was a pleasant": Tibbets, *Tibbets Story*.

**Hiroshima**

"It was a clear": Osada, *Children of Hiroshima*.

"We were eight minutes": Tibbets, *Tibbets Story*.

"Put on your goggles": Toland, *Rising Sun*.

"With the release": Tibbets, *Tibbets Story*.

"I saw a red dragonfly": Osada, *Children of Hiroshima*.

257

"The view, where a moment": Hachiya, *Hiroshima Diary*.

"I had unconsciously": Osada, *Children of Hiroshima*.

"They stagger exactly": Kelly, *Manhattan Project*.

"They moved as though": Hachiya, *Hiroshima Diary*.

"If I live a hundred years": Rhodes, *Atomic Bomb*.

"Now that I knew": Tibbets, *Tibbets Story*.

"a pot of boiling black": Rhodes, *Atomic Bomb*.

"A feeling of shock": Tibbets, *Tibbets Story*.

## Reaction Begins

"I'm proud of you": Bird, *American Prometheus*.

"Keep your seats": McCullough, *Truman*.

"An American airplane": Truman, *Statement by President*.

"Attention please": Bird, *American Prometheus*.

"very considerable elation": Sykes, *No Ordinary Genius*.

"There was a sudden noise": Frisch, *What I Remember*.

"Thank God it wasn't a dud": Conant, *109 East Palace*.

"Of course they were": Frisch, *What I Remember*.

"I was involved in this": Sykes, *No Ordinary Genius*.

"The reaction has begun": Smith, *Letters and Recollections*.

"Hahn was completely": Powers, *Heisenberg's War*.

"The guests were": Bernstein, *Uranium Club*.

"Stalin had a tremendous": Rhodes, *Dark Sun*.

"The whole city": Jungk, *A Thousand Suns*.

"drastically alters the whole": Toland, *Rising Sun*.

"I decided at a glance": Jungk, *A Thousand Suns*.

"I felt that we ought": Stimson, *Memorandum*.

"Back on Tinian": Tibbets, *Tibbets Story*.

"Two additional runs": Rhodes, *Atomic Bomb*.

"We'll go on to secondary": Toland, *Rising Sun*.

"People were saying": Rhodes, *Atomic Bomb*.

"should be ready": Norris, *Racing for the Bomb*.

"I cannot endure": Rhodes, *Atomic Bomb*.

## End Game

"I stopped somewhere": Rhodes, *Dark Sun*.

"We drove out": Haynes, *Spies*.

"He himself was rather": Rhodes, *Dark Sun*.

"Meet openly as friends": *Scope of Soviet Activity*.

"After a period of anxious": Rhodes, *Dark Sun*.

"Things might turn out": Albright, *Bombshell*.

## Father of the Bomb

"a nervous wreck": Herken, *Brotherhood.*

"Father of the Atomic Bomb": Conant, *109 East Palace.*

"Can we make them more": Rhodes, *Atomic Bomb.*

"The safety of this nation": Smith, *Letters and Recollections.*

"Tell Dr. Oppenheimer": Herken, *Brotherhood.*

"I neither can nor will": Rhodes, *Atomic Bomb.*

"His eyes were glazed": Bird, *American Prometheus.*

"It is our hope that": Smith, *Letters and Recollections.*

"I never saw a man": Blum, *Price of Vision.*

"When will the Russians": Davis, *Lawrence and Oppenheimer.*

"I feel I have blood": Bird, *American Prometheus.*

"Never mind": Davis, *Lawrence and Oppenheimer.*

"Don't worry": Bird, *American Prometheus.*

## Fallout

"It really happened so": *Scope of Soviet Activity.*

"Well, well": Rhodes, *Dark Sun.*

"On top of the tower": Holoway, *Stalin.*

"It worked": Rhodes, *Dark Sun.*

"Our atomic monopoly": Bird, *American Prometheus.*

"Had the Russian scientists": Lamphere, *FBI-KGB.*

"Were you not in touch": Moss, *Klaus Fuchs.*

"Even before they showed": *Scope of Soviet Activity.*

## Epilogue: Scorpions in a Bottle

"You don't know what": Moss, *Klaus Fuchs.*

"Every time you squeeze": Roberts, *The Brother.*

"I am calm": *Scope of Soviet Activity.*

"You don't have any microphones": Albright, *Bombshell.*

"We believe a super": Bird, *American Prometheus.*

"I believe the most important": Jungk, *A Thousand Suns.*

"Can the Russians do it": Bird, *American Prometheus.*

"We keep saying": McCullough, *Truman.*

"If successful, radioactive": Jungk, *A Thousand Suns.*

"We may be likened": Rhodes, *Dark Sun.*

"I think to a certain extent": Bird, *American Prometheus.*

# ACKNOWLEDGMENTS

THIS BOOK began as a conversation with Deirdre Langeland, my awesome editor at Roaring Brook. We were discussing an article we'd both read about an obscure World War II spy, and gradually that grew into the idea of doing an ambitious global thriller about the birth of the bomb. Thanks to Deirdre for hashing out the story with me, and for her surgically precise touch in shaping and tightening the narrative. Thanks to Simon Boughton for bringing me onto the Roaring Brook team, and to my agent, Ken Wright, for all of his advice and encouragement—when Ken gets behind an idea, it really gives a guy confidence.

Thanks to Robert Norris, author of *Racing for the Bomb*, for sharing his vast knowledge of Manhattan Project espionage, and to Joseph Albright for talking to me about Ted Hall—Albright and his wife Marcia Kunstel actually interviewed Hall before he died, and somehow coaxed a statement from him about the thoughts that inspired him to become a spy. Their book, *Bombshell*, is a must-ave.

Special thanks to the best friends of every nonfiction writer: libraries and librarians. Many of the sources I needed to research this book were found and read in the New York Public Library. And thanks to the Saratoga Springs

Public Library, especially the beautiful second floor, with its history books and quiet tables. Most of this book was written there.

I'm grateful to my critique group partners, Eric Etkin, Vicki Tremper, and Gail Aldous, for offering insightful advice. And thanks most of all to my wife, Rachel. She will always be my first and most trusted reader, and nothing goes out the door until she says it's okay.

# PHOTO CREDITS

Front cover: Foreground © 2013 by Tristan Elwell, background courtesy of U.S. National Archives; Back cover: Courtesy of Los Alamos National Laboratory; Interior pages: frontispiece: Courtesy of Los Alamos National Laboratory; 4–5 (clockwise from top left): Norwegian Resistance Museum, Bettmann/Corbis/ AP Images, AP Images/Henry Griffin, AP Images, AIP Emilio Segré Visual Archive/Brittle Books Collecion, AP Images, AP Images; 7: AP Images; 42–43 (clockwise from top left): Courtesy of Los Alamos National Laboratory, AP Images, Norwegian Resistance Museum, Getty Images, Bettmann/Corbis/AP Images, The Norwegian Resistance Museum, Courtesy of Thos. Powers; 44: AP Images; 88–89: Courtesy of Los Alamos National Laboratory, AP Images, SPL/ Photo Researchers, Inc., The Norwegian Resistance Museum, Courtesy of Los Alamos National Laboratory, Bettmann/Corbis/AP Images; 90: Courtesy of Los Alamos National Laboratory; 142–43: Bettman/Corbis/AP Images, AP Images, Russian Archives/Museum of Foreign Intelligence Services of Russia, AP Images, AP Images, Bettmann/Corbis/AP Images; 144: Bettmann/Corbis/AP Images 227: AP Images, 236–37: Courtesy of Los Alamos National Laboratory

261

# INDEX

Numbers in **bold** indicate pages with illustrations.

Arms race, 215–217, 231–233, 235–236

Atomic bombs: American monopoly on atomic bombs, 135, 220; destruction from, 194–197, 199–200, 203, 204, 206, 208–209, 232, 236, **241–242**; power and energy of, 31; race to build, 22, 46, 118, 150, 163, 235–236

Atoms, 13–15. *See also* fission (atom splitting)

Berg, Moe, **143**, 150–153

Chicago pile and Chicago pile team, **42**, 70–74, 98, 163, **240**

Churchill, Winston, **44**, 45–46, 103–104, 187–188, 189

Cohen, Lona, **143**, 207–208, 209–211

Communism, 24, 25, 30, 41, 64, 229

Eifler, Carl, **42**, 117–120, 149–150

Einstein, Albert, **5**, 18–21, 232, 238–239

*Enola Gay*, **142**, **144**, 190–201

Fat Man and Nagasaki, 205–206

FBI (Federal Bureau of Investigation): Americans, surveillance of, 30, 41, 49–50, 233–235; Soviet spies, surveillance of, 29, 41, 128, 138

Fermi, Enrico, **43**, 70–74, 75, 93, 98, 163, 238, **240**

Feynman, Richard, 69, **89**, 121, 122–124, 178, 181, 183

Fission (atom splitting): bomb making and, 17, 19; chain reaction of plutonium, 133–134; chain reaction of uranium, 71–74, 98, 123–124; discovery of, 13–15, **15**, 19, 200; energy release during, 14, **15**, 71–74; graphite and, 72–73, 75, 98, **240**; plutonium, 124; study of, 71–72; zip rod, 73–74

Frisch, Otto, 14–16, **15**, 182, 199, 200

Fuchs, Klaus: appearance of, 127, 168; character and personality of, 141; death of, 228; photo of, **42**; spying activities, 60–62, 106, 127–130,

141, 158–159, 168–169, 208–209, 211–212, 221–223; trial and sentencing of, 227–228

Germany: Allied forces attacks on, 150, 162; blitzkrieg, 20, 27; bomb development by, 19, 20–21, 22, 34, 39, 150–151, 155–156, 162–164, 238–239; Great Britain, bombing of, 26–27, 51; invasion of other countries, 17, 20, 26–27, 35; Potsdam meeting of Truman and Stalin, 171–172, 187–188; Soviet Union, agreement not to fight, 25, 26, 27; Soviet Union, fighting against, 39, 103, 150, 162; Soviet Union, invasion of, 27; surrender of, 166; territorial claims by, 12, 17, 20; uranium supply of, 163

Gold, Harry: character and personality of, 23, 25; confession of, 228–229; death of, 229; FBI investigation and search of home, 1–3, 223–225, 228; Pennsylvania Sugar Company, stealing information about, 24–26, 27; photos of, **4, 226**; Soviet contacts, meetings with, 25–26, 27, 106–107; spying activities, 23, 25–26, 219, 223–225; trial and sentencing of, 228–229

Graphite, 72–73, 75, 98, **240**

Great Britain: bomb, agreement to keep secret, 103–104; bomb development and testing, 46, 235; British and US attack on Germany, call for by Stalin, 103; German annexation of, 12; German bombing of, 26–27, 51; German territorial claims to, 17, 20; Germany, fighting against, 150, 162; secrets, passing to ally, 227–228; Special Operations Executive (S.O.E.), 51–54, 76

Greenglass, David, **142**, 169–170, 228

Groves, Leslie: character and personality of, 47–48; Los Alamos laboratory site selection, 66–67; Pentagon, construction of, 47; photo of, **42**; plutonium bomb, design of, 158; plutonium bomb testing, 167, 171–172,

176–177, 178, 179–180, 182, 184, 186, 187–188, **242**

Hahn, Otto, **5**, 13–14, 15, 19, 163–164, 172, 200–201, 202

Hall, Theodore "Ted": appearance and character of, 131, 134–135, 137; death of, 230; education of, 131; photo of, **88**; plutonium and implosion process, 157–158; plutonium bomb testing, 179, 181, 184; spying activities, 135–139, 155, 158, 159, 209–212, 229–230; U-235 sample, experiment with, 132–133

Haukelid, Knut: appearance of, 35, 110; ferry Hydro and transport of heavy water, 110–115; in Great Britain, 37, 51–53; Norwegian Nazi sympathizer, throwing off ferry, 35–36; photo of, **4**; resistance group and spying activities, 36–37, 86–87, 116; in Sweden, 37, 115–116; Vemork Hydroelectric, Gunnerside mission to destroy, 75–79, 81–83, 85–87

Heavy water, 53, 59, 75, **89**, 109–110, 111–115, 163

Heisenberg, Werner, **89**, 116–120, 149–150, 151–153, 162–163, 172–173

Helium atoms, 231

Hitler, Adolf: bomb development and use by, potential for, 19, 20–21; rise of, 11; Soviet Union, invasion of, 27; Stalin, agreement not to fight, 25, 26, 27; suicide of, 166; US, declaration of war against, 33

Hydro, **89**, 110, 111–115

Hydrogen bombs, 231–233, 235

Implosion principle and process, 156–158, 159

Japan: bomb development and war with, 166–167; bomb use against, 173, 184, 189; Fat Man and Nagasaki, 205–206; Little Boy and Hiroshima bombing, 190–201, 202, 203–204; Pearl Harbor attack by, 31–33, 205;

Japan (*continued*)
  Potsdam Declaration, 189–190, 203–205; surrender of, 203–205, 206; Tokyo, bombing of, 188; US declaration of war against, 33; US invasion of, plans for, 188–189

KGB (Soviet intelligence agency): agent cultivation, 39, 41, 63; Amtorg, 136–137; British agents, 60–61; FBI surveillance of agents, 29, 41, 128, 138; information from Fuchs, 106, 127–130, 141, 158–159, 168–169, 208–209, 211–212, 221–223; information from Greenglass, 169–170; information from Hall, 135–139, 155, 158, 159, 209–212; scientists, list of for agent cultivation, 41, 63
Kistiakowsky, George "Kisty," **142**, 156–157, 167, 171, 172, 174, 180, 182, 184
Kurchatov, Igor, **89**, 106, 159, 202–203, 219–220

Little Boy, 190–201, 202, 203–204
Los Alamos laboratory: censors and mail, 121, 154–155; construction of, 97, 98, 100; living conditions at, 100, 134, 141, 171; main gate and gaining entrance to, **90**, 100; rumors about activities at, 93–96; scientists, arrival of in Santa Fe, 92–93, 132; scientists, code names for, 93; scientists, recruitment of for, 67–69, 102, 106, 131–132; site selection, 66–67

Manhattan Project, 47–50, 106, 124–125, 127–130, 161–162, 198
McKibben, Dorothy, **88**, 91–92, 96, 132, 167–168
Meitner, Lise, **5**, 14–15, **15**

Neutrons, 13–15, 16, 53, 71–74, 123–124
New Mexico, 2–3, 165–166, 169–170, 186, 228. *See also* Santa Fe

Norway: British glider missions, 54, 57–59; German bomb factory in, 37; German invasion of, 26, 35; Hardanger Plateau, 54, 57, 76, 77; Nazi sympathizers in, 35–36; Norwegians in Britain, return to Norway for secret mission, 51–59; resistance group activities in, 36–37, 86–87, 116; Vemork Hydroelectric, Gunnerside mission to destroy, **43**, 75–87, 109; Vemork Hydroelectric, Poulsson and glider mission to demolish, 53–59; Vemork Hydroelectric saboteurs, hiding out by, 87, 108–109
Nucleus, 13, 14–15, **15**, 53

Oak Ridge, Tennessee, 122–125, 128, 132, 134
Oppenheimer, Frank, 167, 182, 183, 199–200, **242**
Oppenheimer, Robert: appearance and character of, 10, 49, 50, 120; bomb, development of, 34, 38–39; childhood and early life of, 8–9; CIC surveillance of, 101–102, 104–105; Communism, interest in by, 30, 49–50, 64; death of, 235; education of, 9; FBI surveillance of, 30, 49–50, 233–235; forgetfulness of, 7–8; health of, 8, 50, 120, 156; hydrogen bombs, 231–233; Little Boy and Hiroshima bombing, 198, 200; Los Alamos laboratory recruitment, 68–69, 102; Los Alamos laboratory site selection, 66–67; loyalty of, 49–50, 101, 104–105, 233–234; Manhattan Project director, 48–50, 198; opinions about, 9, 11, 49, 92, 120–121; photos of, **42**, **88**; physics, passion for, 9–11; plutonium bomb, design of, 133–134, 156–158; plutonium bomb testing, 167, 171–172, 173–185; political events, interest in, 11–12; Princeton University, teaching at, **6**, 231, 235; recognition of as Father of Atomic Bomb,

213; resignation of, 214; scorpions in a bottle, 233; security clearance of, 49–50, 233, 234; Soviet agent, attempt to recruit as, 63–65, 105, 234; Truman, meeting with, 216–217; University of California, Berkeley, teaching at, 10–11; Uranium Committee membership, 31, 48

Physicists and scientists: German scientists, US round up of, 163–164; German scientists at Farm Hall, 172–173, 200–202; Jewish scientists in Europe, escape of, 11, 19, 93; Little Boy and Hiroshima bombing, reaction to, 199–202; Los Alamos, recruitment for, 67–69, 102, 106, 131–132

Plutonium and plutonium bombs: bomb, completion of, 167; bomb, testing of, 167–168, 171–172, 173–186, 187–188, 219–220, **240–242**; bomb design for, 133–134, 156–158, 159; chain reaction, 133–134; Fat Man and Nagasaki, 205–206; fission, 124; gun assembly design and method, 133–134, 159; implosion principle and process, 156–158, 159; plastic explosives for bomb, 171, 172; production of, 124, 134; sample for Los Alamos, 133

Poulsson, Jens, **42**, 53–59, 76, 77, 78, 85–86

Protons, 13, 15, 53, 123–124

Roosevelt, Franklin Delano (FDR): bomb, agreement to keep secret, 103–104; bomb danger, letter to about, 20–21, 238–239; bomb danger, reaction to, 21–22; Churchill, meeting with, **44**, 45–46; death of, 160–161; driving abilities of, 45–46; photos of, **4**, **44**; secrecy of Manhattan Project, 124

Santa Fe, 2–3, 92–96, 132, 159, 168

Sax, Saville, 132, 136, 138, 139, 154–155, 158, 207

Semyonov, Semyon "Sam," 27, 29, 30, 39, 128, 136

Serber, Robert, 33–34, **89**, 94–95, 97–99, 132, 183, 190

Soviet Union: bomb development by, 38–39, 106, 202–203, 207, 212; bomb information and scientists, keeping secret from, 163–164; bomb testing, reaction to, 219–221; Communism in, 24, 25; Enormoz project, 39–41, 61–65, 106; German invasion of, 27; Germany, agreement not to fight, 25, 26, 27; Germany, fighting against, 39, 103, 150, 162; hydrogen bombs, 231–233, 235; Japan, declaration of war against, 204; plutonium bomb testing, 219–220; secrets, passing to ally, 227–228; spying to steal US bomb plans, 39–41, 61–65, 106; US, relationship with, 30, 38–39; US aid to, 30, 103–104. *See also* KGB (Soviet intelligence agency)

Stalin, Joseph: bomb development by Soviets, 202–203, 207; British and US attack on Germany, call for, 103; Hitler, agreement not to fight, 25, 26, 27; Little Boy and Hiroshima bombing, reaction to, 202–203; opinions about, 139; plutonium bomb, reaction to information about, 188; plutonium bomb, report on testing of, 220; Truman, Potsdam meeting with, 171–172, 187–188

Stimson, Henry, 67, 125, 161–162, 166–167, 187–188, 190, 199, 204–205

Szilard, Leo, **5**, 18–20, 73, 238

Tibbets, Paul, **142**, **144**, 145–148, 175, 186–187, 190–194, 197–198, 205

Trinity Test Site, **143**, 167–168, 171–172, 173–186, 219, **240–242**

Truman, Harry: Japan, third atomic bomb for, 206; Japanese surrender, demand for,

265

Truman, Harry (*continued*)
204–205; Little Boy and Hiroshima bombing, reaction to, 204; Little Boy and Hiroshima bombing, report to, 198–199; Manhattan Project, secrecy of, 124–125, 161–162; Oppenheimer, meeting with, 216–217; photos of, **88**, **142**; plutonium bomb, reaction of Stalin to information about, 188; plutonium bomb, report on outcome of testing of, 187–188; Potsdam Declaration, 189, 204–205; Roosevelt's death, news about, 160–161; Stalin, Potsdam meeting with, 171–172, 187–188; US invasion of Japan, plans for, 188–189; as vice president, 160

United States (US): bomb, development of, 34, 38–41; bomb, US–British development of, 46; British and US attack on Germany, call for by Stalin, 103; Germany, fighting against, 150, 162; Hitler's declaration of war against, 33; Italy, fighting against, 103; Japan, declaration of war against, 33; Japan, fighting against, 103, 188–189; monopoly on atomic bombs, 135, 220; Pearl Harbor, attack on, 31–33, 205; Potsdam Declaration, 189–190, 203–205; Red Scare and hunt for Communists, 229; Soviets, aid to, 30, 103–104; Soviets, relationship with, 30, 38–39
Uranium and uranium bombs: amount needed for bomb, 48, 99, 133, 134; atom splitting,

discovery of, 13–15, **15**, 19, 200; atom splitting and bombs, 17, 19; bomb, testing of, 167; chain reaction, 71–74, 98, 123–124, 194–195; Czechoslovakian mining of, 21; energy release during splitting of, 14, 15; German supply of, 163; gun assembly design and method, 98–99, **99**; Little Boy bomb and Hiroshima bombing, 190–201, 202, 203–204; number of atoms in an ounce of, 15; Oak Ridge preparation of, 122, 123–124, 128, 134; plutonium, production of, 124; size of atoms of, 15; U-235 sample, experiment with, 132–133; U-238 and U-235, separation of, 123–124, 128

Vemork Hydroelectric: Gunnerside mission, **43**, 75–87, 109; heavy water production at, 53, 59, 75, 109–110, 163; location of, 53, 75, 79; photo of, **43**; Poulsson and glider mission to demolish, 53–59; rebuilding of, 109; sabotage plans against, 111

Wigner, Eugene, **5**, 18–20, 73, 74
World War II: Allied Powers, 33; atomic bombs and loss of, 134, 153; Axis Powers, 33; beginning of, 17, 20; end of, 206; German-Japanese alliance, 31; German surrender, 166; Japan, surrender of, 203–205, 206; Pearl Harbor, attack on, 31–33, 205; Potsdam Declaration, 189–190, 203–205; US declaration of war against Japan, 33